MW00830034

Global Business Strategy

Global Business Strategy

Cornelis A. de Kluyver and John A. Pearce II

Global Business Strategy

Copyright © Business Expert Press, LLC, 2021.

Cover design by Charlene Kronstedt

Interior design by Exeter Premedia Services Private Ltd., Chennai, India

All rights reserved. No part of this publication may be reproduced, stored in a retrieval system, or transmitted in any form or by any means—electronic, mechanical, photocopy, recording, or any other except for brief quotations, not to exceed 400 words, without the prior permission of the publisher.

First published in 2021 by
Business Expert Press, LLC
222 East 46th Street, New York, NY 10017
www.businessexpertpress.com

ISBN-13: 978-1-63742-042-3 (paperback)
ISBN-13: 978-1-63742-043-0 (e-book)

Business Expert Press Strategic Management Collection

Collection ISSN: 2150-9611 (print)
Collection ISSN: 2150-9646 (electronic)

First edition: 2021

10 9 8 7 6 5 4 3 2 1

Description

Global Business Strategy looks at the opportunities and risks associated with staking out a global competitive presence and introduces the fundamentals of global strategic thinking. The authors demonstrate how a company should change and adapt its domestic business model to achieve a competitive advantage as it expands globally.

Our framework includes a company's business model, the strategic decisions a company needs to make as it globalizes its operations, and globalization strategies for creating a competitive advantage. A business model has four principal dimensions: market participation, the value proposition, the supply chain infrastructure, and its management model.

Keywords

global strategy; global competitive advantage; business model; value creation; value proposition; market participation; supply chain infrastructure; global management model; global industry; global branding; innovation; outsourcing; offshoring; global management

Contents

Preface

This book introduces the fundamentals of global strategic thinking. We begin by analyzing the growing number of global business changes and the increased uncertainty they have brought with them. With nationalism on the rise in the Western world, the tariff wars between the United States and China, the shift of the commercial center of gravity to Asia, the worldwide COVID-19 coronavirus pandemic, and the opportunities and risks associated with staking out a global competitive presence have increased substantially.

Underestimating risk can lead to strategies that neither defend against the threats nor take advantage of the opportunities that higher uncertainty levels may provide. At the other extreme, assuming that the world is entirely unpredictable can lead managers to abandon the analytical rigor of their traditional planning processes altogether and base their strategic decisions primarily on instinct.

We define crafting a global strategy in terms of change; how and when a company should change or adapt its core (domestic) business model to achieve a competitive advantage as it expands globally. This definition's conceptual framework has three fundamental building blocks: a company's core *business model*, the various *strategic decisions* a company faces as it globalizes, and a range of *globalization strategy options* for creating a global competitive advantage.

Organization of the Book

The book is organized in three parts. Part 1—*The Global Competitive Environment*—has four chapters. Chapter 1 assesses how global the world economy has become and what its implications are for companies. We analyze globalization in terms of four dimensions—*economic, technological, political,* and *cultural* globalization. We also discuss the growing complexity of the global competitive environment, the shift of the center of gravity of global trade to Asia, and the *persistence of distance*.

Chapter 2 looks at the globalization pressures on companies and the globalization of competitive advantage. We use the well-known *AAA triangle framework* to describe three generic approaches to global value creation. *Adaptation* strategies seek to increase revenues and market share by tailoring one or more components of a company's business model to suit local requirements or preferences. *Aggregation* strategies focus on achieving economies of scale or scope by creating regional or global efficiencies. They typically involve standardizing a significant portion of the value proposition and grouping together development and production processes. *Arbitrage* is about exploiting economic or other differences between national or regional markets, usually by locating separate parts of the supply chain in different places.

Chapter 3 deals with the globalization of opportunity and risk. We consider the attractiveness and risks associated with entering emerging markets. We note that the sheer size of the consumer markets now opening up in emerging economies, especially in India and China, and their rapid growth rates will shift the balance of business activity far more than at any time before. Next, we consider how many megatrends such as climate change, urbanization, and new technologies change the global competitive environment. Finally, we look at arguments for and against protectionism in regulating global trade.

Chapter 4 deals with the globalization of corporate social responsibility, reflecting the changes in societal expectations worldwide. Companies are expected to pay greater attention to so-called environmental, social and corporate governance (ESG) factors today—the environment, social issues, and governance. A primary cause of the dramatic increase in businesses' attention to the physical environment is societies' concern about climate change and global warming. ESG has emerged as an important source of corporate risk and can directly or indirectly affect firms' financial performances, including profitability. ESG disclosures have become an increasingly anticipated component of company reports.

Part II of the book—*Global Strategy Development*—has three chapters. Chapter 5 focuses on how managers can identify the key company resources and capabilities they need to build successful global strategies. The resource-based view (RBV) of a firm is an important framework for conducting this type of analysis. We also review the concept of *core competencies* and their relation to strategy formulation and the development of a global competitive advantage. We next discuss benchmarking against existing competitors in global industries as a basis for gauging the likelihood of success when entering a new global market. The balance of the chapter deals with several issues, including a global mindset, talent, financial resources, and a commitment to *open* innovation.

Chapter 6 introduces the business model concept to define global strategy formulation as *changing or adapting a company's core (domestic) business model to achieve a competitive advantage, as it globalizes its operations or presence.* A *business model* is simply a description of how a company does business. It has four principal components: (1) *market participation*—who its customers are, how it reaches them and relates to them; (2) *the value proposition*—what a company offers its customers; (3) *the supply chain infrastructure*—with what resources, activities, and partners it creates its offerings; and finally, (4) its *management model*—how it organizes and coordinates its operations. A second, complementary view of global strategy development takes a *capabilities* perspective and looks at exploiting existing capabilities, creating new capabilities, and enhancing capabilities. We conclude this chapter with a discussion about creating sustainable global business models.

Chapter 7 considers decisions regarding which foreign markets to enter, why, when, and how—the key dimensions of target market selection and the timing and mode of market entry. We discuss how companies gradually escalate their commitment to global markets as they move from exporting and licensing to strategic partnerships to wholly owned subsidiaries. The section on the timing of entry deals with first-mover advantages and disadvantages and the benefits of fast-follower strategies.

Chapter 8 discusses the globalization of the company's core value proposition and introduces a value proposition globalization matrix to guide strategic thinking. Next, we consider the benefits of combining aggregation and adaptation through global product and service platforms, combining adaptation and arbitrage in global product development, and using all three strategies in creating a global innovation capability.

Part III of the book—*Global Strategic Management*—has three chapters. Chapter 9 addresses global branding and positioning. We look at issues such as a global brand structure, country of origin effects in global branding, assigning custody for key strategic brands, and corporate branding benefits. We conclude with a discussion of global brand value.

Chapter 10 deals with the globalization of the value chain infrastructure—from research and development (R&D) to product development to manufacturing to distribution to after-sale service. As part of this discussion, we look at outsourcing and offshoring. Next, we identify some new manufacturing trends, including reshoring in the wake of rising costs associated with manufacturing overseas and security concerns. The final section deals with sustainability issues in global supply chains.

Chapter 11 rounds out the business model framework by looking at the globalization of a company's management model. We identify four elements that are key to globalizing a management model: (1) the presence of a clear corporate strategy that guides product development, market choice, and entering strategies; (2) the involvement of an experienced global finance function; (3) access to a global talent pool; and (4) global ecosystem management. We conclude the book with a section on *lessons learned in going global*.

The book includes several mini-cases to illustrate the various concepts and strategies discussed. Instructors adopting the book can request a full set of slides from the publisher. Finally, we note that although this is substantially a new book, several sections and paragraphs were adapted or taken from the first author's earlier book *Fundamentals of Global Strategy: A Business Model Approach*, Business Expert Press, 2010.

Acknowledgments

From Kees de Kluyver

Writing this book was inspired by recent events. As a retired Dean and Distinguished Professor Emeritus of the Lundquist College of Business at the University of Oregon, I have the good fortune of being invited periodically to teach in graduate and executive programs around the world and was scheduled to teach in Europe in April of this year. Accordingly, I had prepared—in the form of lecture notes and slide material—a complete, new course on global strategy. When the COVID-19 coronavirus pandemic hit and the course was canceled, I decided to spend my time in self-isolation refining this material and writing this book.

I have a lot of people to thank. My coauthor, Jack Pearce, helped develop the perspective of the book; provided many additions and examples; and was the best critic, supporter, and friend an author could wish for. My dear friends Alan Eliason and Doug Bales encouraged me all the way and were always ready to discuss specific issues of interest. Vijay Sathe, my former colleague at the Peter F. Drucker and Masatoshi Ito Graduate School of Management, and I collaborated in a number of executive programs over the years. These experiences provided me with new perspectives on strategy development. Rob Zwettler, former Executive Director at *Business Expert Press*, and Scott Isenberg, current Executive Director, have been extremely supportive of this effort. And, of course, I am indebted to the late Peter F. Drucker. His guidance and friendship meant a lot to me. Considered by many the *father of modern management*, Peter's unique perspectives on modern capitalism, on the role of the private sector, nonprofits, and the government have helped shape the thinking of CEOs, academics, analysts, and commentators alike. I hope this book contributes to this process.

Finally, as aspiring authors quickly learn and seasoned writers already know, writing a book is a mammoth undertaking. Fortunately, I had a lot of encouragement along the way from my family and friends and take this opportunity to thank them all for letting me spend the time and for their words of encouragement. I am grateful to all of them and hope the result meets their high expectations.

Cornelis A. de Kluyver (Kees)
Retired Dean and Distinguished Professor Emeritus
Lundquist College of Business
University of Oregon,
Eugene, OR, 97403

From Jack Pearce

Kees' invitation to join him in creating a book on global business strategy came at a perfect time. The wonderful and rewarding experience of coauthoring five books with him combined with the success that Richard B. Robinson, Jr., and I had in publishing 38 books gave me confidence that Kees and I could produce a valuable manuscript in the rapidly advancing field of global strategy. By combining Kees' awareness of executive action on the international stage and our knowledge of multinational and domestic plan design and implementation, I believed we could produce a book of useful insights for practicing and aspiring executives.

The distinguishing characteristic of this new book is our emphasis on business practice. It is common when writing about business planning to begin with discussions of conceptual models. These models have value for firms with local or regional markets and corporations with global reach. The main difference is that global firms' managers rely far more heavily on learning from the experience of competitors than do companies with a narrow market scope. Therefore, to serve the needs of present and future global leaders in Global Business Strategy, we highlight strategies that have made notable impacts. By sharing the results of our study of enacted strategies, we believe that our readers can shorten their learning curves to have greater corporate success.

In addition to my responsibilities as the VSB Endowed Chair in Strategic Management and Entrepreneurship at Villanova University, I have committed to being involved as a professor and mentor to Ph.D. students of Organizational Leadership in the College of Business and Leadership at Eastern University. As the Distinguished Scholar in Residence, I am given the rare opportunity to engage with colleagues and students at an extremely high level of academic scholarship. Happily, working on Global Business Strategy is very synergistic with the full range of my professional obligations.

I want to express my great appreciation to my family, colleagues, and friends who have helped me satisfy diverse commitments while working on this book. The organizational and marketing support that we receive from *Business Expert Press* and Scott Isenberg is excellent.

I most fervently hope that in reading this book, you find understanding and insight that advances your career.

John A. Pearce II (Jack)

VSB Endowed Chair in Strategic Management and Entrepreneurship

Villanova School of Business

Villanova University

and

Distinguished Scholar in Residence

College of Business and Leadership

Eastern University

PART I

The Global Competitive Environment

CHAPTER 1

The Globalization of Markets and Competition

Introduction

This first chapter considers the economic, political, technological, and cultural dimensions that have propelled globalization, as well as factors that are checking its progress. Second, we discuss the shift of the center of gravity of global competition from the West to Asia and consider how global competition is evolving. Third, we deal with industry globalization and assess the growing complexity of the global competitive environment. We conclude the chapter by looking at the benefits and costs of globalization.

Defining Globalization

The integration of national economies into a global economic system has been one of the most important developments of the last century. This integration process, called *globalization,* has resulted in remarkable growth in trade between countries. Globalization is manifested as a growing economic interdependence among countries at a macro level, reflected in the increasing cross-border flow of goods, services, capital, and technical knowledge. At the company level, globalization refers to the increasing percentage of revenues and profits derived from foreign markets.

Economic globalization started as countries lowered tariffs and nontariff barriers, and international trade and foreign direct investment (FDI) grew. As more and more countries embraced free-market and anti-protectionist policies, the globalization of production and markets ensued. The globalization of production allowed companies to spread parts of their manufacturing operations worldwide to reduce costs. The globalization of markets has led to an increased focus on the world as a huge global marketplace rather than a collection of local markets, which has produced a measure of convergence in consumers' tastes and preferences.

Among the growth-enhancing factors that come from greater global economic integration are (1) competition: companies that are not focused on innovation and cost-cutting are likely to be replaced by more dynamic firms; (2) economies of scale: firms that export to the world have lower unit costs, which allow them to be more competitive; and (3) learning: companies that operate internationally are more knowledgeable about global competition, innovations, and evolving industry standards.

The globalization of production and markets has had enormous implications for companies. First, it has forced companies to recognize that industry boundaries no longer stop at national borders, and competition can originate abroad. Second, as relatively protected national markets became segments of a more integrated global market, they noted competitive rivalry increased because many firms competed with each other for market share and profits around the globe. Third, with a larger number of competitors, suppliers, customers, and a greater diversity of needs and preferences, the rate of innovation increased, compressing product life cycles and increasing consumer choice.

As globalization increased, it also became more complex. Beyond economics, its dimensions have grown to include technological, political, and cultural considerations that increasingly impact the decisions of nations, companies, and individual consumers. Globalization has brought down prices, increased choice, and provided growth opportunities. Simultaneously, as different areas of the world have become more integrated, the world economy has become more vulnerable to global shocks—from global warming to a financial crisis and, more recently, the global COVID-19 coronavirus pandemic. These changes have made it imperative for companies to understand how they should deal with the growing complexity of the global economic, technological, political, and cultural landscape.

Globalization or Regionalization?

While the term *globalization* is widely used, from an economic perspective, it is more accurate to speak of *semiglobalization* or *regionalization* because global trade and investment is largely concentrated in three sets of relationships—between the United States and the European Union (EU), the EU and Asia, and Asia and the United States, frequently referred to as the Triad. The EU and the United States have the largest bilateral trade and investment relationship in the world. EU and U.S. investments are the principal drivers of the transatlantic relationship, contributing to growth and jobs in both the E.U. and the United States.[1]

Asia and Europe are leading trade partners, with 1.5 trillion U.S. dollars of annual trade in goods. The two continents are moving quickly to build and strengthen ties, with a firm commitment to agree to Sustainable Development Goals (SDGs). Sustainable connectivity has become a focal point of the Asia-Europe Meeting (ASEM), an intergovernmental cooperation forum between 30 European and 21 Asian countries. Trade within Europe and Asia is four times higher than the trade between the two regions. However, the trade between the Asian and European regions is still higher than that between any other world region. Russia is the third-largest trader in the ASEM group of countries; it exports twice as much to Europe as Asia.[2]

Foreign Direct Investment (FDI) in 2015 to 2017 (the latest years for which accurate statistics are available) between Asia and Europe reached close to 90 billion U.S. dollars annually—nearly the same level as FDI flows within Europe. Over half of European investments in Asia come from the United Kingdom and Germany. Similarly, China and Japan are the principal investors from Asia in Europe, while India and China account for around half the total European foreign investment.

U.S. trade with Association of Southeast Asian Nations (ASEAN) was 272.0 billion U.S. dollars in total (two way) goods trade during 2018. Goods exports totaled 86.2 billion U.S. dollars; goods imports totaled 185.8 billion U.S. dollars. The U.S. goods trade deficit with ASEAN was 99.6 billion U.S. dollars in 2018. Trade in services with ASEAN countries (exports and imports) totaled 55 billion U.S. dollars in 2017 (latest data available). Exports were 33 billion U.S. dollars; services imports were 22 billion U.S. dollars. The U.S. services trade surplus with ASEAN countries was 10 billion U.S. dollars in 2017 (latest data available). U.S. FDI in ASEAN countries (stock) was 328.8 billion U.S. dollars in 2017 (latest data available), up 5.6 percent from 2016. U.S. direct investment in ASEAN countries is led by the nonbank holding companies, manufacturing, and wholesale trade sectors.[3] This evidence supports the notion that global trade is still largely *semiglobal* or regional is likely to remain that way for some time.

Globalization's Four Underlying Dimensions

Globalization has grown in complexity to include four sets of drivers: (1) ongoing changes in the *economic* arena, (2) advances in *technology*, (3) the convergence of *political* ideas, and more recently, (4) the growing integration of *values and cultures* around the world (see Exhibit 1.1):

The economic dimension. The economic dimension of globalization is rooted in free trade. Chapter 3 reviews the principal economic and regulatory constructs that define the current global trading environment. For many companies, foreign sales have become an increasing or even dominant portion of their total sales. Market size is of particular importance to companies that produce goods and services that have a high research and development (R&D) intensity or capital expenditures. If their potential customer base is small, developing and producing a product is significantly costlier. Growth of markets abroad helps firms spread development and production expenditures over a larger revenue base. This is often referred to as the scale benefit of globalization.

Globalization has created opportunities for specialization. Specialization makes it easier to enter new markets, especially when it is not necessary to be

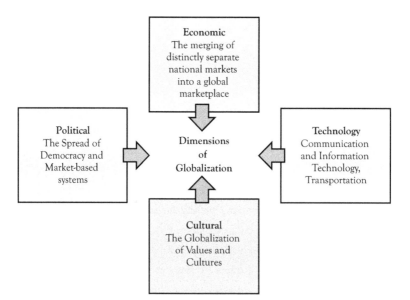

Exhibit 1.1 Dimension of globalization

large with strong existing ties to customers. Specialized markets usually have greater space for new companies and can compete based on new technologies and ideas. For example, a high-quality producer of automobile engine components does not need to compete with larger firms such as Ford and Toyota in the end customer market. Rather, it can allocate all of its resources to become even more competitive in designing engine components. That means, among other things, that resources (e.g., staff and technology investments) can become more specialized. *Greater Human Capital*

Companies that can leverage the benefits from trade, such as scaling up and specializing production, also create better-paying jobs that demand greater skills. These benefits tend to be strongest in economies that are open to trade and investment. While outsourcing and off-shoring sometimes lead to unemployment, wages and employment levels tend to be higher because trade enhances human resources efficiency. When some parts of the production are off-shored, companies can specialize and invest more in human capital.

Globalization has resulted in lower consumer prices and increased living standards. While this benefit has primarily accrued to Western economies, developing countries are catching up due to freer and higher levels of trade in the world.

Consumer choice and product variation have increased. Between 1972 and 2001, the number of goods in the U.S. economy doubled to 16,000, while the median number of countries from which a good was imported rose to 12.[4]

Globalization has also promoted economic efficiency in the world economy.[5] Economies of scale and specialization have improved resource use in the economy. As a consequence, labor productivity has increased.[6] Moreover, the fragmentation of value chains has boosted productivity through lower-cost imports of inputs.[7] Trade and investment improve the technology of sectors and economies by forcing greater competition upon incumbent firms. The top 10 percent of U.S. firms in productivity is twice as productive as the bottom 10 percent.[8] In Europe, the top 10 percent of firms are three times as productive as the bottom 10 percent.[9]

Globalization has reduced inflation in Western economies and increased *real* wages by lowering the cost of consumption. Many goods that previously were affordable by only a few—for example, a mobile phone or car—are common in many households. Globalization also has stimulated the spread of new technologies, making economies greener and more productive. Finally, globalization has helped reduce gender wage discrimination, provide new opportunities to women, and improve management and working conditions.

Two impending changes in globalization's economic dimension are noteworthy. First, trade in commercial services is growing faster than the trade in goods. Second, the demand for goods and services is gradually shifting eastward. By 2030, developing countries, led by China, are expected to account for more than half of global consumption.

These changes are creating new challenges for companies and nations alike. Companies will have to (1) carefully monitor how these global trends affect their business model(s), target markets, and how value creation is shifting within their industry; (2) enhance service offerings; (3) build closer and more digital supplier relationships; and (4) focus on costs, risks, speed, flexibility, and resilience in their strategy development.[10] Nations face equally serious challenges. Countries will need to (1) strengthen their service sectors, (2) embrace automation in all value chains, (3) deepen regional ties, and (4) invest in R&D and skill development. Countries have already begun to specialize. Analysis by McKinsey and Company shows how countries are focusing their trade on specific sectors of the economy and are assuming specific roles in the value chain. For example, Germany, Japan, and South Korea are *innovation providers* in automobiles, pharmaceuticals, and chemicals. The United States, France, and the United Kingdom are *service providers* in financial intermediation, telecom, and information technology (IT). Other countries can be classified as *regional processors* (e.g., Finland for paper), *resource providers* (e.g., Australia for mining), or *labor providers* (think of China in textiles).[11]

According to the McKinsey Global Institute (MGI), developing a robust global *digital identification* system for individuals and companies will be key to unlocking future global growth. Many people in the world do not have any form of identification that is usable in the digital world and cannot access important governmental or economic services. Individuals will be the major beneficiaries of digital identification (ID) through (1) increased access to and use of financial services, (2) improved access to employment opportunities, (3) greater agricultural productivity from formalized landownership, and (4) time savings by reducing the need to travel. Public and private institutions stand to benefit through (1) cost savings; (2) less fraud; and (3) higher sales, productivity, and tax revenue. ✓ *Account ?*

Some systems have already been launched in Argentina, Canada, Estonia, Sweden, India, and the United Kingdom—either by the public sector or as partnerships with private entities. Adoption rates have been encouraging, but a lot of work remains to be done. Ultimately, a convergence of these systems toward a universally recognized and honored system will be necessary to unlock their full potential.[12]

The technology dimension. Whereas the lowering of trade barriers made globalization of markets and production a theoretical possibility, *technology* has made it a reality through advances in communication, information processing, and transportation. Several new technologies are about to disrupt global trade once again: (1) blockchain, (2) artificial intelligence (AI) and machine learning, (3) trading services via digital platforms, (4) three-dimensional (3D) printing, and (5) mobile payments.

Blockchain. A blockchain is a growing list of records, called *blocks*, linked by *cryptography*. Each block contains a cryptographic jumble of information of the previous block, a timestamp, and transaction data. By design, a blockchain is resistant to modification of the data.[13] It is "an open, distributed ledger that can record transactions between two parties efficiently and in a verifiable and permanent way."[14] This new tool will have a tremendous impact on global trade supply chains by reducing costs and improving transparency and security. Blockchain-based solutions also are changing the world of trade financing. For example, blockchain is used to simplify the long process of obtaining a letter of credit (LoC), a payment mechanism used in international trade.[15]

AI and machine learning. AI is the idea of machines using *smart* technology to carry out tasks. By contrast, machine learning is an application of AI to provide machines with access to data and learn for themselves. AI and machine learning can be used to optimize trade transportation, manage marine and truck traffic at ports, and translate Internet-based queries from one language into another, thereby facilitating inventory management.

Trading services via digital platforms. Technology has revolutionized the *go-to-market* strategy of modern businesses using digital platforms. Fundamentally, a *digital platform* is a technology-enabled business model that facilitates exchanges between multiple groups, has open connectivity, and is easily scaled. For example, digital platforms like Upwork allow users to find service providers from all over the globe for a wide range of services.

3D printing. 3D printing, sometimes called additive manufacturing, creates a 3D object from a computer-aided design (CAD) model or a digital 3D model. The term *3D printing* refers to various computer-controlled processes in which material is deposited, joined, or solidified to create a 3D object. Some studies predict that once high-speed 3D printing is mass-adopted and cheap enough, global trade may decrease by as much as 25 percent because 3D printing requires less labor and reduces the need for imports. Others maintain that such views are too optimistic and do not account for mass manufacturing's complexity and reality.[16]

Mobile payments. Mobile payments are money payments made for a product or service through a tablet or cellphone. This new technology can also be used to send money to friends or family members, such as PayPal and Venmo. Mobile payment technology connects more people to market opportunities, especially in emerging economies.

The political dimension. Globalization's political dimension concerns the growth of the global political system, both in size and complexity. That system includes governmental and intergovernmental organizations, as well as nongovernmental organizations (NGOs) and social movement organizations, which increasingly impact companies' strategic postures in foreign countries.

Protectionism, political uncertainty, and trade wars impede the globalization process. All have increased or intensified in recent years. Examples include the recent U.S. withdrawal from the Trans-Pacific Partnership, tariff wars with China, trade conflicts with Mexico, Canada, other key trading partners, and the UK's withdrawal from the EU (Brexit).

History also shows that globalization goes through cycles. The slowing growth in global trade suggests that the globalization process may have reached another turning point. *The coronavirus pandemic and the efforts underway to control its effects* have brought economic growth to a temporary standstill in many parts of the world. However, there is no evidence that a sustained process of deglobalization has begun, as some suggest.[17] World trade has steadily increased in recent years despite variations in the growth rate.

Moreover, most globalization and trade measures focus primarily on manufactured goods, even though services comprise the fastest-growing and dynamic sector of the global economy. The deglobalization argument also does not account for the rapid growth in the number of middle- and lower-class consumers—especially in emerging markets. This has allowed local firms that focused largely on export markets to turn inward because of a growing domestic market. Nevertheless, the current increase in global uncertainty has threatened jobs and dissuaded many companies from expanding and innovating.

The cultural dimension*. Cultural* globalization is the transmission of ideas, meanings, and values from country to country and its impact on social relations between people. Knowledge of other cultures enables individuals to participate in extended social relations that cross national and regional borders. Cultural globalization involves adopting shared norms and knowledge with which people associate their individual and collective cultural identities. It thereby brings increasing interconnectedness among different populations and cultures.

The cultural dimension of globalization has always been controversial. Supporters maintain that cultural globalization (1) has united millions of people, (2) increased multiculturalism, (3) redefined human rights and environmental values, and (4) enhanced our understanding of global cultural diversity. They note that globalization represents free trade, promotes global economic growth, creates jobs, and makes companies more competitive. This lowers prices for consumers and provides developing countries with a chance to develop economically. Through infusions of foreign capital and technology, conditions are created in which prosperity can spread and respect human rights, and the environment can flourish.

Critics are more diverse in their arguments and have formed an active *anti-globalization movement* or *counter-globalization movement*.

Members share their opposition to multinational corporations (MNCs) having unchecked political power, exercised through trade agreements, and deregulated financial markets. They also accuse corporations of aiming to maximize profits at the expense of work safety conditions and standards, labor hiring and compensation standards, and environmental conservation principles. In light of the large economic gap between rich and developing countries, they claim that free trade without measures to protect the environment and workers' health and well-being will merely increase industrialized nations' power.

Companies are beginning to respond to these concerns. A growing number recognizes that being responsive to environmental, social, and governance (ESG) issues are key to creating a sustainable competitive advantage. Worldwide, younger generations of customers, employees, and other stakeholders have grown up with increased awareness about ESG issues and expect companies to reflect their values and aspirations. If companies fail to address these issues, they may not attract and retain the customers and employees they need to grow. What is more, companies that do not act risk falling behind their competitors.

The finance sector of the global economy also has begun to heed ESG concerns. It encourages businesses to change their corporate mission from a shareholder to a more inclusive stakeholder perspective. A growing number of mission statements explicitly state that the company seeks to optimize for social and business value, using the core business to deliver the financial returns expected by its owners and help society meet its most significant challenges.

The Persistence of Distance[18]

While globalization has brought the world's citizens closer in many respects, it would be wrong to conclude that *distance* no longer matters. The CAGE (cultural, administrative, geographic, and economic) model offers a broad view of distance and shows how distance persists in various forms. This framework defines distance in terms of four principal dimensions—*cultural, administrative, geographic, and economic*[19]:

Cultural distance. A country's culture shapes how people interact with each other and with organizations. Differences in religious beliefs, race, social norms, and language quickly can become barriers, that is, *create distance*. A common language, for example, makes trade much easier and, therefore, more likely. Social norms, the set of unspoken principles that strongly guides everyday behavior, are mostly invisible. For example, Japanese and European consumers prefer smaller automobiles and household appliances, reflecting a social norm that highly values space. The food industry must concern itself with religious attributes; Hindus do not eat beef because their religion forbids it. Thus, cultural distance shapes preference and, ultimately, choice.

Administrative or political distance. Administrative or political distance is created by differences in governmental laws, policies, and institutions, including international relationships between countries, treaties, and membership in international organizations. The greater the distance, the less likely it is that extensive trade relations develop. Over the last half century, the EU's integration is probably the best example of deliberate efforts to reduce administrative distance among trading partners. Additionally, bad relationships can increase administrative distance. Although India and Pakistan share a colonial past, land borders, and linguistic ties, their long-standing mutual hostility has reduced official trade to almost nothing.

Countries can also create administrative and political distance through unilateral measures. Indeed, policies of individual governments pose the most common barriers to cross-border competition. In some cases, difficulties arise in a company's home country. For companies from the United States, domestic prohibitions on bribery and the prescription of health, safety, and environmental policies have a dampening effect on their international businesses. More commonly, though, it is the target country's government that raises barriers to foreign competition: tariffs, trade quotas, restrictions on FDI, and preferences for domestic competitors in the form of subsidies and favoritism in regulation and procurement.

Geographic distance. Geographic distance is about more than how far away a country is in miles. Other geographic attributes include the country's physical size, average within-country distances to borders, access to waterways and the ocean, and topography. They also include human-made elements such as a country's transportation and communications infrastructure. Geographic attributes most directly influence transportation costs and therefore are particularly relevant to businesses with low value-to-weight or bulk ratios, such as steel and cement. Likewise, the costs of transporting fragile or perishable products become significant across large distances. Intangible goods and services can be affected by geographic distance as well. For example, cross-border equity flows between two countries drop significantly as the geographic distance rises. This decline directly results from differences in infrastructure such as telephone, Internet, and banking services.

Economic distance. Disposable income is the most important economic attribute that creates distance between countries. Rich countries engage in proportionately higher levels of cross-border economic activity than poorer ones. The greater the economic distance between a company's home country and a host country, the greater the likelihood of making significant adaptations to its business model. Walmart in India, for instance, is a very different business from Walmart in the United States. But, Walmart in Canada is virtually a carbon copy of its operations in the United States.

CAGE differences are likely to matter most when one or more of the CAGE distances are great. That is, when CAGE differences are small, there will likely be a greater opportunity for business to be conducted across borders. The impact of CAGE differences also varies by product and industry. Some products (fashion items) are more culturally sensitive than others (laptops). Similarly, some countries favor certain industries or support *national champions*, thereby raising the administrative distance dimension. Finally, when considering the geographic distance, ask how sensitive products or shelf life is to climate differences.

Global Competition's New Center of Gravity

Developing countries are a key force reshaping the global competitive environment. Emerging economies are experiencing significant growth rates in Gross Domestic Product (GDP), trade, and disposable income. A large consumer market is opening up in emerging economies, especially in India and China. Their rapid growth rates will shift the balance of business activity eastward.

This shift in the global competitive landscape will have a great impact in the years to come. Consider, for example, the growing number of companies from emerging markets that appear in the *Fortune* 500. It is expected that half will come from emerging markets in the not-too-distant future.

Consider also the significant increase in the number of emerging market companies acquiring established Western businesses and brands, proof that *globalization* is no longer just another word for *Americanization*. For example, Budweiser, the maker of America's favorite beer, is currently part of the MNC Anheuser-Busch InBev and is produced in various breweries worldwide.

Lenovo, the Chinese computer-maker, became a global brand in 2005 when it paid around 1.75 billion U.S. dollars for IBM's PC business—including the ThinkPad laptop range. Lenovo had the right to use the IBM brand for five years, but dropped it two years ahead of schedule; such was its confidence in its brand.[20] This new phase of globalization creates huge opportunities and threats—for developed-world multinationals and new competitors from developing countries.

The Evolution of Global Competition

There are two main approaches to introducing a product globally: *standardization*, also referred to as *aggregation*, and *customization*, often called *adaptation*. Standardization calls for introducing an established product, service, technology, brand image, and messages into new markets. The continually improving online communication technology leads to an ever-more-homogenous global customer base that allows for strategic success with a standardized offering in some industries.

Standardization performed exceptionally well until the early 2000s, when global brand owners began to see their share prices drop as consumers reached for local products that were better aligned with their cultural identities. The change in customer purchase behavior was the beginning of an evolution in international strategy. Since then, standardization has been steadily replaced by customization, which requires the development of modified products, services, and technologies and the use of somewhat tailor-made messages, to meet the requirements of a more focused market segment or local population.

Aware of global corporations' strategic opportunities and the obstacles that can stall their progress, executives in almost every industry monitor global markets' evolution. The largest 20 U.S.-headquartered MNCs all derive more than 50 percent of their total sales *outside the United States.* These companies are led by Intel (80.0 percent of its total revenue is derived from foreign operations), Mondelez (75.8 percent), Coca-Cola (70.0 percent), ExxonMobil (65.4 percent), Apple (63.2 percent), and GE (62.1 percent).[21]

According to these data, Alphabet leads U.S. corporations in the percentage of its global workforce that is employed outside the United States (87 percent), followed by DowDuPont (73.8 percent) and Procter and Gamble (73.4 percent). It also reveals that the U.S. corporations with the highest percentage of assets (property, plant, and equipment) located in foreign countries are Coca-Cola (92.4 percent), followed by Mondelez (84 percent) and Johnson and Johnson (75 percent). Although the financial results vary slightly from year to year, the important take away from the table stays impressively constant. Major U.S. corporations invest throughout the world wherever they see an opportunity to improve their operations over the long term and expand their customer base.

Understanding the myriad and sometimes subtle nuances of competing in global markets or against global corporations is a required competence of strategic managers. This requirement's scope and complexity need to match the organizations' scope and complexity that they direct.

Industry Globalization

An important consideration in formulating a global strategy is *how* global an industry is or is likely to become. Virtually, all industries are global in some respects. However, only a handful of industries can be considered truly global today or are likely to become so in the future. Many more will remain hybrids, that is, global in some respects, local in others. *Industry globalization, therefore, is a matter of degree.* What counts is which industry segments are becoming global and how they affect strategic choice.

In approaching this issue, we must focus on industry globalization drivers and think about how these elements shape strategic choice.

We must also distinguish between three concepts: *industry globalization*, *global competition*, and the degree to which a *company has globalized* its operations. In traditionally global industries, competition is mostly waged worldwide, and the leaders have created global corporate structures. But, the fact that an industry is not truly global does not prevent global competition. And, a competitive global posture does not necessarily require a global reorganization of every aspect of a company's operations. Economies of scale and scope are among the most important drivers of industry globalization; in global industries, the minimum volume required for cost efficiency is simply no longer available in a single country or region. Global competition begins when companies cross-subsidize national market share battles in pursuit of global brand and distribution positions. A global company structure is characterized by production and distribution systems in key markets around the world that enable cross-subsidization, competitive retaliation on a global basis, and world-scale volume.

Industry Globalization Drivers[22]

Four sets of *industry globalization drivers* define conditions in each industry that create the potential for that industry to become more global and, consequently, for the potential viability of a global approach to strategy.

- *Market drivers* include the extent to which (1) customer needs converge around the world, (2) customers procure on a global basis, (3) worldwide channels of distribution develop, (4) marketing platforms are transferable, and (5) *lead* countries can be identified in which most innovation takes place. They all define how customer behavior distribution patterns evolve.
- *Cost globalization* drivers such as the opportunity for exploiting (1) global scale or scope economies, (2) sourcing efficiencies reflecting differentials in costs between countries or regions, and (3) technology advantages shape the economics of the industry.

- *Competitive* drivers are defined by the actions of competing firms, including the extent to which (1) competitors from different continents enter the market, (2) they globalize their strategies and corporate capabilities, and (3) they create interdependence between geographical markets.
- *Government* drivers are comprised of factors such as (1) favorable trade policies, (2) a benign regulatory climate, and (3) common product and technology standards.

Market drivers. One aspect of globalization is the convergence of customer needs. As customers in different parts of the world increasingly demand similar products and services, opportunities for scale arise through the marketing of more or less standardized offerings. How common needs, tastes, and preferences will become varies greatly by product or service and depends on the importance of cultural variables, levels of disposable income, and the degree of homogeneity in the conditions in which the product is consumed used. Coca-Cola offers similar, but not identical, products around the world. While adapting its product line to local tastes and preferences, McDonald's has standardized many elements of its operations. Software, oil products, and accounting services increasingly look alike, no matter where they may be purchased. The key to exploiting such opportunities for scale lies in understanding which elements of the product or service can be standardized without sacrificing responsiveness to local preferences and conditions.

Global customers have emerged as needs continue to converge. Large corporations demand the same level of quality in the products and services they buy, no matter where in the world they are procured. In many industries, global distribution channels are emerging to satisfy an increasingly global customer base, further causing a convergence of needs. Finally, as consumption patterns become more homogeneous, global branding and marketing will become increasingly important to global success.

Cost drivers. The globalization of customer needs and scale and standardization opportunities have fundamentally altered many industries' economics. Economies of scale and scope and exploiting differences in factor costs for product development, manufacturing, and sourcing in different parts of the world have become important global strategy determinants. A single market is no longer large enough to support a competitive strategy globally in many industries.

Global scale and scope of economics can have far-reaching effects. The more economies of scale and scope shape incumbents' strategies in global industries, the harder it is for new entrants to develop a significant competitive threat. Thus, barriers to entry in such industries will get higher. Simultaneously, the rivalry within such industries is likely to increase, reflecting the broadening scope of competition among interdependent national and regional markets and the fact that true differentiation in such a competitive environment may be harder to achieve.

Competitive drivers. The globalization potential of an industry is also affected by factors such as (1) the degree to which total industry sales are made up by export or import volume, (2) the diversity of competitors in terms of their national origin, and (3) the extent to which major players have globalized their operations. High levels of trade, competitive diversity, and interdependence increase the potential for industry globalization. Industry evolution plays a role too. As the industry's underlying characteristics change, competitors will respond to enhance and preserve their competitive advantage. Sometimes, this causes industry globalization to accelerate. At other times, as in the worldwide major appliance industry, the globalization process may be reversed.

Government drivers. Government globalization drivers include factors such as (1) the presence or absence of favorable trade policies, (2) technical standards, (3) economic policies and regulations, and (4) government-operated or subsidized competitors or customers. They all shape the global competitive environment in an industry. In the past, multinationals almost exclusively relied on governments to negotiate the rules of global competition. As global competition's politics and economics become more closely intertwined, multinational companies are beginning to pay greater attention to the so-called nonmarket dimensions of their global strategies aimed at shaping the global competitive environment to their advantage. This broadening of the scope of global strategy reflects a subtle but real change in the balance of power between national governments and MNCs and is likely to have important consequences for how differences in policies and regulations affecting global competitiveness will be settled in the years to come.

The Growing Complexity of the Global Competitive Environment

Global strategy formulation is more complicated than purely domestic planning. Five factors contribute to this increase in complexity[23]:

- Global companies face multiple political, economic, legal, social, and cultural environments and various rates of change. A complicating factor is that governments work in concert with their militaries to advance economic aims in developing countries. In such situations, international firms must resist the temptation to benefit financially from opportunities that compromise their values. For example, a company would choose not to align with an oppressive regime in a foreign country, even though such an arrangement could produce highly favorable financial contracts with the host government when packaged with side payments.
- Interactions between the national and foreign environments are complicated by an increased number of national sovereignty issues and widely differing economic and social conditions.
- Geographic separation, cultural and national differences, and business practice variations tend to make communication and control efforts between headquarters and overseas affiliates difficult.
- Global firms face extreme competition because of differences in industry structures within and among countries.
- Global firms are sometimes restricted in their competitive options by various regional blocs and economic integrations, such as the European Economic Community, the European Free Trade Area, and the Latin American Free Trade Area.

Despite the growing complexity of the global competitive environment, several favorable global industry factors attract entry by major competitors, including

- The opportunity to create economies of scale
- The need to spread R&D expenditures over several markets to recover development costs
- The trend in many industries toward predominantly global firms that expect consistency of products and services across markets
- The evolution toward more homogeneous product needs across markets reducing the requirement of customizing the product for each market
- The presence of a small group of highly visible global competitors
- A low level of trade regulation and regulation regarding FDI

Benefits and Costs of Globalization

As this chapter has shown, globalization is a complex and sometimes controversial issue. Exhibit 1.2 summarizes its impact on the global economy. The benefits of globalization include:

1. *Increased trade has delivered a greater choice of goods. Free trade* has allowed countries to specialize in producing goods wherever they have a comparative advantage. When countries specialize, benefits include lower prices for consumers, increased choice of products, bigger export markets for domestic manufacturers, economies of scale, and increased competition.

2. *Free movement of labor.* Increased labor migration benefits both workers and recipient countries. If a country experiences high unemployment, there are increased opportunities to look for work elsewhere.

3. *Increased economies of scale.* Globalization enables goods to be produced in different parts of the world, thereby lowering average costs and prices for consumers.

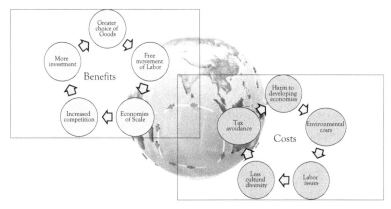

Exhibit 1.2 The benefit and costs of globalization

4. *Fostered greater competition.* Domestic monopolies used to be protected by a lack of competition. However, globalization means that firms face greater competition from foreign firms.

5. *Increased investment.* Globalization has made it easier for countries to attract short- and long-term investment. Investment by multinational companies can play a big role in improving the economies of developing countries.[24]

The costs of globalization include:

1. *Free trade can harm developing economies.* Developing countries often have trouble competing with developed countries fueling the argument that free trade benefits developed countries more. As a consequence, industries in developing countries may need protection from free trade to develop. On the other side, developing countries are often harmed by tariff protection imposed by Western economies on agricultural products.

2. *Environmental costs.* Globalization has increased the use of nonrenewable resources and contributed to increased pollution and global warming. Firms have also outsourced production to countries with less strict environmental standards.

3. *Labor issues.* Globalization enables workers to move more freely around the world. Some countries find it difficult to hold onto their best-skilled workers, attracted by higher wages elsewhere.

4. *Less cultural diversity.* Globalization has reduced cultural diversity. At the same time, it has also led to more options for some people.

5. *Tax competition and tax avoidance.* Multinational companies like Amazon and Google can set up offices in countries like Bermuda and Luxembourg with low corporate tax rates and then transfer profits through their subsidiaries. As a result, these firms pay little or no tax in the countries where they do most of their business, making it necessary for governments to increase value-added tax (VAT) or income taxes. This benefit to global companies can also be seen as unfair competition for domestic firms that do not have access to the same tax avoidance measures. The greater mobility of capital means that countries have sought to encourage inward investment by offering the lowest corporation tax (e.g., Ireland offers a very low tax rate). This has encouraged lower corporation taxes, which leads to higher forms of other taxes.[25]

CHAPTER 2

The Globalization of Companies and Competitive Advantage

Introduction

This chapter considers the globalization of companies and the primary sources of competitive advantage. We begin by considering the pressures on companies to expand globally. Next, we discuss three generic strategies for creating value in a global context: *adaptation, aggregation, and arbitrage.*[1] Finally, we consider how and why companies globalize in stages. In the first stage of globalization, companies move from a *domestic* to an *international* strategy. In the second stage of globalization, commitment to overseas markets increases, and the company adopts a *global* or a *multidomestic* strategy. Adopting a *transnational* strategy defines the final stage of company globalization.

Globalization Pressures on Companies

As shown in Exhibit 2.1, there are five main *imperatives* that drive companies to become more global: *to pursue growth, to increase efficiency, to secure knowledge or talent, to meet customer needs better, and to pre-empt or counter competition.*[2]

Growth. International expansion offers companies a chance to conquer new markets and reach more consumers, thereby increasing sales. Many industries in developed countries are maturing rapidly, thereby reducing growth opportunities. Consider household appliances. In the developed part of the world, most households own appliances such as stoves, ovens, washing machines, dryers, and refrigerators. Industry growth is, therefore, largely determined by population growth and product replacement.

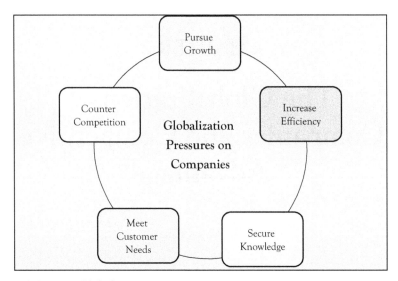

Exhibit 2.1 Globalization pressures on companies

By contrast, in developing markets, household penetration rates for major appliances are still low compared to Western standards, thereby offering significant growth opportunities for manufacturers.[3]

Extending a product lifecycle can be an important consideration in overseas expansion. Product sales generally go through four phases: launch, growth, maturity, and decline. An overseas expansion strategy can extend the cycle significantly. What is more, companies get a chance to reimagine strategic products or services they think will excel in a new market. A new, foreign market thereby allows the revitalization of products or services that may be close to maturity in other markets.

Global expansion is not just an option for large corporations. *Lemonade* is a New York-headquartered insurance company that offers renters insurance and home insurance policies. The company was founded in 2015 and made its initial public offering in 2020 on the New York Stock Exchange (NYSE). *Lemonade* takes a flat 25 percent fee from the *premium* that customers pay to cover its expenses. The company uses any amount above this fee to cover claims and make reinsurance purchases. The remaining proceeds, if any, are donated to a nonprofit organization of the customer's choice. The distribution of proceeds is in line with its mission of "transforming necessary evil into social good." Part of *Lemonade*'s appeal is that it provides insurance policies that customers feel good purchasing.

Since 2018, Lemonade has had a stated goal of expanding globally, responding to consumers' needs that are increasingly cosmopolitan in their views. By 2020, the company was operating across the U.S. and had established toeholds in Germany and the Netherlands. To ease their transition into new countries, Lemonade introduced Policy 2.0, which is software designed to meet European consumers' specific needs and make Lemonade's product as plain and as simple as possible to understand and use.[4]

Lemonade is continuing its expansion across Europe. It is taking advantage of the fact that European countries are bound by agreements that favor business expansion on the continent. A business license facilitates the global growth that Lemonade acquired in Holland that allows it to operate in 28 other European countries.

Efficiency. A global presence automatically expands a company's operations scale, giving it larger revenues and a larger asset base. A larger scale can help create a competitive advantage if a company undertakes the tough actions needed to convert scale into *economies of scale* by (1) spreading fixed costs, (2) reducing capital and operating costs, (3) pooling purchasing power, and (4) creating critical mass in a significant portion of the value chain. Whereas economies of scale primarily refer to efficiencies associated with supply-side changes, such as increasing or decreasing the scale of production, *economies of scope* refer to efficiencies typically associated with demand-side changes, such as increasing or decreasing the scope of marketing and distribution by entering new markets or regions, or by increasing the range of products and services offered. The economic value of global scope can be substantial when serving global customers with coordinated services and leveraging a company's expanded market power.[5]

Outsourcing and offshoring are strategies aimed at reducing costs. Under an outsourcing strategy, a company contracts with a party outside a company to perform services or manufacture products traditionally created in-house. Offshoring involves relocating a business activity to another country, generally to take advantage of labor cost differentials. While outsourcing and offshoring can reduce a firm's costs of doing business, its home country's job losses can devastate local communities, leading to negative publicity.

Knowledge and talent. Greater cross-border competition means that there is no firm capable of staying competitive by relying entirely on its internal resources and capabilities. While accessing external resources is common to firms in all sectors, the need to collaborate with external partners—suppliers, customers, competitors, universities, or institutions—is even more evident in technological sectors. More must be done with stretched research and development (R&D) budgets, as products and services increasingly involve multiple technologies. The need for a growing breadth of competencies has raised the costs and the associated risks of new product development. At the same time, firms must innovate faster to maintain their competitiveness in the market. As a result, for many companies, technological or R&D alliances are no longer viewed as an option but as a strategic necessity. Accessing external knowledge through R&D alliances can help firms reduce time-to-market and develop new product innovations that they could not have done internally. R&D alliances also can improve the quality and efficiency of new products and processes and facilitate access to new markets.

Foreign operations can be a reservoir of knowledge. Some locally created knowledge is relevant across multiple countries and, if leveraged effectively, can yield significant strategic benefits to a global enterprise such as (1) faster product and process innovation, (2) lower cost of innovation, and (3) reduced risk of competitive preemption. For example, Procter and Gamble's (P&G's) liquid Tide was developed as a joint effort by the company's U.S. employees (technology to suspend dirt in water), its Japanese subsidiary (cleaning agents), and its Belgian operations (agents that fight mineral salts found in hard water). Realizing the full potential of transferring and leveraging knowledge across borders is difficult. Significant geographic, cultural, linguistic distances often separate subsidiaries. The challenge is to create systematic and routine mechanisms to uncover opportunities for knowledge transfer.

Another major reason for going global is the opportunity to access new talent pools. In many cases, international labor can offer companies unique advantages in increased productivity, advanced language skills, diverse educational backgrounds, and more. For example, when Netflix expanded to Amsterdam, the company praised the city for enabling Netflix to hire multilingual and internationally minded employees who can expertly "understand consumers and cultures in all of the territories across Europe."

Also, international talent may improve innovation output within a company. That is one reason why foreign markets that welcome global entrepreneurs and skilled workers often have denser and more successful startup climates.

Globalization of customer needs and preferences. Through technology and experience, individual customers have become more aware of the rich variety of products and services available worldwide and want to buy them. Global travelers insist on consistent worldwide service from airlines, hotel chains, credit card companies, television news, and others. Global companies such as General Electric (GE) or DuPont insist that their suppliers—from raw material suppliers to advertising agencies to personnel recruitment companies—also globalize their approach and serve them whenever and wherever required. These trends force companies to adapt to changing customer needs and preferences and may require them to globalize their operations.

The globalization of competitors. Just as the globalization of customer needs and preferences compels companies to consider globalizing their business model, so does the globalization of one or more major competitors. Companies may use international expansion to gain a competitive edge over their opponents. For example, businesses that expand in markets where their competitors do not operate sometimes have a first-mover advantage, allowing them to build strong brand awareness with consumers before their competitors. International expansion can also help companies acquire access to new technologies and industry ecosystems, which may significantly improve their operations.

Finally, international business can also increase a company's perceived image. Global operations can help build name brand recognition to support future business scenarios, such as contract negotiations, new marketing campaigns, or additional expansion.

Other reasons to expand abroad include diversification and investment potential.

Countries and regions vary in terms of their stage of development, with different growth rates and potential. Companies may prefer not to concentrate all their efforts in a limited number of countries and wish to spread their risk. Such firms will look for markets that are different from those they already serve in terms of economic parameters such as growth rate, size, affluence of customers, stage of market development, and so on. Serving a portfolio of different markets can make revenues and profits more consistent and investment requirements more balanced.

Finally, companies considering international expansion should not forget about the additional investment opportunities that foreign markets can offer. For example, many firms can develop new resources and forge important connections by operating in global markets. Companies with multinational operations can sometimes benefit from lucrative investment opportunities that may not exist in their home country. For example, many governments around the world offer incentives for companies looking to invest in their country.

Mini-Case 2.1: Harley-Davidson—Globalizing to Survive[6]

Harley–Davidson is an American motorcycle brand with a rich history and loyal brand following. The company has traditionally focused on heavyweight motorcycles with engine displacements greater than 700 cm^3 but—to remain competitive—recently has broadened its product offerings to include mid-sized and smaller motorcycles. Due to Harley-Davidson's customers' passion for the brand, it has successfully licensed a wide range of other products, including apparel, home decor, toys, accessories, and more.

In the last few years, the company has been challenged by changes in its primary market's socio-cultural environment—the United States—and the legal environment internationally and domestically in the form of trade barriers. In the United States, *gas-guzzling hogs* are no longer appealing to younger consumers. In response, the company has (1) opened assembly plants in India to get around some of the tariffs and (2) entered Brazil to take advantage of the free trade zone. However, the company is still facing the impact of steel tariffs on U.S. imports, which has added millions to Harley-Davidson's costs.

Harley-Davidson is also eying growth abroad. Developing countries represent an increasingly attractive opportunity as improved infrastructures in these countries allow for better distribution and motorcycles usage.

The *AAA* Global Strategy Framework[7]

Pankaj Ghemawat offers three generic approaches to developing a global competitive advantage (see Exhibit 2.2). *Adaptation* strategies seek to increase revenues and market share by tailoring one or more components of a company's business model to suit local requirements or preferences. *Aggregation* strategies focus on achieving economies of scale or scope by creating regional or global efficiencies. They typically involve standardizing a significant portion of the value proposition and grouping together development and production processes. *Arbitrage* is about exploiting economic or other differences between national or regional markets, usually by locating separate parts of the supply chain in different places.

Adaptation. Adaptation—creating global value by changing one or more elements of a company's business model to meet local requirements or preferences—is probably the most widely used global strategy. The reason is that some degree of adaptation is essential or unavoidable for virtually all products in all parts of the world. A good example is provided by McDonald's. This global company adapts its menus to the locations

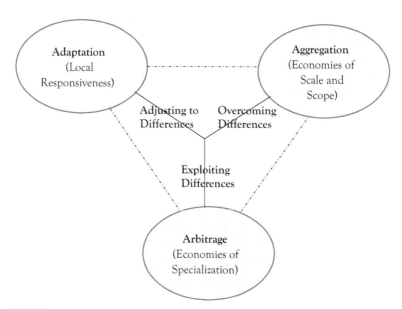

Exhibit 2.2 Adaptation, aggregation, and arbitrage Adapted from Ghemawat, P. 2007. Redefining Global Strategy. Harvard Business School Press.

the brand is targeting. For example, there are many kosher restaurants in Israel and Argentina and halal branches in Pakistan, Malaysia, and other predominantly Muslim countries worldwide. In India, no beef or pork products are sold in deference to Hindu and Islamic beliefs and customs. Also, consider the construction adhesive industry. The packaging in the United States informs customers how many square feet it will cover; the same package in Europe must do so in square meters. Even commodities such as cement are not immune; its pricing in different geographies reflects local energy and transportation costs and what percent is bought in bulk.

Adaptation strategies can have many foci, including *variation, focus, externalization, design, and focus* (see Exhibit 2.3).

Variation strategies involve making changes in *products and services* and adjusting *policies, business positioning,* and *success expectations.* For example, Whirlpool offers smaller washers and dryers in Europe than in the United States, reflecting the space constraints prevalent in many European homes. The need to consider adapting *policies* is less obvious. An example is Google's dilemma in China to conform to local censorship rules. Changing a company's overall *positioning* in a country goes well beyond changing products or even policies. Initially, Coke did little more

Adaptation	Aggregation	Arbitrage
Variation		Performance Enhancement
Focus: Reduce Need for Adaptation	Economies of Scale	
Externalization: Reduce Burden of Adaptation		Cost Reduction
Design: Reduce Cost of Adaptation	Economies of Scope	
Innovation: Improve on Existing Adaptation		Risk Reduction

Exhibit 2.3 AAA strategies and their variants

than *skim the cream* off big emerging markets such as India and China. It successfully changed to a "lower margin—higher volume" strategy that involved lowering price points, reducing costs, and expanding distribution to boost volume and market share. For example, changing expectations with investors or partners about a particular country's growth rate is also a prevalent variation.

The second type of adaptation focuses on particular products, geographies, or vertical stages of the value chain, or market segments to reduce the impact of differences across regions. A *product* focus recognizes that wide differences can exist *within* broad product categories in the degree of variation required to compete effectively in local markets. Action films such as *The Gentlemen* or *Bad Boys for Life* need far less if any adaptation than local newscasts, for example. Restriction of *geographic* scope can focus on countries where relatively little adaptation of the domestic value proposition is required. A *vertical* focus strategy involves limiting a company's direct involvement in the supply chain's specific steps, while outsourcing others. Finally, a *segment* focus involves targeting a more limited customer base. Using this strategy, a company realizes that it will appeal to a smaller market segment or different distributor network from those in the domestic market, unless it modifies its products. Many luxury goods manufacturers employ this approach.

Whereas focus strategies overcome regional differences by narrowing the scope, *externalization* strategies transfer responsibility for specific parts of a company's business model to partner companies to accommodate local requirements, lower cost, or reduce risk. Options for achieving externalization include *strategic alliances, franchising, user adaptation, and networking.* Eli Lilly, for example, extensively uses *strategic alliances* abroad for drug development and testing. McDonald's growth strategy abroad uses *franchising* as well as company-owned stores. And, software companies depend heavily on user adaptation and networking to develop applications for their basic software platforms.

The fourth type of adaptation focuses on *design* to reduce costs. Manufacturing costs can often be achieved by introducing design *flexibility* to overcome supply differences. Introducing standard product *platforms* and *modularity* in components also helps to reduce costs.

The fifth approach to adaptation is *innovation,* aiming to enhance adaptation efforts' effectiveness through cost reduction or value enhancement. For instance, IKEA's flat-pack design, which has reduced the geographic distance by cutting transportation costs, has helped the company expand more effectively into foreign markets.

Aggregation. Aggregation is about creating *economies of scale or scope* as a way of dealing with differences. The objective is to exploit similarities among geographies rather than to adapt to differences. Complete standardization destroys concurrent adaptation approaches. Therefore, the key is to identify ways to introduce economies of scale and scope into the global business model without compromising local responsiveness. For example, Walmart's economies of scale are derived from buying its merchandise in bulk, usually at significant discounts. To do business with Walmart is important to suppliers—its products are seen by millions of shoppers each day across the globe. This benefit allows Walmart to force suppliers to accept low prices to remain in its good standing.

Adopting a *regional* approach to globalizing the business model is probably the most widely used aggregation strategy. As discussed earlier, *regionalization* or *semiglobalization* applies to many aspects of globalization—from investment and communication patterns to trade. Even when companies have a significant presence in more than one region, competitive interactions are often regionally focused. Nestle is a good example of a company that uses regionalization. The company's Indian subsidiary—Nestle India—has adopted a regional cluster-based approach to developing tailor-made brand, marketing, and distribution strategies to address the needs of consumers in specific geographies. The company has created virtual teams for each cluster responsible for tailor-made strategies for brands, distribution, channel strategy, marketing, and promotion relevant to each region.[8] Dutch electronics giant Philips created a global competitive advantage for its Norelco shaver product line by centralizing global production in a few strategically located plants. By locating plants in each part of the triad, the company realized significant economies of scale.

Global corporate branding over product branding is another powerful way to create economies of scale and scope. A global brand is the brand name of a product that has worldwide recognition. Economies of scope are realized to the extent a brand is recognized, accepted, and trusted across borders. Some of the world's most-recognized brands include Coca-Cola, IBM, Microsoft, GE, Nokia, McDonald's, Google, Toyota, Intel, and Disney. As these examples show, geographic aggregation strategies have potential applications for every major business model component.

Geographic aggregation is not the only way to generate economies of scale or scope. Other, nongeographic dimensions of the CAGE framework—*cultural, administrative or political, and economic*—also lend themselves to aggregation strategies. For example, major book publishers publish their bestsellers in just a few languages, knowing that readers will accept a book in their second language (*cultural* aggregation). Pharmaceutical companies seeking to market new drugs in Europe must satisfy a few selected countries' regulatory requirements to qualify for a license to distribute throughout the European Union (EU) (*administrative* aggregation).

Arbitrage. A third generic strategy for creating a global advantage is *arbitrage*. Arbitrage is about exploiting differences between national or regional markets, usually by locating separate parts of the supply chain in a different country. Exploiting differences in labor costs—through outsourcing and offshoring—is probably the most common form of *economic* arbitrage. This strategy is widely used in labor-intensive (garments) and high-technology (flat-screen TVs) industries. Another form of economic arbitrage is the exploitation of differences in knowledge. Many Western companies have established R&D and software development centers in India because of the availability of relevant talent. Finally, an arbitrage strategy can improve a company's risk profile by spreading operations over several countries or regions.

Favorable effects related to country or place of origin have long supplied a basis for *cultural arbitrage*. For example, an association with French culture has long been an international success factor for fashion items, perfumes, wines, and foods, whereas Italian products connote a high level of stylishness. Similarly, fast-food products and drive-through restaurants are mainly associated with U.S. culture.

Legal, institutional, and political differences between countries or regions create opportunities for *administrative* arbitrage. Administrative arbitrage encompasses all the measures that companies take regarding taxes and regulations, including environmental regulations. Taxation is a major factor in companies' geographic decisions because of the large variations in tax rates worldwide.

As globalization advances, the scope for *geographic* arbitrage—the leveraging of geographic differences—has been diminished but not fully eliminated. For example, air transportation has created a global flower market where flowers from favorable growing regions can be auctioned year-round in Aalsmeer, the Netherlands, and flown to customers worldwide while still fresh.

Which A Strategy Should a Company Use?[9]

A company's financial statements can be a useful guide to signaling which of the *A* strategies will have the greatest potential to create global value. Consumer goods manufacturers with large marketing budgets use adaptation strategies to improve their market share abroad. Firms that engage heavily in R&D and have high levels of fixed costs, such as pharmaceutical companies, should consider centralizing and locating their laboratories in talent-rich, cost-effective locations worldwide. Firms that rely heavily on branding and do a lot of advertising, such as food companies, often need to engage in considerable adaptation to local markets. For firms whose operations are labor-intensive such as apparel manufacturers, arbitrage will be of particular interest because labor costs can vary greatly from country to country.

Which *A* strategy a company emphasizes also depends on its globalization history. Companies that start their globalization on the supply side of their business model, that is, seeking to lower cost or access new knowledge, typically focus on aggregation and arbitrage to create global value. Firms that start their globalization by exporting are immediately faced with adaptation challenges.

P&G is an example of a company that has successfully applied all three A strategies in different parts of its business model in a coordinated manner. P&G's global business units sell-through market development organizations that are aggregated up to the regional level. It adapts its value proposition to important markets and competes—through global branding, R&D, and sourcing—based on aggregation. Its use of arbitrage—mostly through outsourcing activities invisible to the final consumer—is important to keeping costs under control and enhancing P&G's global competitive advantage.

Moving From A to AA to AAA

From an A to AA strategy. Although most companies start by focusing on just one *A* at any given time, increased competition has forced companies to pursue two or even all three of the As. Doing so presents special challenges because there are inherent tensions between all three approaches. Companies focused on aggregation seek economies of scale and scope through standardization of products and processes and centralization of decision making. On the other hand, companies using adaptation strategies need to tap local knowledge and involve local creative partners in adapting their business model to suit local needs and preferences. As a result, companies seeking adaptation are less concerned with economies of scale and scope and often more decentralized. These tensions show that the pursuit of *AA* strategies or even an *AAA* approach requires considerable organizational and managerial flexibility.[10]

International business machines (IBM) addressed the tensions between *adaptation and aggregation* by using different As of the AAA framework at *various points in expanding globally.* The company uses adaptation to enter the various international markets it operates in—now more than 170 countries.[11] Typically, IBM enters international markets by launching a mini IBM in the foreign country targeted that guides the adaptation strategy to match its customers' local needs and preferences. Once established, it begins to look regionally for aggregation opportunities through economies of scale and scope.

Tata Consultancy Services (TCS), headquartered in Mumbai, India, successfully combined *aggregation and arbitrage* within its business model. The company uses an arbitrage strategy by exporting software service export to countries where labor costs are high. It has supplemented this strategy with an *aggregation* component by developing a new global delivery structure based on three types of software development centers. Global centers in India cater to large accounts; regional centers based in Hungary and Brazil specialize in language and cultural aspects of software support, while Phoenix and Boston centers support U.S. technology corridors with a close location.[12]

Developing a AAA strategy. As shown in Exhibit 2.4, organizational tensions between the three A strategies seriously constrain companies to use all three simultaneously with great effectiveness. The different A strategies are focused on different sources of competitive advantage. Two of them (adaptation and aggregation) seek to minimize CAGE effects, whereas the other (arbitrage) seeks to exploit them. The implementation of the different A strategies calls for different loci of coordination and has different organization champions. Finally, there are considerable differences associated with the strategy levers associated with each A strategy. As a consequence, attempts to implement all three strategies at the same time (1) stretch a firm's managerial bandwidth, (2) force a company to operate with multiple corporate cultures, and (3) can create opportunities for competitors to undercut a company's overall competitiveness.

	Adaptation	Aggregation	Arbitrage
Competitive Advantage	Local Responsiveness	Economies of Scale and Scope	Economies of Specialization
Configuration	Country Selection: Reduce CAGE effects		Exploit CAGE effects
Coordination	By country	By business or region	By function
Threats	Too much localization	Too much standardization	Narrowing spreads
Change Blockers	Entrenched country heads	Powerful business unit or region heads	Heads of key functions
Corporate Diplomacy	Apply discretion with country heads	Avoid homogenization or HQ dominance	Address displacement of key suppliers
Strategy Levers	Variation Decentralization Partnership Flexibility Innovation	Regions Product or Business Platforms Confidence	CAGE factors

Exhibit 2.4 Differences among the A strategies

Thus, to consider an AAA strategy, a company must find ways to mitigate the tensions between adaptation, aggregation, and arbitrage.

Companies that have successfully adopted a combination of all three As typically spent years in trial-and-error mode. P&G is a good example. P&G started its global expansion with an adaptation–arbitrage strategy. The company focused extensively on locational R&D and creating autonomous mini P&G branches in each location. Meanwhile, it outsourced a certain part of the production process to cheaper locations. Later, when this localization strategy started to create too much redundancy across regions, P&G added aggregation by adopting a matrix organization structure to focus on exploiting synergies across regional business units and product lines.[13]

Pitfalls and Lessons in Applying the AAA Framework

As noted, the implementation of the AAA framework presents considerable challenges. As a consequence, companies should consider:

1. *Focusing on one or two of the As.* While it is possible to make progress on all three As, companies or business units or divisions usually have to focus on one or at most two A's to build competitive advantage.

2. *Making sure the new elements of a strategy are a good fit organizationally.* If a strategy introduces new elements, companies should pay particular attention to how well they work with other things the organization is doing. IBM has grown its staff in India much faster than other international competitors such as Accenture. But quickly molding this workforce into an efficient organization with high delivery standards and a sense of connection to the parent company is a critical challenge.

3. *Employing multiple integration mechanisms.* The pursuit of more than one of the As requires creativity and breadth in thinking about integration mechanisms. Given the stakes, these factors cannot be left to chance.

4. *Thinking about externalizing integration.* IBM and other firms illustrate that some externalization is a key part of most

ambitious global strategies. Externalization can take several forms such as (1) joint ventures in advanced semiconductor research, development, and manufacturing; (2) links to and support of Linux and other efforts at open innovation; (3) outsourcing of hardware to contract manufacturers and services to business partners; and (4) IBM's relationship with Lenovo in personal computers.

5. *Knowing when not to integrate.* Some integration is usually good, but more integration is not always better.

Mini-Case 2.2: SoFi—Adaptation and Arbitrage at Work

Social Finance (SoFi) is an online personal finance company whose business strategy was originally centered on refinancing student education loans. Outstanding student debt in the United States had been growing tremendously, reaching 1.54 trillion U.S. dollars in early 2020. Financial technology (fintech) solutions helped meet student loan needs, explaining the industry's rapid growth in the preceding decade. SoFi generated revenue by charging a small fee to merchants for the use of their cards, by earning interest on money in consumer spending accounts, and by selling loan packages to institutions that acted as third-party investors. The company generated over 400 million U.S. dollars in revenue in 2019 and had raised over three billion U.S. dollars in equity financing. By 2020, SoFi had acquired over a million members.

SoFi helped refinance and consolidate student loans, both federal and private. Customers applied through a simple online process, and they benefited from SoFi's seven-day a week customer support. It allowed borrowers to defer their loans if they were enrolled at least part time in a graduate program or actively serving in the military. SoFi offered low-interest rates and enabled its customers to pay fixed amounts for their loans ranging from 5,000 to 100,000 U.S. dollars.

Customers also benefited from SoFi's flexibility because the financial institution tried to meet their needs and make it easier for them to get the money they needed. For example, if customers lost their job, SoFi would defer their payments and even help them find a new job. In addition to loans, bank accounts, mortgages, and payments infrastructures, SoFi also provided insurance. The company offered several insurance products (life insurance, auto insurance, homeowners' and renters' insurance) through partnerships with several third-party insurance companies.

The typical credit score of an approved borrower or cosigner was 700 or higher. There was no minimum income required for approval, but SoFi studied the borrower's free cash flow to determine eligibility. Generally, applicants were U.S. citizens or permanent residents, and they had graduated with an associate degree or higher.[14] Nearly 400,000 graduate students had refinanced their student debt through SoFi. The company also helped them pay for graduate school, offering private student loans at a competitive rate.

SoFi's success was particularly impressive because it was achieved after overcoming a major setback. In 2018, the Federal Trade Commission (FTC) filed a complaint against Sofi, claiming that the company misled customers regarding how much they could save with SoFi's services. SoFi settled with the FTC. Although it avoided paying penalties, it was barred from making any claim about how much the consumer would save that was not backed with clear evidence.

Encouraged by its profitability in fintech, SoFi reformulated its corporate strategy to diversify its offerings. Customers were increasingly drawn to SoFi for mortgages, loans, debit cards, and cryptocurrency trading. In 2020, the company announced its plan to expand globally. As a financial capital in Asia and a renowned financial center, Hong Kong stood out as a great location to start the global expansion.[15] SoFi's first move toward this goal was acquiring 8Securities, a trading platform based in Hong Kong.[16] Many businesses and individuals, including investors in Hong Kong, could take advantage of the SoFi offerings. As part of the expansion plan, the company launched SoFi Invest in Hong Kong, the only investing platform that offered full access to a wide range of services, from brokerage and exchange traded funds (ETFs) to automated investing, all commission-free.

With the changes prompted by the COVID-19 pandemic in 2020, the global shift toward remote work, and the need for additional online-based tools, SoFi decided to expand into nonconsumer-facing services. It acquired Galileo Technologies, which provided payment infrastructure for multiple companies in the financial technology industry, such as Robinhood, Chime, or TransferWise. Galileo offered debit, credit, prepaid and virtual cards, cryptocurrency, contactless payments, mobile technology, fraud protection, and advanced analytics. Adding the company under SoFi's umbrella broadened the array of services that SoFi offered, enabling them to capture a larger customer base. The acquisitions also supported SoFi's plan to expand internationally while diversifying its revenue streams to reduce its investment risk.

Stages in the Globalization of Companies

Going global is often described in incremental terms as a more or less gradual process, starting with increased exports or global sourcing, followed by a modest international presence, growing into a multinational organization, and ultimately evolving into a global posture. This appearance of gradualism, however, is deceptive. It obscures the key changes globalization requires in a company's mission, core competencies, structure, processes, and culture. Consequently, it leads managers to underestimate the enormous differences between managing international operations, a multinational enterprise, and managing a global corporation.

A domestic focus is much simpler to implement than pursuing international business objectives. Domestic operations are subject only to a domestic set of rules and requirements. Market analysis has a narrower focus when coping with fewer regions than predicting several cultures' needs and preferences across various countries. As a result, domestic businesses can often establish and capitalize on a market niche. Domestic businesses follow the home country's securities laws and generally construct their financial reports according to the country's generally accepted accounting principles. Domestic businesses manage their balance sheets without considering the currency, tax regulations, and financial reporting differences of other countries like an international company would.

International business requires dealing with foreign stakeholders, employees, consumers, and governments. Therefore, managers need to consider many factors when conducting business in global markets, such as customers' local needs and preferences, the competitive environment, supply chain management challenges, government rules and regulations, and marketing issues. To successfully expand their consumer base and increase profitability through internationalization, companies need to spend the necessary time and resources to understand global market opportunities and choose the proper international business strategies.

Doing business internationally, therefore, is different from doing business at home. New skills need to be learned and knowledge acquired about the countries a company wishes to enter. Firms need to learn about the different laws and regulations, customer needs and preferences, buying habits, and adapt their business model to appeal to the new countries they are targeting. Key differences include:

- *Politics or government or legal systems.* Although competing in international markets offers important potential benefits, such as access to new customers, the opportunity to lower costs, and the diversification of business risk, going overseas also presents considerable challenges. Political risk refers to the potential for government upheaval or business interference. For example, the term *Arab Spring* has been used to refer to a series of uprisings in 2011 in the Middle East. Political instability makes it difficult for firms to plan for the future. Over time, a government could become increasingly hostile to foreign businesses by imposing new taxes and new regulations. In extreme cases, a firm's assets in a country are seized by the national government. For example, in recent years, Venezuela has nationalized foreign-controlled operations in the oil, cement, steel, and glass industries. Countries with the highest levels of political risk tend to have governments that are so unstable that few foreign companies are willing to enter them. That said, high levels of political risk are also present in several of the world's important emerging economies, including India, the Philippines, Russia, and Indonesia. The dilemma for firms is that these high-risk countries also offer enormous growth opportunities. Finally, no two countries have the same political and legal systems. Each government has its policies related to the presence of foreign firms and products. The key is to understand that once a company enters a foreign market, it must abide by the country's rules and laws, not the ones in its home market. These laws and regulations can severely impact the potential long-term success of a business.[17,18]

- *Cultures.* Cultural risk refers to the risks posed by differences in language, customs, norms, and customer preferences. The history of business has many examples of cultural differences that undermined companies. For example, a laundry detergent company was surprised by its poor sales in the Middle East. Executives believed that their product was promoted using print advertisements that showed dirty clothing on the left, a box of detergent in the middle, and clean clothing on the right. However, unlike English and other Western languages, the languages used in the Middle East, such as Hebrew and Arabic, involve reading from right to left. To consumers, the implication of the detergent ads was that the product could be used to take clean clothes and make them dirty. As this example shows, understanding both the social and business culture in another country is key to success. Therefore, it is important to include research on the country's culture(s) a firm intends to sell before entering the market.[19]

- *Level and nature of competition.* The level of competition a company will experience in foreign markets is likely to be more dynamic and complex than in domestic markets. Competition may exist from various sources, and the nature of competition may change from country to country. Competition may be encouraged or discouraged in favor of cooperation, and buyer–seller relationships may be friendly or hostile. When companies compete for access to the latest technology, the technological innovation level can be an important aspect of the competitive environment.

- *Transportation infrastructure and media.* Business infrastructure in foreign markets is likely to be at different levels of development. This can impact a firm's ability to get products to market. It is important to research a new target market and understand how goods are moved within the country before a company commits to that market. If advertising and promotion are critical components of a firm's business model, it is important to know the types of media available and the kinds of media the target market uses to gain information about products and services offered. In many regions of the world, only a limited number of potential customers are connected to the Internet, and not every customer can read and write. This means firms need to research the most appropriate media for the chosen target market.

The Bartlett–Ghoshal Matrix

A frequently used framework to distinguish between four types of international companies is the Bartlett and Ghoshal matrix. It characterizes firms based on two criteria: *global integration* and *local responsiveness* (see Exhibit 2.5). Businesses that are highly globally integrated seek to reduce costs as much as possible by creating economies of

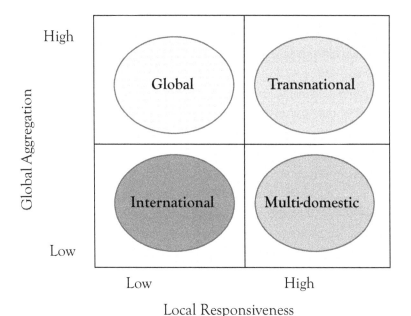

Exhibit 2.5 Bartlett–Ghoshal matrix

scale through a more standardized product offering worldwide. Companies that are locally responsive seek to adapt products and services to specific local needs. Although these strategic options appear to be mutually exclusive, some companies are trying to be both globally integrated and locally responsive. Together, these two factors define four types of strategies that internationally operating businesses can pursue: *international, multidomestic, global, and transnational* strategies.[20]

International companies. An *international* strategy is focused on exporting products and services to foreign markets or importing goods and resources from other countries for domestic use. Companies that employ an international strategy are often headquartered exclusively in their country of origin and typically do not invest in staff and facilities overseas. However, this model is not without significant challenges, like establishing sales and administrative offices in major cities internationally, managing global logistics, and ensuring compliance with foreign manufacturing and trade regulations.

As shown in Exhibit 2.5, *international* companies typically operate with a low degree of integration and local responsiveness. Firms that mainly export or license have little need for local adaption and global integration. Products are produced in the company's home country and shipped to customers all over the world. If subsidiaries operate, they function more like local channels through which the products are being sold to the end-consumer.

An international strategy may be the most common strategy because it requires the least amount of overhead. As a company's globalization develops further, many international companies evolve into multidomestic, global, or transnational companies. The international model is unsophisticated and unsustainable if the company further globalizes and therefore is usually transitory. In the short term, this organizational form may be viable when the need for localization and local responsiveness is very low. The potential for aggregation economies is also low. Large wine producers are good examples of international companies.

Multidomestic companies. For a business to adopt a *multidomestic* business strategy, it must establish its presence in one or more foreign markets and tailor its products or services to the local customer base.

In moving from an international to a multidomestic strategy, a business typically starts by establishing a presence in one or more foreign market(s) and adapting its products or services to a local market. As opposed to marketing foreign products to customers who may not initially recognize or understand them, companies modify their offerings and reposition their marketing strategies to meet local needs and preferences. A complicating factor is that they may need distinctive strategies for each of these markets because customer demand and competition are different in each country. Competitive advantage, therefore, is determined *separately for each country.*

Multidomestic businesses usually keep their company headquarters in their country of origin. Often, they establish overseas subsidiaries, which are better equipped to offer foreign consumers region-specific versions of their products and services. Multidomestic companies typically employ country-specific strategies with only modest international coordination or knowledge transfer from the central headquarters. Each country subsidiary typically makes key decisions about local strategy, resource allocation, decision making, knowledge generation, transfer, and procurement with little value-added from the corporate headquarters. Consequently, the pure multidomestic organizational structure ranks high on local adaptation and low on global aggregation. Like the international model, the traditional multidomestic organizational structure is not well suited to a globally competitive environment in which standardization, global integration, and economies of scale and scope are critical. However, this model is still viable in situations where local responsiveness, local differentiation, and local adaptation are important. There are limited opportunities for global knowledge transfer, economies of scale, and economies of scope. As with the international model, the pure multidomestic company sometimes represents a transitory organizational structure.

Multidomestic strategies are frequently used by food and beverage companies. For example, the Kraft Heinz Company makes a specialized version of its ketchup for customers in India to match the nation's preferences for a different blend of spices. However, these adjustments are often expensive and can incur a certain financial risk level, especially when a company wishes to launch unproven products in a new market.

Companies, therefore, only utilize this expansion strategy in a limited number of countries.

Global companies. Companies following a global strategy seek to leverage economies of scale to boost their reach and revenue. Global companies attempt to standardize their products and services as much as possible to minimize costs and reach as broad an international customer base as possible. Global companies tend to maintain a central office or headquarters in their country of origin while also establishing operations worldwide. Pharmaceutical companies such as Pfizer can be considered global companies.

Even when they try to keep essential aspects of their products and services intact, companies using a global strategy typically have to make some practical small-scale adjustments to penetrate international markets. For example, software companies need to adjust the language used in their products. By contrast, fast-food companies may add, remove, or change the name of certain menu items to suit local markets better while keeping their core items and global message intact. Thus, a traditional *global* company is the opposite of a traditional multidomestic company. It describes companies with globally integrated operations designed to take advantage of economies of scale and scope by the following standardization and exploiting global efficiencies.[21] By globalizing operations and competing in global markets, these companies aim to reduce cost—in R&D, manufacturing, production, procurement, and inventory. They also seek to enhance customer preference through global products and brands and obtain competitive leverage. Key strategic decisions are typically made at corporate headquarters. In the global aggregation or local adaptation matrix, the pure global company scores high on global aggregation (integration) and low on local adaptation (localization).

Transnational companies. A *transnational* business strategy can be seen as a combination of global and multidomestic strategies. Typically, a transnational company keeps its headquarters and core technologies in its country of origin, but also considers allows establishing full-scale operations in foreign markets. The decision-making, production, and sales responsibilities are evenly distributed to individual facilities in these different markets, allowing companies to have separate marketing, research, and development departments to respond to local consumers' needs.

A transnational company aims to maximize local responsiveness but also to gain benefits from global integration. Even though this appears contradictory, this is made possible by considering the entire whole value chain. Transnational companies often seek to create economies of scale upstream in the value chain and use more locally adaptive approaches in downstream activities such as marketing and sales. In terms of organizational design, a transnational company typically has an integrated and interdependent network of subsidiaries worldwide. These subsidiaries have strategic roles and act as centers of excellence. Because of efficient knowledge and expertise exchange between subsidiaries, a transnational company can meet both strategic objectives.

A transnational company's biggest challenge is identifying the best management tactics for achieving positive economies of scale and increased efficiency. Having many inter-organizational entities collaborating in dozens of foreign markets requires a significant start-up investment. Costs are driven by foreign legal and regulatory concerns, hiring new employees, and buying or renting offices and production spaces. Therefore, this strategy is more complex than others because pressures to reduce costs are combined with establishing value-added activities to gain leverage competitiveness in each local market.[22] Larger corporations—such as Unilever, GE, and P&G—employ a transnational strategy to invest in research and development in foreign markets and establish production, manufacturing, sales, and marketing divisions in these regions.

The Extended Bartlett–Ghoshal Matrix

Given the limitations of each of the aforementioned strategies in terms of either their global competitiveness or their implementability, many companies have settled on hybrid strategies that are more easily managed than the pure transnational model but still target the simultaneous pursuit of global integration and local responsiveness. Two of these have been labeled *modern multidomestic* and *modern global* models.

Exhibit 2.6 shows that the *modern multidomestic* model is an updated version of the traditional (pure) multidomestic model, including a more significant role for the corporate headquarters. Its major characteristic is a matrix organizational structure focusing on operational decentralization,

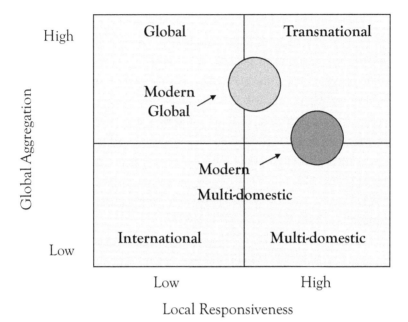

Exhibit 2.6 Extended Bartlett–Ghoshal matrix

local adaptation, product differentiation, and local responsiveness. The resulting model, in which national subsidiaries have significant autonomy, allows companies to maintain their local responsiveness and their ability to differentiate and adapt to local environments. Simultaneously, in the modern multidomestic model, the center is critical to enhancing competitive strength. Whereas the subsidiary's role is to be locally responsive, the center's role is to enhance global integration by developing global corporate and competitive strategies. The center is also actively involved in resource allocation, selecting markets, developing strategic analysis, mergers, and acquisitions, decisions regarding R&D and technology matters. An example of a modern multidomestic company is Nestlé.

The *modern global* company is rooted in the traditional global form but gives a more significant role in decision making to the country's subsidiaries. Headquarters is focused on creating a high level of global integration by pursuing low-cost sourcing options, opportunities for global scale and scope, product standardization, and global technology sharing. Modern global companies operate with an explicit, overarching global corporate strategy. But unlike the traditional (pure) global model, a modern global company makes more effective use of its subsidiaries to provide local responsiveness. As traditional global firms evolve into modern global enterprises, they tend to focus more on strategic coordination and integration of core competencies worldwide. Protecting home country control becomes less important. Modern global corporations may disperse R&D, manufacture and production, and marketing around the globe. This helps ensure flexibility in the face of changing factor costs for labor, raw materials, exchange rates, and hiring talent worldwide. P&G is an example of a modern global company.

CHAPTER 3

The Globalization of Opportunity and Risk

Introduction

The rise of emerging markets (EMs) has created major opportunities—for the West as well as developing countries. The term *emerging markets* refers to economies that experience considerable economic growth and possess some, but not all, characteristics of a developed economy. Therefore, EMs are transitioning from the *developing* phase to the *developed* phase.

As global opportunities have increased, so has global risk. Climate change, global warming, environmental pressures, and resource scarcity all have increased substantially—in part due to globalization. In addition, several megatrends in nature, technology, and society—some beyond environmental, social, and cultural factors—increasingly influence and shape the world. Sometimes referred to as *global tectonics*, they shift the ground beneath our feet, much like the earth's tectonic plates, and with it, the global competitive landscape. These forces are global, sustained, and will impact the future of business, the economy, society, culture, and our personal lives.

We conclude the chapter with an overview of the global regulatory climate—the institutions, laws, and treaties that govern global economic activity.

Emerging Markets: Engines of Global Growth

EMs have become the world's primary drivers of global growth and wealth accumulation. They cover a dominant share of the world's population and natural resources and are home to the world's largest pool of future consumers.[1] Many developing countries that were once associated with high volatility and risk levels have liberalized their policies and instituted reforms in their economies, infrastructure, and governance. The world's economy is often depicted as consisting of three parts of a pyramid: maturing developed economies with the smallest number of consumers and high per capita income levels, high-growth EMs with a growing middle class and rising per capita incomes, and the *bottom (or base) of the pyramid* (BOP) economies, which are home to the vast majority of people and still struggling with high levels of poverty.

By adopting new technologies and manufacturing techniques, countries such as China, Brazil, and India have become important production locations. As their purchasing power continues to increase, these countries are becoming important consumer markets. At the same time, they are also becoming formidable competitors. As developed countries are increasingly faced with limited growth options in the developed world, EMs offer attractive growth opportunities. Analyzing EMs and identifying opportunities within these markets has become a major priority for many companies.

The term *emerging market* was coined by Antoine van Agtmael, an economist at the World Bank, to refer to fast-growing economies with rapid industrialization.[2]

Of the nearly 200 countries globally, more than 160, or 80 percent, are classified as *emerging*, based on their per capita gross domestic product (GDP). The International Monetary Fund (IMF) maintains a useful list of emerging and developing economies. At the same time, the World Bank references those countries that may be considered low-income, lower-middle-income, or upper-middle-income.[3,4] Such definitions are useful but do not fully reflect their dynamism and rapid development, however.[5]

In addition to per capita GDP, a second key factor defining EMs, is the degree of development of these countries' financial markets. It is not always the case that per capita GDP correlates with financial depth or sophistication. Several countries with high GDP per capita but relatively underdeveloped financial markets are frequently classified as EMs, including several oil-rich Middle Eastern countries. The focus on financial development is critical, as the evolution of EMs (including financial institutions and instruments) correlates highly with economic development.

The lists of EMs have changed in recent years, as the countries included are often selected according to growth indicators and projections annually. The lists also vary between institutions, reflecting the use of different indicators and growth projections. BRICS is an acronym created by Goldman Sachs for the combined economies of Brazil, Russia, India, China, and South Africa. In 2020, Morgan Stanley updated its Emerging Market Index list to include 26 countries as EMs: Argentina, Brazil, Chile, China, Colombia, Czech Republic, Egypt, Greece, Hungary, India, Indonesia, Korea, Malaysia, Mexico, Pakistan, Peru, Philippines, Poland, Qatar, Russia, Saudi Arabia, South Africa, Taiwan, Thailand, Turkey, and the United Arab Emirates.

Comparing Emerging and Developed Economies

EMs are countries or regions that are transitioning from developing to developed markets. Markets that have (1) started an economic reform process aimed at alleviating poverty, poor infrastructure, and overpopulation; (2) achieved steady growth in the gross national product (GNP) per capita; and (3) increased their integration in the global economy, qualify as EMs.

EMs can be compared along several dimensions. Standards of living, literacy rates, and the quality of infrastructure are higher in developed nations. Growth rates, unemployment, and poverty levels are generally higher in developing countries. On the other hand, emerging nations are less stable in economic and political terms and are, in many ways, a *work in progress*. Economic and political frameworks are being developed, infrastructure is under construction, government influence is great, and some cultural resistance may exist. However, there is an enormous upside potential as the economy grows and a middle class of consumers begins to develop.

Many factors govern the trade relationships between developed and emerging economies. In developed nations, foreign trade policy drivers include (1) new jobs associated with export activity, (2) competition from other countries, (3) low domestic GDP growth, and (4) foreign trade imbalances. In other words, companies are motivated to expand globally because of growth opportunities and competitive pressures. Emerging

Not Value add?

economies represent (1) a huge internal market potential, (2) high GDP growth, (3) growing political ambitions, and (4) opportunities for export subsidies. Most of all, emerging countries seek to develop rapidly and improve their standards of living. The balance between these forces is governed by advances in technology, the growth in the number of multinational corporations, and the business environment's globalization.[6]

Characteristics of Emerging Markets

EMs are very different from developed countries in *demographics, economic* and *political, market* factors, and *cultural* characteristics.

Demographic factors. Except for Russia, *the population in EMs is typically younger than that of developed economies.* This implies that EMs all have sizeable working-age populations. Simultaneously, economic growth within these markets has increased the average education of the labor force, thereby creating a valuable source of human talent.

Major strides have also been made in life expectancy, infant mortality, and other key development metrics. Expectations of quality of life have risen as well, driven by domestic economic growth, global communication, and access to technology.[7]

An increase in urbanization is a direct result of economic growth and a focus on industrialization. Growth in urbanization results from the movement of people from low-income agricultural work to higher-income industrial jobs. This demographic trend also increases the demand for infrastructure, housing, and services in cities. Finally, the relatively lower old-age dependency ratios of the BRICS indicate these markets' potential to become major consumers.

Political and economic factors. Historically, EMs were characterized by protected domestic firms, high tariffs, and weak institutions. A turbulent political climate made the entry of multinational corporations difficult. Toward the end of the 20th century, developing nations started to adopt structural reforms to create stability and growth.[8] As a consequence, EMs have become a powerhouse of the global economy.

Economic growth in EMs remains high. In 2018, economic growth in most developed countries, such as the United States, Germany, Mexico, and Japan, was less than 3 percent.[9] Growth in Egypt, Poland, Bolivia, and Malaysia was 4 percent or more. China, Vietnam, and India saw their economies grow by around 7 percent. Economic growth forecasts prepared by the IMF suggest that the GDP in EMs will continue to grow much faster than those in developed markets economies in the foreseeable future.[10] The so-called *growth premium*—the difference between the growth rates of developed and emerging economies—is forecast to increase as well in the coming years. The growth premium reflects an increased growth rate in Latin America, the Middle East, and Sub-Saharan Africa, and a stagnant growth rate in developed economies.[11]

External and internal influences have facilitated economic reforms in EMs. Trade institutions such as the World Trade Organization (WTO) and the IMF have contributed significantly to the reform process. They have (1) recommended and enforced the liberalization of trade, (2) supported regulations that contribute to a stable economic environment, and (3) fostered fairness and efficiency in the market system. As a result, many state-owned enterprises have been privatized, industries deregulated, borders opened, and adopted fiscal and monetary reforms.[12]

In part because of these actions, *EM countries have accumulated a significant amount of wealth.* EM countries now control about three-fourths of all global foreign exchange reserves. This accumulated wealth provides important insurance against unanticipated global high-risk events and flexibility in the event of currency volatility.[13]

This wealth accumulation reflects sustained and increased economic growth, an expansion of the *middle class*, and the growth in savings and investment. *Increased wealth leads to increased consumer spending*, increasing the demand for consumer products, improved housing, and other products and services demanded by a growing middle class. The Organization of Economic Cooperation and Development (OECD) estimates that middle-class spending in EMs will increase from 25 percent of global consumption in 2009 to nearly 70 percent by 2030, with the bulk of the growth occurring in Asia.[14]

The rapid development of financial markets and increased access to global capital markets have played a key role in encouraging capital efficiency.

EM countries and corporations increasingly have access to financing in both hard currencies, for example, USD, EUR, and local currency. This development provides flexibility and the ability to search for the most cost-effective market to raise capital. It also gives governments and corporations a more efficient tool to balance revenues and income with expenditures and interest.[15]

Lastly, Western companies have discovered that *EMs have begun to drive global innovation.* More and more, firms are finding that EMs allow them to innovate at a lower cost and leverage local talent and knowledge.

Market factors. EMs share some market characteristics that are potential barriers to entry. First, *business systems are often more are more relationship-based* than in developed countries. Second, family businesses and informal arrangements between companies based on family ties are also more prevalent. Third, relations with the government are frequently more important than in developed nations.[16]

Manufacturers or importers control wholesale distribution in many developing countries, also creating formidable barriers to entry. Wholesalers tend to control the product portfolios and finances of retail outlets. These market imperfections result in highly controlled markets in which consumers must purchase whatever is offered. What is more, the power of these natural monopolies often remains unchallenged because of their traditional ties to the government and each other.

Cultural factors. Many emerging economies have very different cultures and traditions compared to developed countries. What is common and accepted for a professional from one country could be very different overseas in an international business context. Recognizing and understanding how culture affects international business in three core areas—communication, etiquette, and organizational hierarchy—helps avoid misunderstandings with executives and clients abroad.[17]

The Bottom of the Pyramid: New Target Markets?[18]

While the growing middle class in emerging economies is an attractive strategic target for small and large companies alike, the so-called

BOP markets in underdeveloped economies constitute a much greater challenge. C.K. Prahalad and Kenneth Lieberthal first challenged Western multinational companies to tailor their operations more effectively to the unique conditions of EMs. Arguing that hundreds of millions of people in China, India, Indonesia, and Brazil are ready to enter the marketplace, they observed that multinational companies typically target only a tiny segment of affluent buyers in these Ems—those who most resemble Westerners. They suggested that developing countries simply as new places to sell old products is shortsighted. Still, it causes them to miss out on much larger market opportunities further down the socioeconomic pyramid, often seized by local competitors.[19]

Prahalad and Hart argued that the four billion poor people worldwide represented a vibrant consumer market, that this market could best be tapped with *for-profit* models, and that the poor had to be partners in the process.

The idea of combining profit and purpose at the *BOP* captured the imagination of corporations and the development community alike. Almost two decades after Prahalad and Hart introduced their ideas, businesses continue to pursue profits at the BOP. Global cellphones are widely available, proving that poor people will buy cell service if it is made available at low prices. Single-serve packages of products such as shampoo and toothpaste can be bought from small stores in rural villages.[20]

Arguably, the BOP market leader is *Unilever*, which generates more than half of its sales from developing markets. Its main BOP product is Pureit, a countertop water-purification system sold in India, Africa, and Latin America. It is saving lives, but it is not making money for shareholders. Doing business at the BOP is complex and costly because customers are hard to reach and often make very small purchases.[21]

A litany of failures illustrates the difficulty. *Procter and Gamble* invented a water-purification powder called PUR for BOP markcts, but it was a commercial failure. A philanthropic enterprise now distributes it. In 2007, *SC Johnson* launched Community Cleaning Services, a BOP business to create employment in Kibera, part of Nairobi, Kenya. The venture lost money, and the project was eventually spun off into a non-profit. *DuPont's* Solae unit tried to alleviate malnutrition and open new markets by selling soy-fortified snack foods in India's pilot program but was forced to discontinue it because it saw no path to profitability.[22]

Nonetheless, there are a few notable successes. *Grameen Bank* pioneered the concept of microcredit in commercial banking. It provides a means for providing small loans to the poor by extending credit opportunities for often poor borrowers. Many live in remote, underdeveloped, rural villages; never had any money; and depend on a barter economy to meet their basic needs. The microcredit approach is unique, as members of the borrower's community provide the loans. This creates pressure within the group for borrowers to return the loan on time. As of December 2018, it has 9.08 million members, 97 percent of whom are women. With 2,568 branches, Grameen Bank offers services in 81,677 villages, more than 93 percent of the total villages in Bangladesh.[23] The success of the microcredit program in Bangladesh encouraged similar programs in other developing countries, including Bolivia and Indonesia. Today, two innovative spin-offs of Grameen Bank, Grameen Telecom—a village phone service provider—and Grameen Shakti—a developer of renewable energy sources—support Grameen Bank by building technological infrastructure to automate its processes.[24]

SABMiller also has a strong commitment to BOP consumers. It supports small businesses as suppliers, distributors, and retailers. In Mozambique, SABMiller sells beer made from cassava, while in Uganda, it sells a beer brewed with sorghum. Local crops like cassava and sorghum meet local preferences, provide employment for local farmers, and reduce costs. A SABMiller project in Colombia called Oportunidades Bavaria (named after the local beer, called Bavaria) supports small-scale retailers with micro loans for things like fixing up or expanding a store, or sending a child to college. The program has helped more than 10,000 shopkeepers.[25]

Climate Change and Other Mega Trends[26]

Several primary environmental, social, political, and technical global megatrends have major implications for society, markets, and cultures. Analysis of these megatrends constitutes an important component of global strategy formulation as they impact different industries and regions differently.

Global warming and climate change[27] Whereas global warming specifically refers to the warming of the planet due to increased greenhouse gas emissions, the term *climate change* covers the full range of changes caused by human activity, including global warming, rising sea levels, melting glaciers, and more.

Scientists have reached both positive and negative conclusions about globalization's effects on climate change and the environment. On the one hand, more integrated supply chains have produced efficiency gains and lowered stresses on the world's water resources. On the other hand, globalization has led to increased carbon emissions due to global transportation by land, sea, and air.[28]

According to the United Nations Human Rights Council, climate change will disproportionately affect the health of vulnerable population groups, including those living in developing countries. Extreme weather, disease transmission, and water quantity deterioration are all more prevalent in developing countries. The World Health Organization estimates that by 2030, climate change could put an additional 100 million people worldwide in extreme poverty.[29]

Climate change affects companies in several ways. On the one hand, it creates a series of new business risks. First, there are physical risks, such as the operational impacts of extreme weather events or supply shortages caused by water scarcity. Second, companies are exposed to transition risks related to society's response to climate change. Such responses include changes in technologies, markets, and regulations that can increase business costs, reduce the viability of existing products or services, or adversely affect asset values.[30] Another climate-related risk for companies is the potential liability for emitting greenhouse gases. An increasing number of legal cases have been brought directly against fossil fuel companies and utilities in recent years, holding them accountable for climate change's damaging effects.[31]

Climate change also offers business opportunities. First, companies can target improvements in their resource productivity, for example, by increasing energy efficiency. Second, climate change can spur innovation and lead to the development of new products and services that are less carbon-intensive. Third, companies can enhance their supply chains' resilience by shifting toward renewable energy. Together, these actions can foster competitiveness and open new market opportunities.

Water, food, and energy will be high on the list of resource allocation concerns in the decades to come. Water is becoming increasingly scarce. Although produced at a rate to feed the entire world, food cannot reach the necessary locations. Energy, a key force in the global economy, faces an uncertain future. Businesses must invest in strategic resources to position themselves to succeed as these forces unfold.

Urbanization. With industrialization, more people have started to move from villages into towns and then into cities. The effects of urbanization have begun to appear in terms of decreased quality of life, increased pollution, water scarcity, and traffic jams. This inevitably leads to increased stress, less healthy lifestyles, and a significant increase in violence.

Increasing urbanization, especially in the developing world, will have a massive impact on the future of mobility, working life, and societies. The populations of Jakarta, Delhi, Manila, Seoul-Incheon, Shanghai, Karachi, Beijing, Guangzhou/Foshan, and Sao Paolo now all exceed 20 million. As urban growth continues, three concepts of urbanization are emerging: megacities, megaregions, and mega-corridors. *Megacities* integrate core cities with suburbs and house over five million people; *Megaregions* combine two or more megacities and house over 12 million people; *mega-corridors* are transport corridors connecting two or more megacities or megaregions.

With more technology and infrastructure development, there will be a shift from the *green* to a *smart* concept. Some of the *smart* initiatives will find their way into energy, technology, grids, cars, buildings, utilities, and infrastructure.

Emerging transportation corridors are expected to produce economic and technology clusters. These integrated hubs will be the future centers of innovation, research and development (R&D), and technical excellence attracting massive investment and government support.

A *zero concept* world will drive technologies and applications to *innovate to zero*. Development of zero-emission technologies such as wind power, traveling wave reactor (TWR), Solar photovoltaic (PV), third-generation biofuels will be the emerging trend gaining considerable interest.

Other trends. Finally, some socio-cultural, societal, and governmental megatrends are likely to influence our future.

Disease and globalization. The spread of epidemics was once limited by geography. However, the proliferation of high-speed global transport of people and livestock have opened the floodgates for disease transmission. Private businesses must find answers to responding to disease outbreaks.

Knowledge dissemination knowledge—the production and dissemination of context-dependent information—plays an important role in wealth generation worldwide. In this economy, ideas and know-how prove to be as valuable as capital, land, and labor. China and India are already riding this new economic wave.

Conflict. From domestic, religious, and ethnic disputes to worldwide terrorism, conflict is shaping the global economy. As the global economy strengthens through foreign direct investment and monetary integration, nation-states' interdependence makes violent conflicts more likely. Problems arising from ethnicity, religion, and ideology are intense and are often seen as irreconcilable.[32]

Governance: The rise of non-governmental organizations (NGOs). Information technology and its results touch every aspect of our lives. Statistics reveal that information technology (IT) will be an ever more vital and multidimensional part of our daily lives. While the opportunities are obvious, the challenges are often hidden.[33]

New trade zones. Governments are entering into new trade agreements, which will encourage the development of new trading hubs and increase trade volume. These trade agreements will ultimately produce lower tariffs, particularly for countries in Asia, Africa, and Latin America.

Future Fortune Global 500. Companies in developing economies, particularly Asia, will see a higher rate of economic progress than their Western counterparts. We can expect a substantial increase in the number of Asian companies in the Global 500 companies list, cementing the shift of economic growth from Europe and the United States to developing India and China regions. At the same time, an increasing number of Fortune Global 500 Companies will be headed by women. Women will have more power over finance and business development and be more prominent in boardrooms.

Some of these forces will have a gradual impact; others will be more disruptive. The effects will also vary by industry and region. Nevertheless, executives should monitor these and other emerging forces for the opportunities and challenges they create.

Global Trade—Free Trade or Protectionism

Throughout history, *free trade* has been an important factor in the prosperity of different civilizations. Adam Smith pointed to increased trade as the primary reason for the flourishing of the Mediterranean cultures such as Egypt, Greece, Rome, and Bengal (East India), and China. Classical economist David Ricardo made one of the strongest arguments for free trade in his analysis of *comparative advantage*. Comparative advantage occurs when different parties (countries, regions, or individuals) have different opportunity costs of production. The theory is that free trade will induce countries to specialize in making products where they have a competitive advantage. By specializing, they will maximize the total wealth produced.

Adopting *free trade* means supporting and protecting (1) the trade of goods without taxes (including tariffs) or other trade barriers such as quotas on imports or subsidies for producers, (2) trade in services without taxes or other trade barriers, (3) the absence of *trade-distorting* policies— taxes, subsidies, regulations, or laws that give some firms or factors of production an advantage over others, (4) free access to markets and market information, (5) efforts against firms trying to distort markets through monopoly or oligopoly power, and (6) the free movement of labor and capital between and within countries.

Opposition to free trade, generally known as *protectionism*, is based on the idea that the advantages of free trade are outweighed by considerations such as (1) national security, (2) the importance of nurturing infant industries, (3) preventing the exploitation of economically weak countries by stronger ones, or (4) of furthering various social goals.

Free trade is sometimes also opposed by domestic industries threatened by lower-priced imported goods. If the U.S. tariffs on imported sugar were reduced, for example, U.S. sugar producers would have to lower their prices and sacrifice profits, benefiting U.S. consumers. Economics informs us that, collectively, consumers would gain more than the domestic producers would lose. However, as only a few domestic sugar producers, each one could lose a significant amount. This explains why domestic producers may be inclined to mobilize against the lifting of tariffs, or more generally, why they often favor domestic subsidies and tariffs on imports in their home countries while objecting to subsidies and tariffs in their export markets.

Economic policy-based protectionism is about restraining trade between nations. Methods used include tariffs on imported goods, restrictive quotas, and various other restrictive government regulations designed to discourage imports and prevent foreign takeover of local markets and companies. This policy is closely aligned with anti-globalization. The term is mostly used in economics, where protectionism refers to policies or doctrines that *protect* businesses and workers within a country by restricting or regulating trade between foreign nations. USMCA

Many other initiatives besides tariffs, quotas, and subsidies have been called protectionists in the modern trade arena. For example, some scholars, such as Jagdish Bhagwati, see developed countries' efforts in imposing their own labor or environmental standards as forms of protectionism.[34] The imposition of restrictive certification procedures on imports can also be seen in this light. Others point out that free trade agreements often have protectionist provisions such as intellectual property, copyright, and patent restrictions that benefit large corporations. These provisions restrict trade in music, movies, drugs, software, and other manufactured items to high-cost producers with quotas from low-cost producers set to zero.

Arguments for Protectionism

Opponents of free trade argue that the comparative advantage argument for free trade has lost its legitimacy in a globally integrated world—in which capital is free to move internationally. Herman Daly, a leading voice in the discipline of ecological economics, has stated that although Ricardo's theory of comparative advantage is one of the most elegant theories in economics, its application to the present day is illogical:

> Free capital mobility totally undercuts Ricardo's comparative advantage argument for free trade in goods, because that argument is explicitly and essentially premised on capital (and other factors) being immobile between nations. Under the new globalization regime, capital tends simply to flow to wherever costs are lowest— that is, to pursue absolute advantage.[35]

Others criticize free trade as *reverse protectionism in disguise*; of using tax policy to protect foreign manufacturers from domestic competition. By ruling out revenue tariffs on foreign products, the government must fully rely on domestic taxation to provide its revenue, which falls heavily on domestic manufacturing. Or, as Paul Craig Roberts puts it:

> [Foreign discrimination of U.S. products] is reinforced by the US tax system, which imposes no appreciable tax burden on foreign goods and services sold in the U.S. but imposes a heavy tax burden on U.S. producers of goods and services regardless of whether they are sold within the U.S. or exported to other countries.[36]

Other defenses of *protectionism* include the idea that protecting newly founded, strategically important, infant industries by imposing tariffs allows those domestic industries to grow and become self-sufficient within the international economy once they reach a reasonable size. For example, a country may wish to protect technology innovations, especially if they have application in national defense.

Arguments Against Protectionism

Most economists fundamentally believe in free trade and agree that protectionism reduces welfare. They argue that free trade helps third-world workers, even though they may not be subject to developed countries' stringent health and labor standards. This occurs because the growth of manufacturing and the other jobs that a new export sector creates have a ripple effect throughout the economy, which creates competition among producers, thereby lifting wages and living conditions.

Regulation of International Trade

Traditionally, international trade was regulated through bilateral treaties between the two nations. After the Second World War (WWII), as free trade emerged as the dominant doctrine, multilateral treaties like the *General Agreement on Tariffs and Trade* (GATT) and WTO became the principal regime for regulating global trade.

The WTO, created in 1995 as the successor to the GATT, is an international organization charged with overseeing and adjudicating international trade. Headquartered in Geneva, Switzerland, the WTO has more than 150 members, representing more than 95 percent of total world trade. The WTO deals with the rules of trade between nations at a near-global level. It is responsible for negotiating and implementing new trade agreements and policing member countries' adherence to all the WTO agreements. Additionally, the WTO has to review the national trade policies and ensure trade policies' coherence and transparency through global economic policy-making surveillance.

Regional arrangements such as Mercosur in South America, the United States–Mexico–Canada Agreement (USMCA) (formerly known as North American Free Trade Agreement (NAFTA)) between the United States, Canada and Mexico, Association of Southeast Asian Nations (ASEAN) in Southeast Asia, and the European Union (EU) between 27 independent states constitute a second dimension of the international trade regulatory framework.

The *EU* is an economic and political union of 27 member states. Committed to regional integration, the EU was established by the Treaty of Maastricht on November 1, 1993, upon the foundations of the pre-existing European Economic Community. With almost 500 million citizens, the EU combined generates an estimated 30 percent share of the nominal gross world product.

The EU has developed a single market through a standardized system of laws that apply in all member states, ensuring the freedom of movement of people, goods, services, and capital. It maintains common policies on trade, agriculture, fisheries, and regional development. A common currency, the euro, has been adopted by 16 member states known as the eurozone. The EU has developed a limited role in foreign policy, having representation at the WTO, G8 summits, and the UN. It enacts legislation in justice and home affairs, including the abolition of passport controls between many member states. Twenty-one EU countries are also members of North Atlantic Treaty Organization (NATO), those member states outside NATO being Austria, Cyprus, Finland, Ireland, Malta, and Sweden. In January of 2020, The United Kingdom (UK) became the first and only country to formally leave the EU and voluntarily withdraw from an economic and monetary union of countries (although the UK never adopted the euro).

Mercosur is a regional trade agreement among Argentina, Brazil, Paraguay, and Uruguay, founded in 1991 by the Treaty of Asunción, which was later amended and updated by the 1994 Treaty of Ouro Preto. Its purpose is to promote free trade and the fluid movement of goods, people, and currency. Bolivia, Chile, Colombia, Ecuador, and Peru currently have associate member status. Venezuela signed a membership agreement on June 17, 2006, but before becoming a full member, its entry must be ratified by the Paraguayan and the Brazilian parliaments.

USMCA. The agreement between the United States, Mexico, and Canada, commonly as the USMCA, is the successor of the NAFTA. The agreement has been characterized as *NAFTA 2.0* or *New NAFTA*, as many provisions from NAFTA were incorporated, and its changes were seen as largely incremental. On July 1, 2020, the USMCA entered into force in all member states.

ASEAN is a geo-political and economic organization of 10 countries located in Southeast Asia, formed on August 8, 1967, by Indonesia, Malaysia, the Philippines, Singapore Thailand. Since then, membership has expanded to include Brunei, Burma (Myanmar), Cambodia, Laos, and Vietnam. Its aims include the acceleration of economic growth, social progress, cultural development among its members, and the protection of the region's peace and stability.

In November 2020, Asia Pacific nations, including China, Japan, and South Korea, signed the world's largest regional free-trade agreement, encompassing nearly a third of the world's population and GDP. Called the *Regional Comprehensive Economic Partnership (RCEP),* this new trade agreement includes 15 nations, including China, Japan, South Korea, Australia, New Zealand, and 10 members of the ASEAN. The agreement provides for eliminating at least 92 percent of tariffs on traded goods among participating countries and stronger provisions to address nontariff measures and enhancements in areas such as online consumer and personal information protection, transparency, and paperless trading.

CHAPTER 4

The Globalization of Corporate Social Responsibility

Introduction

Whether it is called corporate social responsibility (CSR), environmental, social and corporate governance (ESG) or sustainability, a common understanding is emerging worldwide: a company's long-term financial success is increasingly tied to its social responsibility record, environmental stewardship, and corporate ethics.

As business has become global, so has the idea and practice of corporate responsibility.

Importantly, several trends indicate that corporate sustainability is here to stay:

1. *Transparency*. Transparency is hard to reverse: demands for reporting and disclosure will continue to grow, driven by improved information access, higher public interest, and regulatory changes.
2. *Trust.* The growing impact of business on society means that citizens and consumers expect corporate power to be exerted responsibly. Consequently, the corporate community will have to be proactive and thorough in explaining how a company views its responsibilities and impacts on society and manages its operations accordingly.
3. *Community participation.* Companies are expected to do more in areas that used to be the exclusive domain of the public sector—ranging from health care and education to community investment and environmental stewardship. Natural resources are now recognized to be finite and under stress. Companies need to

collaborate with scientists, civil society, and public regulators and show that they are part of the solution.

4. *Accessing new markets responsibly.* With economic growth migrating to Asia and other parts of the world, foreign direct investment is increasingly directed at building and gaining access to new markets and less about exploiting low-cost inputs. Overcoming barriers to growth, such as an uneducated workforce and unsustainable energy sources, is becoming imperative for business.

5. *Initiatives to engage companies.* Engaging in corporate sustainability is becoming easier. Initiatives, standards, and consultancies are growing rapidly at national and global levels. For example, the UN Global Compact is engaging 8,000 companies in more than 145 countries on human rights, labor standards, the environment, and anti-corruption.[1]

Businesses realize that ESG responsibilities are becoming integral to success. While most companies have yet to commit to this trajectory, there is a strong upward growth curve in actively engaged companies. What is more, engaged companies have benefited financially and socially. Investors, boards of directors, and other stakeholders have come on board to actively guide the transition from a shareholder economy to a stakeholder economy in which ESG factors are central to a company's mission.

Expanding the Definition of Performance for Global Corporations

The *ESG* framework is a generic concept used in capital markets and by investors to evaluate corporate behavior and forecast companies' future financial performance. *Environmental* issues require companies to critically analyze the sources of energy and energy usage that impact their industries. The concerns determine how a company impacts the natural world, primarily through its sustainability investments and commitment to stakeholder capitalism. *Social* concerns require that companies maintain positive relations with their domestic and global business partners. Specific issues include promoting employee and management diversity, ensuring broad representation in employment, customer perspectives, and social representation through inclusion awareness. Social assessments involve a business's relationships with its employees, suppliers, customers, and the communities where it operates. *Governance* refers to the internal system of practices, controls, and procedures that a company adopts to help align decision making throughout the company consistent with its sustainability and ethical objectives.[2] An assessment of a company's governance considers various factors, such as its board diversity, executive pay, gender makeup, internal controls, leadership, and shareholder rights. The following examples evidence the breadth and scope of global initiatives by companies to advance ESG priorities:

1. *Amgen Inc.* is a California biopharmaceutical industry. In 2018, Amgen committed two million U.S. dollars to support recovery efforts in Puerto Rico, including rebuilding educational institutions, after the island was devastated by Hurricane Maria in the fall of 2017. The donation came on the heels of an initial three million U.S. dollars in immediate relief distributed through Americares, Direct Relief, the International Medical Corps, and others.[3]

2. *Coca-Cola Company*, a beverage manufacturer and retailer, headquartered in Atlanta, Georgia, developed a *5-by-20* initiative in 2010. This initiative had the goal of economically empowering five million women to assume company roles by the end of 2020. The program assists women entrepreneurs in overcoming social and economic barriers by attending business skills training, mentoring and networking opportunities, and accessing financial services. As of 2018, over 3.2 million women in 92 countries had participated in the program and subsequently worked for the company. Their employment involved suppliers to retailers, producers, artisans, and more.[4]

3. *Ford Motor Company* is an automaker headquartered in Dearborn, Michigan. In 2018, Ford's global named Operation Better World initiative awarded 250 grants totaling over 12 million U.S. dollars to nonprofits in over 60 countries. The project enables local Ford teams to work with community leaders to support communities worldwide where Ford has a presence. One such project was the Argentinatón, which was created to deliver free,

three-dimensional (3D)-printed prosthetic hands and limbs to hundreds of Argentinians in need.[5]

4. *JPMorgan Chase*, an investment bank headquartered in New York, sourced renewable energy for 22 percent of its global energy use as of year-end 2018. To reduce energy usage, the firm installed 2,570 U.S.-manufactured solar panels at Chase branches to provide 30 percent of the energy consumed on-site. They also retrofitted all Chase-owned branches with light-emitting diode (LED) lighting to halve their lighting energy consumption and installed energy-efficient building management systems at 900 Chase branches.[6]

5. *VF Corporation*, one of the world's largest apparel companies, manages brands, including Timberland, The North Face, and Vans. As part of their *Made for Change* strategy, the Colorado-headquartered firm attempts to reduce its impact on the environment and to help people in need. Across their brands, VF collects unwanted clothing and footwear at 150 retail and outlet stores, sometimes offering discounts on the purchase of new products when an item is donated. The donated items are then redistributed for reuse and recycling, with over 47 tons of clothing donated as of 2018.[7]

A wide range of investors and stakeholders globally have increased their demands on businesses to focus on ESG practices that protect consumers and foster sustainability. According to a JPMorgan report, the United States and Europe account for about 80 percent of the world's investments in sustainability, and Japan accounts for about 6 percent more.[8] ESG is now viewed as a major source of corporate risk that can directly or indirectly affect a firm's financial performance.

ESG measures are based on multiple indicators of performance. The ratings of a company's performance on the various indicators are summed to provide three component scores (E, S, G) that reflect a company's breadth and scope of involvement. The number of indicators included in each component score is shown as follows in parentheses:

- The environment score is comprised of indicators of the company's resource use (19 indicators), emissions created in the operations of the company (22), and innovations by the company that improve environmental conditions (20).

- The social score consists of the concern by the company leadership about their management practices (34), shareholders (12), and CSR (8).
- The governance score is comprised of indicators of the company's concern for its workforce (29), human rights (8), community (14), and product responsibility (12).
- When summed to produce an overall grade (E+S+G), the ESG score indicates the strength and results of the company's sustainability strategy, enhances the firm's reputation, and influences the public's perception of the industry.[9]

ESG's contribution to value creation is inferred from the company's top-line growth, cost reductions, limited regulatory and legal interventions, employee productivity increases, and investment and asset optimization. Improvements in these measures, if they occur, differ among competitors, industries, and nations.[10]

NextEra Energy, Inc received a best-in-class preparedness assessment and a final ESG Evaluation score of 86 in S&P Global Ratings' ESG Evaluation.[11] NextEra's environmental goal is to lower CO_2 emissions by 67 percent by 2025. Since 2001, the company's investment in infrastructure has cut costs by nearly 10 billion U.S. dollars by making its electricity power plants more fuel-efficient. NextEra's initiative included contributing more than 85,000 employee work and personal hours to local communities in company-sponsored projects. NextEra also invested in its employees' future by funding more than 1.1 million hours in continuing education. The company's ESG initiatives result in that NextEra was the top-scoring company in the S&P 500 Utilities Index for the 15th consecutive year, with a combined ranking in the companies' 82nd percentile in the S&P 500.[12]

Climate Change—A Key Factor

The primary cause of the dramatic increase in businesses' attention to the physical environment is societies' concern about climate change and global warming. In 2015, the popular press alerted the world to scientific research that warned of high and rising global temperature levels that jeopardized human well-being.[13] Research on the physical hazards and socioeconomic impacts of climate change studies generated distressing predictions. Based on the rise of global temperatures by 2.0 degrees Celsius above preindustrial levels, and up from 1.1 degrees as of 2020, many aspects of life are predicted to deteriorate drastically.[14] Specific predictions on climate change by 2050 include drought throughout Northern, Central, and South America, sharp decreases in surface water supplies among many countries. Consequently, rising ocean temperatures will reduce fish yields by 35 percent, steep declines in beef production, and lethal heatwaves annually.

The World Economic Forum in Davos, Switzerland, produced a risk map that determined that the five top economic risks in 2020 were related to global environmental change.[15] Many conference attendees pledged their help through their ESG investments. For example, Salesforce.com announced it would plant a trillion trees over 10 years. Bank of America showed that it had achieved carbon neutrality, and Starbucks committed to a 50 percent reduction in emissions. Several companies pledged to divest from fossil fuels, most notably BlackRock, which committed to limiting its investments in coal companies.

Mini-Case 4.1: Why It Makes Business Sense to Flatten the Global Warming Curve[16]

Globally, COVID-19 lockdowns have temporarily stemmed pollution. The coronavirus pandemic provides a stark reminder of how important it is for countries to flatten the upward curve of global warming and safeguard the ecosystem. It also has created a major incentive for governments and businesses to develop postpandemic *green* recovery plans.

Investors will have to play an important role in facilitating this. They can promote real economic action by realigning portfolios and urging companies to make investment choices that deliver positive, measurable, and enduring changes for a better environment. Investors increasingly base their capital allocations and support to portfolio businesses on the condition of climate commitments to achieve zero emissions.

There is a growing consensus that ESG investing will positively influence corporate behavior and governance. Encouraging companies to comprehensively report their climate-related risks and address them will lead to greater transparency and better solutions.

Given the magnitude of the challenge, investors will need to join forces with each other, governmental institutions, scientists, academics, and nongovernmental organizations (NGOs) to consider and adopt sustainable principles and practices. For example, the UN-Convened Net-Zero Asset Owner Alliance—a coalition of 23 international asset owners (comprising insurance companies and pension funds with total investments of about 4.6 trillion U.S. dollars)—is a real game-changer. This alliance is an example of how investors and scientists can cooperate to protect the people and the planet by using their influence to help companies realize opportunities the crisis presents.

ESG Increases Stock Prices

Research to determine the financial performance consequences for a firm of investing in ESG produces some important agreements. Initially, articles written on the topic tended to base their conclusions on anecdotal materials, consultant testimonials, and opinion surveys. Fortunately, there were notable exceptions to this trend.[17] In a large-scale database study conducted in India, researchers examined the performance of three sustainability indexes, including the S&P ESG India Index, the Nifty, and the S&P CNX 500.[18] The S&P ESG India Index includes only firms with a strong sustainability focus.

The research sought to understand the value of resources that firms might be advised to allocate to support ESG initiatives. The research's principal finding was that there was no statistical difference in returns to investors between indices composed of firms actively invested in ESG and those that have not declared their allocations or intentions. The results suggest that the cost of investing in ESG is counterbalanced by some combination of greater investor support and improved functionality by the firm. Other researchers reported similar findings and added that ethical investors receive returns that match investors who use other selection criteria.[19,20]

Several academic researchers have studied the relationship between ESG investment and a company's financial performance. Reviews of the significant findings conclude that studies of multinationals in developed markets can be separated into three groups.[21] Some studies found that investing in ESG activities improves financial performance.[22] The second group of researchers found negative effects.[23] Finally, the third group of researchers concludes that there is, in fact, no relation between the ESG score and financial performance.[24]

Taken together, these large dataset empirical research efforts suggest that investment in ESG may initially add to market value because of positive investor evaluations of their support for ESG.[25] Firms known for their ESG investments may also benefit from their ability to offset negative volatility within their industry and achieve ethical pursuits. When companies incorporate sustainability practices, they build public and investor support that increases their company's stock price compared to competitors that are less invested in sustainability.[26]

ESG Market Impact

In the early days of the ESG movement, a major barrier to company acceptance of the approach was the lack of data and analytical tools needed to give not-yet adopters the confidence to reallocate resources to additional sustainability programs. However, by 2020, the situation had improved greatly. The Global Reporting Initiative (GRI) was an early source of credibility for companies that wanted to be recognized for ESG programs. GRI is an independent organization that operates internationally to establish standards that facilitate communications between businesses and their stakeholders on the progress and impact on ESG issues through sustainability reporting. Their annual sustainability reports include 93 percent of the world's largest 250 corporations.[27] GRI's main appeal results from recognizing the value of ESG information, which is expected and increasingly required by investors.[28]

Other rating approaches have emerged that further validate the value of ESG investments and disclosures. The International Integrated Reporting Initiative (IIRC) and the U.S.-based Sustainability Accounting Standard Board (SASB) have achieved similar stature by advancing industry sector reporting.

Viewed as members of the ESG rating industry, these firms' participation adds further legitimacy to ESG disclosures, especially when they are packaged with traditional financial reporting. They also provide evidence of the value derived by companies that elevate ESG criteria to the level of long-term business objectives. The percentage of publicly listed companies reporting environmental, social, and corporate governance data is growing exponentially. Of the largest 100 companies in each of 49 countries, only 12 percent issued sustainability reports in 1993. By 2017, the participation rate grew to 75 percent.[29]

Central to the emergence of the ESG rating industry is the availability of comparative competitive performance data. The credibility of ESG ratings increases with the quality and quantity of the data on which the ratings are determined.[30] In recognition of this fact, Moody's Investors Services invested in building investor confidence in the value of ESG ratings. In 2019, Moody's acquired two companies that specialize in collecting and analyzing data to measure and assess companies' sustainability and ethical investments. Named Vigeo Eiris and Four Twenty-Seven, the acquisitions add legitimacy to Moody's ESG evaluations and benefit companies whose rating recognizes the benefits of their efforts to contribute beyond economic returns.

Five Ways ESG Creates Value

Researchers for McKinsey and Company reviewed the studies that provide evidence of businesses' value when adopting ESG.[31] They found that value creation took place in five important ways:

1. *Top-line growth*

   When the marketplace appreciates a company's ESG investments, it is likely to experience a heightened sales level. Consumers are attracted to products and services that are acknowledged to be environmentally sensitive. A company's supply chain participants and governments also tend to prefer companies with a strongly stated and publicly announced ESG proposition. Specifically, the research shows that ESG investments are associated with comparatively higher social capital and customer approvals levels.

2. *Cost reductions*

ESG often plays a role in helping a business work to limit rising operating costs. A popular target among new ESG investing firms are reductions in its utility, raw material, and waste costs. These efficiency investments provide immediate benefits to the company's bottom line while simultaneously improving its ESG profile.

3. *Reduced regulatory and legal interventions*

A company's ESG investments that produce government-supported changes and improve sustainability can simultaneously reduce public demand for restrictions on company strategy. ESG investments are interpreted as responsible corporate behavior that counters demand for increasing regulatory pressure.

4. *Employee productivity uplift*

The eagerness with which employees identify with their employer is strongly and positively related to the company's ESG reputation. Among the documented benefits of engendering, employee support is higher employee motivation levels, employee retention, productivity, and employee satisfaction.

5. *Investment and asset optimization*

Comparatively high levels of ESG investment have been shown to improve corporate financial performance. A company that enjoys increased revenues, receptive markets, a favorable public image, and even slightly reduced operating costs is attractive to investors because of its ability to benefit from sustainability and expected long-term viability.

The Rise in ESG Disclosures

Investors use ESG disclosures to supplement financial reports for evaluating a company's performance and contributions to sustainability. ESG disclosures are becoming an increasingly anticipated component of company reports. In 2011, 20 percent of S&P 500 companies published reports featuring ESG data, while in 2018, this number jumped to 86 percent.[32] In 2019, 26 percent of professionally managed assets in the United States considered a company's commitment to sustainability before investing, compared to 18 percent five just years earlier.[33] The rapid acceptance of ESG disclosures has become recognized as a key environmental imperative.[34]

Understandably, ESG ratings are problematic. For example, oil and gas companies rank highly on some ESG rating scales because some ESG methods reward a company solely to track and report its sustainability data. This approach can result in companies being awarded scores that mismatch with their cross-industry impact on the environment. As evidence that such shortcomings in ESG ratings sometimes exist, 10 percent of top-rated ESG companies in the European corporate bond index in 2018 were fossil fuel-producing companies.[35] Additionally, some ESG rankings measure social responsibility for a company relative to its industry. This practice allows a few companies with harmful impacts to be ranked highly and qualify for inclusion in a socially responsible portfolio because they are better performers than their worse peers.

On the other hand, the dramatic increase in ESG reporting is a positive sign that businesses and their constituencies pay ever greater attention to environmental concerns. Nevertheless, trying to evaluate the progress of the company by comparing *ad hoc* ESG disclosures is difficult. While judging a company's relative performance to its peers is complicated by differences in resources, strategies, and product market segments, it can be nearly impossible to compare a firm relative to businesses in other industries.[36] As a result, ESG disclosures provide corporate executives with few explicit recommendations about revising their capital structures or investing corporate resources to improve their profitability, reduce societal concerns, or moderate environmental threats.

Fortunately, the data needed to elevate ESG disclosures to universal acceptance and prominence in business practice is rapidly emerging. As more companies engage in ESG investments, more data is collected and analyzed to assess their consequences. The results have internal value in helping each firm determine its progress in attaining its objectives. They have external value in assessing the industry activities that can best serve as benchmarks for advancing its industry's sustainability progress globally.

Exhibit 4.1 presents a list of questions recommended by Invest Europe to guide companies in an initial evaluation of their ESG commitment level.

The following list of questions is recommended by Invest Europe to help co mpanies evaluate their level of ESG commitment:

1. Does the company monitor and report its carbon and other greenhouse gas (GHG) emissions ?
2. Has the company conducted a climate change risk assessment to ascertain whether its operations could be at risk from current/ evolving climate change regulation and physical changes brought about by climate change?
3. What are the company's primary energy (e.g., gas, coal, diesel, heating oil, electricity) and water sources (river/lake or groundwater extraction, public mains) and what initiatives have been put in place to monitor, reduce consumption and improve efficiencies?
4. Does the company have formal processes for undertaking workplace risk assessments, providing communication and training to employees, and conducting audits?
5. Does the company have a policy that supports anti-discrimination?
6. Does the company have a policy that supports diversity and equal opportunity?
7. Does the company have any data security policy?
8. Has the company implemented an IT security management system?
9. Does the company have a responsible purchasing policy/Code of Conduct for suppliers?
10. Does the company conduct supply chain risk assessments involving its procurement, supply chain, and logistics departments?
11. How is diversity taken into consideration when appointing board members?
12. Does the company have a code of ethics?

Exhibit 4.1 Invest Europe *questions for assessing ESG commitment*

An Emphasis on Relevant ESG Factors

Because there are numerous ESG options, it is nearly impossible for a firm to invest in many of them without inevitably depressing companywide returns because the options with the best financial returns are the first options chosen. For this reason, investors seek companies that focus on ESG options that are especially impactful in their industries.[37]

Responding to the need for ESG specificity, the Sustainable Accounting Standards Boards (SABS) developed a materiality map to identify ESG issues by industry and sector.[38] For example, material (i.e., relevant) ESG issues for a company that sells agricultural products include GHG emissions (principally carbon dioxide), energy management, water management, product quality and safety, employee health and safety, and materials sourcing. By contrast, an investment banking and brokerage firm might focus on material ESG issues such as employee engagement, diversity and inclusion, product design and lifecycle management, and business ethics.

The United Nations' Perspective on ESG

Principles for Responsible Investment (PRI) is an organization supported by the United Nations that focuses on responsible investing. It tries to understand the investment implications of ESG factors and support its international network of investors and companies. The PRI de facto establishes the guidelines for ESG issues concerning responsible investing. Investors looking to invest responsibly want to ask themselves the following questions[39]:

1. Does our fiduciary duty extend beyond strictly financial benefits for stakeholders?
2. Is positive real-world impact an explicit part of our primary objective for investment results?
3. Do we view ESG factors as material?
4. Do we incorporate ESG factors into our investment analysis?
5. Do we actively engage with our partners and subsidiary companies?

ESG Initiatives in Different Countries

The factors driving ESG in countries across the globe share several key components.[40] Some specific country-level commitments to ESG are reflected in the following initiatives:

- *Arabian Gulf Region.* After studying the Arabian Gulf Region, PRI reports that Islamic finance and ESG investing are complementary investment approaches with shared principles.[41] Islamic finance refers to investment activities that are compliant with shariah, which prohibits interest payments in favor of shared risk and reward between lender and borrower. Islamic finance also prohibits investment in tobacco, alcohol, and gambling businesses.

- *Australia* has provided evidence that ESG integration can create outperformance in down markets and reduce volatility.[42] Executive research also shows that investors do not count ESG issues against Australian companies in discounting their investments.

- *China*. ESG initiatives in China include a green bond market, support for establishing green funds, and bank lending limitations for companies invested in greater numbers of industrial sectors, including coal mining and steel production. A study from PRI found that while leading Chinese investors have fully integrated ESG factors and tools into their research process, the market as a whole is not advanced widely.[43]

- *Germany*. The DVFA (Deutsche Vereinigung für Finanzanalyse und Anlageberatung, German) issued minimum requirements for use by companies in reporting their ESG activities. The guidelines outline the importance of ESG for corporate strategy and describe how ESG is implemented. Specific recommendations include how businesses develop and publish online reports on ESG strategies, explain the current and future relevance of ESG to the company and its industry, present ESG management system and program to investors, and communicate with stakeholders ESG's relevant matters.[44]

- More generally, *Europeans* express optimism about the benefit of responsible investing.[45] The growth of ESG reporting in Europe has been identified as client demand, risk management, and regulation change.[46]

- *Hong Kong*. The Hong Kong Financial Services Development Council published an ESG strategy, including creating a green finance hub, developing a green bond market and accreditation schemes, and providing funds and tax exemptions.

- *Japan.* The 2014 Japanese Stewardship Code encourages sustainable investing practices through dialogue between investees and clients. In 2015, Japan released a Corporate Governance Code.
- *Singapore*'s central bank launched a Green Bond Grant Scheme to encourage the development of the green bond market in Singapore. A study of ESG integration in the Asia Pacific found that share prices, corporate bond-yields, and sovereign debt interests are affected by ESG factors.[47]

PART II

Global Strategy Development

CHAPTER 5

Assessing a Company's Resource Base and Capabilities for Going Global

Introduction

This chapter focuses on how managers can identify the key company resources and capabilities around which they can build successful global strategies.[1] The resource-based view (RBV) of a firm is an important framework for conducting this type of analysis. This approach examines a variety of specific types of resources and capabilities that all firms possess in some form and then evaluates the degree to which they serve as the basis for creating a sustained competitive advantage based on industry and competitive considerations.

Next, we review the concept of *core competencies* and its relation to strategy formulation and the development of a global competitive advantage. We conclude this part of the chapter by examining how managers can use their performance records and financial prospects to benchmark against existing competitors in global industries as a basis for gauging the likelihood of success when entering a new global market.

The chapter's balance deals with three issues that are critical to global success—a global mindset, talent, financial resources, and a commitment to *open* innovation.

The Resource-Based View of the Firm

Toyota versus Ford is a competitive situation that virtually all of us recognize. Stock analysts look at the two and conclude that Toyota is the clear leader. They cite Toyota's superior intangible assets (newer factories worldwide, research and development (R&D) facilities, computerization, cash, etc.) and intangible assets (reputation, quality control culture, global business system, etc.). They also mention that Toyota leads Ford in several capabilities to use these assets effectively. Examples include managing distribution globally, influencing labor and supplier relations, managing franchise relations, customer-responsive marketing, and using the speed of decision making to take quick advantage of changing global conditions are a few. Combining capabilities and assets creates competencies for Toyota that are vital, durable, and not easily imitated competitive advantages over Ford.

The Toyota–Ford example illustrates several concepts central to the *firm's RBV*. The RBV is a method identifying and analyzing an organization's strategic advantages based on its distinct combination of assets, skills, capabilities, and intangibles as an organization. RBV's underlying premise is that firms differ in fundamental ways because each firm possesses a unique set of resources to use those assets. Each firm develops competencies from these resources, and, when developed exceptionally well, these become the source of the firm's competitive advantages. Toyota's unmatched decisions to enter global markets locally and regularly invest in or build factories in global markets produced a competitive advantage that led to distinctive competencies and a sustainable competitive advantage.

Tangible Assets, Intangible Assets, and Organizational Capabilities

The RBV's ability to create a more focused, measurable approach to internal analysis starts with its delineation of three basic types of resources. *Tangible assets* are the most straightforward resources to identify and are often found on a firm's balance sheet. They include financial resources, raw materials, production facilities, real estate, and computers. Tangible assets are the physical means a company uses to provide value to its customers. *Intangible assets* are resources without a physical quality such as brand names, company reputation, employee morale, technical knowledge, accumulated experience within an organization, patents, trademarks, and copyrights. *Organizational capabilities* are skills—the ability and ways of combining assets, people, and processes—that a company uses to transform inputs into outputs.

What Makes a Resource Valuable?

After managers identify their firm's tangible assets, intangible assets, and organizational capabilities, they can answer four questions to determine the resources contributing to core competencies and ultimately sustain competitive advantage. The RBV argues that resources are more valuable when they satisfy all four of these guidelines.

1. *Is the resource or skill critical to fulfilling a customer's need better than that of the firm's competitors?*

   Walmart redefined discount retailing and outperformed the industry in profitability by emphasizing four resources—store locations, brand recognition, employee loyalty, and sophisticated inbound logistics. These emphases allowed Walmart to fulfill customer needs much better and more cost-effectively than other discount retailers. The insight from this example is that managers need to identify the few resources that contribute to competitive superiority in, especially, valuable ways. Other resources at Walmart contribute little to competitive advantages because they do not help fulfill customer needs better than those of its key competitors. Examples include the restaurant menu, specific products offered, or parking spaces.

2. *Is there a scarce supply of the resource, or is it easily substituted for or imitated?*

   Short supply. When a resource is scarce, it is more valuable. When a firm possesses a critical resource, and few other competitors do, it can become the basis of competitive advantage. Very limited natural resources, a unique location, and skills that are truly rare represent scarce resources.

   Availability of substitutes. A substitute product is one that the customer can purchase instead of ours to do the same task. It is a different product from a different industry, not a different brand of the same industry product. Examples include printers instead of copier machines, cigarettes instead of e-cigarettes, and solar power instead of coal power.

Imitation. A resource that competitors can readily copy can only generate temporary value. It is scarce for only a short time. Competitors will match or better a resource as soon as they can. Thus, the firm's ability to forestall the competitor's imitation is critical. The RBV identifies four characteristics, called *isolating mechanisms*, that make resources difficult to imitate:

○ *Physically unique resources* are virtually impossible to imitate. A one-of-a-kind real estate location, mineral rights, and patents are examples of resources that cannot be imitated. While there are claims that resources are physically unique, this is seldom true in an impactful way.

○ *Path-dependent resources* are challenging to imitate because of the vague and complicated path a competitor must figure out and replicate to recreate the resource. These resources must be created over time in a very expensive manner and always difficult to accelerate. Google's creation of proprietary search algorithms, Gerber Baby Food's reputation for quality, and Steinway's piano manufacturing expertise would take competitors many years and millions of dollars to match. Consumers' experience drinking Coke or using Gerber, or playing a Steinway would also need to be matched.

○ *Causal ambiguity* refers to situations in which it is difficult for competitors to understand precisely how a firm has created the advantage it enjoys. Such causally ambiguous resources are often organizational capabilities that arise from subtle combinations of tangible and intangible assets and culture, processes, and organizational attributes.

○ *Economic deterrence* usually involves large capital investments incapacity to provide products or services in a given market that are scale-sensitive. Economic deterrence occurs when a competitor understands the resources and may even have the capacity to imitate but chooses not to engage because of a limited market size that would not support an additional firm.

3. *Appropriability: Who actually gets the profit created by a resource?*

Because the Walt Disney Company owns the Mickey Mouse copyright, all profits from that valuable resource accrue to Disney. The value of the franchise name, reservation system, and brand recognition are other examples of appropriability that may be critical in generating the business's profits. Also, many appropriability cases result from employee skills and knowledge that develop within the firm and cannot be transferred readily or effectively to another company.

4. *Durability: How rapidly will the resource depreciate?*

The slower a resource depreciates, the longer its value is maintained. Tangible assets are measurable, and the rate of decline in their value can be estimated. It is challenging to estimate intangible resources' future value, even if intellectual property protections cover them. Thus, they present a much more difficult depreciation or amortization challenge. In the increasingly hypercompetitive global economy, distinctive competencies, and competitive advantages can fade quickly, making the durability of a resource a critical test of value.

Core Competencies

A *core competence* is a capability or skill in which a company excels that it can leverage in the pursuit of its overall mission. Core competencies that differ from those found in competing firms would be considered *distinctive competencies.* Apple's competencies in pulling together available technologies, Toyota's pervasive organizationwide pursuit of quality, and Wendy's systemwide emphasis on providing fresh meat each day are examples of unique competencies to these firms and distinctive compared to their competitors. Distinctive competencies enable a firm to provide products, services, and technologies superior to those of competitors, thus becoming the basis for a lasting *competitive advantage* for the company.

Core competencies evolve as a firm develops its business model. Core competencies are sets of skills or systems that create high value for customers at best-in-class levels. To qualify, such skills or systems should contribute to perceived customer benefits, be difficult for competitors to imitate, and allow for leverage across markets. Honda's use of small engine technology in various products—including motorcycles, jet skis, and lawnmowers—is a good example.

Core competencies also benefit innovation. For example, Charles Schwab successfully leveraged its core competency in brokerage services by expanding its client communication methods to include the Internet, telephone, offices, and financial advisors. For further examples of core competencies, see Exhibit 5.1.

Hamel and Prahalad suggest three tests for identifying core competencies: (1) core competencies should provide access to a broad array of markets; (2) they should help differentiate core products and services; and (3) core competencies should be hard to imitate because they represent multiple skills, technologies, and organizational elements.[2]

Few companies have the resources to develop more than a handful of core competencies. Picking the right ones, therefore, is key. "Which resources or capabilities should we keep in-house and develop into core competencies, and which ones should we outsource?" is an important question to ask. Pharmaceutical companies, for example, often outsource clinical testing to focus their resources on drug development.

Company	Core Competencies	Applications
Google	Proprietary algorithms for the Internet	Online search, e-mail, Google maps
Honda	Small, reliable, powerful combustion engines	Cars, boats, lawnmowers
IKEA	Modern functional home furnishings at low prices	Fully furnished room setups, do-it-yourself (DIY)
McKinsey	Developing practice-relevant knowledge, insight, and frameworks	Management and strategy consulting
Starbucks	High-quality beverages served in a unique ambiance	Customized beverages, seasonal drinks, free Wi-Fi
Tesla	High-performance battery-powered motors and power trains	Cars, trucks
UPS	Superior supply chain services at low cost	Package tracking and delivery, ecommerce

Exhibit 5.1 Examples of core competencies

Generally, core competencies focus on long-term platforms to adapt to market circumstances, sources of leverage in the value chain where the firm can dominate, important elements to customers, and key skills and knowledge, not on specific products.

To develop core competencies, a company must take several actions[3]:

- Isolate its key abilities and hone them into organizationwide strengths
- Compare itself with other companies with the same skills to ensure that it is developing unique capabilities
- Develop an understanding of what capabilities its customers truly value and invest accordingly to develop and sustain valued strengths
- Create an organizational roadmap that sets goals for competence building
- Pursue alliances, acquisitions, and licensing arrangements that will further build the organization's strengths in core areas
- Encourage communication and involvement in core capability development across the organization
- Preserve core strengths even as management expands and redefines the business
- Outsource or divest noncore capabilities to free up resources that can be used to deepen core capabilities.

Benchmarking: Comparison With Competitors

A firm's primary focus in determining the value of its resources and competencies is to compare itself with existing and potential competitors. Firms in the same industry develop and rely on similar resources, competencies, and skills in functional areas and operating facilities and locations, technical know-how, brand images, levels of integration, managerial talent, and so on. However, when there are differences in internal resources, they can build relative strengths and essential considerations in strategy formulation.

The largest technology companies in the world are resource-rich, as is required for the production of cellphones and laptop computers. The list of the largest global competitors, based on market capitalization, include Accenture, Adobe, Alphabet, Apple, Broadcom, Cisco, Facebook, IBM, Intel, Microsoft, NVIDIA, Oracle, Qualcomm, Salesforce, Samsung, SAP, Taiwan Semiconductor Manufacturing, Tata Consultancy Services, Tencent, and Texas Instruments. In many cases, these companies are head-to-head competitors in the global tech-services industry. Because they have a shared reliance on many resources and capabilities, benchmarking is a useful tool in determining how a company stands in the race to provide attractive customer segments with the most demanded product characteristics.

For example, New York-based IBM and India-based Tata Consultancy Services are major rivals. Tata focuses on large American and European companies by providing lower-cost information technology (IT) services and business process simplification consulting. By contrast, IBM focuses on helping clients cut costs and emerging market customers build their technology infrastructures.

Tata's strength is its ability to offer low-cost outsourcing options to large firms for their information system operation needs. IBM emphasizes systems design and optimization of the latest technology infrastructure to make systems perform well. IBM also relies on its technical skills and computer technology expertise, where it maintains a relative strength.

These strategies produce a situation where Tata generates half of its global revenue from U.S. clients. By contrast, IBM generates half of its revenue in foreign nations, with particular success in selling tech services in India. Thus, managers in both Tata and IBM have built successful yet fundamentally different strategies. Benchmarking each other, they have identified ways to build on relative strengths while avoiding dependence on capabilities at which the other firm excels.

Benchmarking, which is defined as comparing how a company performs a specific activity with a competitor that does the same thing, is a central concern of managers in quality committed companies worldwide. Managers seek to systematically benchmark the costs and results of all value activities against relevant competitors or useful standards. It has proven to be an effective way to improve that activity continuously.

General Electric's (GE's) approach includes sending managers to benchmark FedEx's customer service practices, seeking to compare and improve its practices within a diverse set of businesses, none of which compete directly with FedEx. It earlier did the same thing with Motorola, leading it to embrace Motorola's Six Sigma program for quality control and continuous improvement.

The Importance of a Global Mindset

Many corporations encounter a common challenge, as they move to globalize their operations can be summed up in one word: *mindset*. Herbert Paul defines a mindset as "a set of deeply held internal mental images and assumptions, which individuals develop through a continuous process of learning from experience".[4] In a global context, a global mindset is "the ability to avoid the simplicity of assuming all cultures are the same, and at the same time, not being paralyzed by the complexity of the differences".[5] As Exhibit 5.2 shows, a global mindset has three main components. *Intellectual capital,* which describes the ability to deal with global complexities. *Psychological capital* defines the capacity and eagerness to deal with an unfamiliar situation. Finally, *social capital* assists in dealing with different cultures and situations requiring a high level of empathy.

The concept of a mindset does not just apply to individuals; it can be extended to organizations as the members' aggregated mindset. At the organizational level, mindset also reflects whether its members interact

Global Mindset

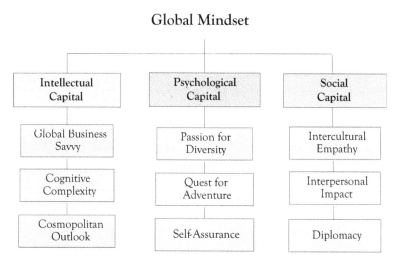

Exhibit 5.2 Elements of a global mindset

mainly formally or informally and whether decision-making processes are hierarchical or informal. The personal mindset of the CEO sometimes is the single most important factor in shaping the organization's mindset.

A corporate mindset determines how corporate challenges, opportunities, capabilities, and limitations are perceived. It also defines how goals and expectations are set and significantly impacts what strategies are considered and ultimately selected and implemented. Recognizing the diversity of local markets and seeing them as a source of opportunity and strength, while at the same time, pushing for strategic consistency across countries lies at the heart of global strategy development.

To understand the importance of a corporate mindset, consider two often quoted corporate mantras: "Think global and act local" and its opposite: "Think local and act global." "Think global and act local" indicates a global approach based on the belief that a powerful brand name combined with a standard product, package, and advertising concept is the best way to succeed in global markets. Contrast this with a "Think local and act global" mindset, which assumes that global expansion, is best accomplished through adaptation to local needs and preferences. In this mindset, diversity is considered a source of opportunity, whereas strategic cohesion plays a secondary role. Such a *bottom-up* approach can offer greater revenue generation possibilities, particularly for companies wanting to grow rapidly.

To become truly global, multinational companies will increasingly have to look to emerging markets for talent. India is recognized as a source of technical talent in engineering, sciences, and software. High-tech companies recruit in India not only for the Indian market but also for the global market. China and other parts of Asia may be next.

As corporate globalization advances, senior management's composition will also begin to reflect the importance of the emerging markets. At present, with a few exceptions, such as Citicorp and Unilever, C-suites are still filled with nationals from the company's home country. As the senior management for multinationals becomes more diverse, decision-making criteria and processes, attitudes toward ethics and corporate responsibility, risk-taking, and team building will likely change. The changes in decision-making priorities may reflect a slow but persistent shift in many multinational companies' attention toward Asia. In many Western countries, decision making is highly participative. In other words, many decisions are made based on a group majority, and participation is encouraged by subordinates and leaders. In many Asian cultures, a more systematic approach to governance and administration is preferred.

Determinants of a Corporate Global Mindset

What factors shape a corporation's mindset? Can they be managed? Given the importance of mindset to a company's global outlook and prospects, these are important questions. Paul cites four primary factors: (1) *top management's view of the world*, (2) *the company's strategic and administrative heritage*, (3) *the company's dominant organizational dimension*, and (4) *industry-specific forces driving or limiting globalization.*[6]

Top management's view of the world. The composition of a company's top management and how it exercises power can influence the corporate mindset. A visionary leader can be a major catalyst in breaking down existing geographic and competitive boundaries. By contrast, leaders with a regional, predominantly ethnocentric vision, are more likely to concentrate on the home market and not be very interested in international growth.

Administrative heritage. The second factor is a company's *administrative heritage*—its strategic and organizational history. This history reflects how the company has grown, what assets it has acquired over the years, the evolution of its organizational structure, the strategies and management philosophies the company has pursued, and its core competencies and corporate culture. In most companies, these elements evolve over several years and increasingly *define* the organization. Changing one or more of these key tangible and intangible elements of a company is an enormous challenge and, therefore, a constraint on its global strategic options.

Organizational structure. The type of *organizational structure* a company has adopted is also a key determinant of a corporate mindset. In a strongly product-oriented structure, management is more likely to think globally as the entire information infrastructure is geared toward collecting and processing product data worldwide. In an organization focused on countries or areas or regions, the managerial mindset tends to be more local because it is primarily oriented toward local and regional needs. In a matrix organizational structure based on both product and geographic dimensions, management's mindset reflects both global and local perspectives.

Industry forces. Industry factors also affect managers' perceptions and outlook. When there are opportunities for economies of scale and scope, global sourcing, and lower transportation and communication costs, managers are pushed toward a global efficiency mindset. Other factors that a global efficiency mindset include are (1) stronger global competition, (2) the need to enter new markets, (3) the globalization of important customers, (4) a trend toward more homogeneous demand, particularly for products in fast-moving consumer goods industries, and (5) more uniform technical standards, particularly for industrial products.

However, another set of industry drivers works in the opposite direction and calls for strategies with a high degree of local responsiveness. Such drivers include strong local competition in important markets and cultural differences, making the transfer of globally standardized concepts less attractive. Issues such as protectionism, trade barriers, and volatile exchange rates may also suggest a national or regional business approach.

Thus, to create the right global mindset, management must understand the different, often opposite, factors that shape it. At the corporate level, managers focused on global competitive strategies typically emphasize increased cross-country or cross-region coordination and more centralized, standardized approaches to strategy formulation. By contrast, country managers frequently favor greater autonomy for their local units because they feel they have a better understanding of the local market and customer needs. Thus, different managers can interpret data and facts differently and favor different strategic concepts and solutions depending on their mindsets.

In practice, two different scenarios can develop. The first is defined by a situation in which one perspective consistently wins at the other's expense. Under this scenario, the company may well be successful initially. However, it is likely to run into trouble when its ability to learn and innovate is impaired as it opts for *short-sighted* solutions. A second scenario occurs when a deliberate effort is made to maintain a *creative tension* between both perspectives. This scenario recognizes the importance of such tension to the company's ability to develop new ways of thinking and look for completely new solutions. A clear corporate vision and a commitment to fair decision-making processes are key to fostering and maintaining such creative tension. A clear corporate vision provides general direction for all managers and employees where the company wishes to be in the future. Accepted and well understood, fair decision processes encourage analysis and discussion of both global and local perspectives and their merits, given specific strategic situations.

Executive Talent Required for Going Global

To be successful in the world of international business demands a special set of skills. Global executives increasingly face a *VUCA* business environment—one that is volatile, uncertain, complex, and ambiguous. The most important skills needed to navigate this new, globalized business landscape are *soft skills*. While strong technical know-how is still essential, the *soft skills* can mean the difference between survival and international business success.[7] Key *soft skills* include (1) *cross-cultural communication skills*, (2) *excellent networking abilities*, (3) *collaboration*, (4) *interpersonal influence*, (5) *adaptive thinking*, (6) *emotional intelligence*, and (7) *resilience*.

Financial Resources

Expanding internationally requires significant financial resources. Financial resources are made up of a company's liquid assets, including cash, bank deposits, and liquid financial investments, such as stocks and bonds. Corporations have three main sources of capital: (1) *business operations,* such as the sale of goods and services; (2) *capital funding,* including issues of shares and capital contributions; and (3) *external sources* such as bank loans or issues of corporate bonds.

Equity. Multinational companies have access to a number of options to raise funds beyond domestic financing. A global company can partner with investment banks to fund its expansion by issuing equity in exchange for cash in markets such as the stock exchanges in New York, Tokyo, London, and Hong Kong.

Debt. A second option is to raise funds by selling debt in the form of bonds. Selling debt products is a complicated process that is governed by strict regulations in most countries. Companies must clear several regulatory hurdles before being granted access to the credit market because holders of debt (creditors) have different legal rights from owners of stock (shareholders) when a company becomes insolvent. In addition to bonds, a global business entity can raise operating funds for its operations by selling commercial paper.

Private lenders. Offering equity or debt products in an open market is not the only way to raise funds from private sources. Private lenders such as banks, insurance companies, hedge funds, and private equity funds can often be more flexible and responsive, leading to faster funding than a well-regulated stock market can offer.

Government funding. Finally, an international company can form a corporation with public assistance. Government subsidies are generally targeted at attracting new businesses to a city or area, creating jobs and improving the local economy. If a corporation meets applicable regulatory requirements and is in an eligible line of business, a government subsidy can help provide much-needed funds for operational expenses.

A Commitment to Open Innovation[8]

In *closed innovation* companies, innovation occurs by using only internal resources. Internally generated new ideas are evaluated, and only the best and most promising ones are selected for their development and commercialization. The ones that show less potential are usually abandoned.

Open innovation companies use external knowledge, cooperate with external partners, and buy and incorporate external technologies and ideas. Innovations generated inside the company can be sold as new technology or industrial property to other companies. This makes sense if they are not applicable within their business model or because they have no capacity or experience to develop the invention.

There are significant advantages to opening the innovation process to the flow of ideas and knowledge in both directions:

- Reduction in the time and cost of innovation projects
- Development of a greater number of solutions, innovations, ideas, patents, products, and technologies
- Due to a lack of ability or strategic limitations, commercial inventions cannot always be introduced to the market

All three are pertinent to global strategy development. Timing can be key to entering a foreign market, as we will discuss in Chapter 8. Most products and services require a degree of adaptation to be accepted in foreign markets. Having local input into key decisions such as the degree and form of adaptation of the product or service, its manufacture and distribution, positioning, and branding can spell the difference between success and failure. Finally, the commercialization of ideas that do not fit with the current strategy provides additional revenue and often yields lasting partnerships with other companies.

Open innovation is based on five fundamental principles[9]:

1. "Not all smart people work for us, so we must find and tap external knowledge and expertise."
2. "External R&D can create significant value; internal R&D is needed to realize some portion of that value."
3. "Our company does not have to originate the research to use it profitably."
4. "If we make the best use of internal and external ideas, we have a better chance to win."
5. "We should profit when other companies use our intellectual property (IP), and we should buy the IP from other firms whenever it advances our business model."

When engaging with universities, start-ups, customers, or suppliers, R&D laboratories developing new products or processes rely heavily on the firm's support functions. However, there cannot be only a single open innovation champion within the organization. Innovation processes are complex and often involve different persons, departments, and disciplines. Therefore, different roles are required to help manage complex innovation projects. Three types of internal roles or *promoters* can help boost open innovation:

1. A *power promoter* drives a project, provides necessary resources, and helps overcome obstacles that might arise during a project.
2. The *expert promoter* is someone with specific technical or market knowledge for the innovation problem at hand and overcomes technical barriers.
3. The *process promoter* is the *glue* between the power promoter, the expert promoter, as well as other project members who contribute to an open innovation project but do not have the permission to do so due to existing internal rules or limited capacity and resources.[10]

GE is a company that employs various open innovation strategies. Its GE open innovation message emphasizes its comprehension of the need to address the world's problems by applying crowdsourcing innovation. The Open Innovation Manifesto of the company highlights the collaboration between entrepreneurs and experts from anywhere to solve problems by sharing their ideas. Based on GE's innovation Ecomagination project that targets to resolve environmental challenges via innovative solutions, the company, over the last decade, has spent 17 billion U.S. dollars on R&D and realized total revenues of 232 billion U.S. dollars.

Samsung adopted an open innovation strategy to build their external innovation strengths through the Samsung Accelerator program. This initiative aims to encourage collaboration between designers, innovators, and thinkers to focus on different solutions. Samsung divides its innovation cooperation projects into four categories: partnerships, ventures, accelerators, acquisitions. Partnerships typically aim for new features or integrations within Samsung's existing products. Ventures can be described as investments into early-stage start-ups. These investments provide access to new technologies. For example, Samsung has invested in Mobeam, a mobile payment company. Accelerators provide start-ups with an initial investment, facilities to work in, and other resources. Products coming from the internal start-ups can become a part of Samsung's product portfolio over time or just serve as learning experiences. Acquisitions are used to bring in start-ups working on innovations that are at the core of Samsung's strategic areas of the future. These acquisitions often remain independent units and can even join the Accelerator program.

Hewlett–Packard (HP) was an early adopter of the ideals of open innovation. It has created an open innovation team that links collaborators with researchers and entrepreneurs in business, government, and universities to develop innovative solutions to hard problems to develop breakthrough technologies.

Procter and Gamble's (P&G's) open innovation with external partners is organized through its Connect+Develop website. Through this platform, P&G communicates with innovators who can access detailed information about specific needs and submit their ideas to the site. Connect+Develop has generated multiple partnerships and produced several new products.

Mini-Case 5.1: Dialing up Innovation at Nestle: Taking Open Innovation to a New Level Through a Multifaceted Approach[11]

By 2050, the world's population is expected to reach almost 10 billion, making the supply of affordable foods more challenging than ever. Consumers are also beginning to demand healthier, natural, and more authentic food products and shift toward a plant-based diet. Sustainability and environmental concerns are putting pressure on natural resources, leading consumers to demand food choices that are good for them and good for the planet.

The only way to meet the needs of this growing population is through disruptive innovation. Nestlé has adopted a multifaceted approach to new ways to innovate.

Globally, the company has 23 R&D centers with 4,200 employees, tasked with discovering and developing innovative products that fuel business growth. It is adopting new ways of working, enabling the company to launch consumer-centric products more quickly. It is simplifying processes, creating a leaner organization, and funding fast-track projects. To ensure the early translation of science into groundbreaking innovations, the company is upgrading its R&D centers to include prototyping facilities and pilot-scale equipment that all its employees can use. Collaborations with suppliers and its commercial operations are being strengthened to bring new products to market faster and more efficiently.

In the first half of 2019, Nestle launched the *Garden Gourmet* plant-based burger, *YES!* snack bars in a recyclable paper wrapper, and a new range of *Starbucks* products. It also rolled out its infant formula with human milk oligosaccharides (HMOs) across 44 markets in just 12 months. It invented the first dark chocolate made entirely from cocoa fruit for its popular *KitKat* brand.

Nestle recognizes the need to collaborate differently with suppliers, researchers, and start-ups. For example, strategic innovation partnerships play a key role in improving the environmental performance of our packaging. It has joined forces with Danimer Scientific partners to develop biodegradable plastic products and PureCycle to deliver the world's first virgin-like recycled polypropylene.

CHAPTER 6

Global Strategy Formulation

Introduction

Strategy is about *positioning* a company for *competitive advantage*. It involves making *choices* about *which markets to participate in, what products and services to offer,* and *how to allocate corporate resources.* Its primary goal is to *create long-term value for shareholders and other stakeholders* by providing *customer value.* Strategy is different from a firm's vision, mission, goals, priorities, and plans. It is *the result of choices executives make about what to offer, where to play, and how to win, to maximize long-term value.*

Choices must be made because there is usually more than one way to compete in every market. The choice of target market(s), the value proposition, capabilities, and management regime must fit together coherently. The *resource-based* perspective of strategy helps make these decisions by defining strategic thinking in building core capabilities that transcend the boundaries of traditional business units. It focuses on creating corporate portfolios around *core businesses* and adopting goals and processes to enhance *core competencies.* This paradigm emphasizes creating value by developing and nurturing key resources and capabilities rather than merely capturing economic value from existing assets and opportunities.

[handwritten margin note: Safe Control]

Corporate, Business Unit, Functional and Global Strategy

A comprehensive set of strategic plans includes a roadmap for the firm's *corporate, business unit,* and *functional* strategies:

- *Corporate strategy* is about determining in what businesses a company should be engaged. Corporate strategy, therefore, delineates the direction the firm is taking and the role each business unit will play in pursuing that direction. It defines how the firm can increase its scale of operation from a single business to a portfolio of businesses operating in multiple international markets.

- *Business unit strategy* seeks to determine how a firm should compete in each of its businesses or regions worldwide. For a single-product firm, the business strategy typically overlaps with the company's corporate strategy. For organizations with multiple businesses or a presence in multiple countries, however, each business unit or region will have its strategy that defines the products or services it will offer and the customers it wants to reach.
- *Functional strategies* are focused on supporting the business unit and corporate strategies. Examples include manufacturing, marketing, human resources, research and development, and finance strategies.

As shown in Exhibit 6.1, *global strategy* is embedded and part of strategy development at each level. As noted in Chapter 2, *global strategy is a generic term covering four areas: the development of international,*

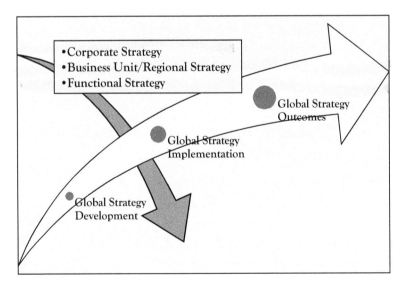

Exhibit 6.1 Corporate, business unit, functional and global strategy

multidomestic (also referred to as multinational), global, and transnational strategies. Each describes a different starting point and a different set of objectives for international expansion. Each area also defines a unique set of opportunities and challenges that need to be considered.

At the corporate level, the key questions are (1) identifying where to expand internationally and why, (2) deciding what products and services to offer, and (2) selecting the best method and timing of entry into a new foreign market. Depending on the firm's current global posture, global strategy at the corporate level can also be focused on determining the degree to which products and processes are standardized across geographic boundaries and on harmonizing business unit or regional strategies into a more homogeneous format. Therefore, the objectives of global strategy development at the corporate level include reducing the complexity of managing diverse markets and achieving an appropriate balance between local responsiveness and economies of scale. International and global business strategies emphasize economies of scale. Multidomestic strategies emphasize local responsiveness. A transnational strategy tries to do both.

Some product categories, such as luxury goods or software, lend themselves to a substantial amount of standardization. By contrast, product categories such as food products or clothing may require a significant adaptation due to differences in customer preferences, climate, language, or local laws. Note that using the word *balancing* when considering standardization and adaptation issues is somewhat misleading. Whenever possible, companies will want to develop strategies that will realize the benefits of both. A good example is provided by transnational companies that exploit economies of scale in one part of the value chain, say research and development (R&D) or sourcing, while using adaptation in another, such as product design or marketing.[1]

At the *business unit or regional* level, global strategy is focused on creating a strategy for each business unit or country in which the firm operates. Global strategy must be sensitive to the national context and be responsive to the local competitive landscape. It defines the products the company will offer and the marketing strategies it will use. National or regional strategies may include country-specific sourcing policies, manufacturing strategies, and human resource procedures. National strategies are key to creating a firm's core competencies, which are later aggregated into global and transnational strategies. When a company operates in several countries, the complexity of handling too many national strategies will lead the firm to introduce a more harmonized global approach.

At the *functional* level, decisions must be made about (1) which functions to perform locally, regionally, or globally and (2) which functions to outsource and why.

Benefits of a Global Strategy

A well-thought-out global strategy can confer many benefits to a company. Among them are:

1. *Economies of scale*: The extra cost savings realized when higher volume production allows unit costs to be reduced—for example, a steel mill that incurs lower steel costs per unit as the mill's size increases.[2]

2. *Economies of scope*: The cost savings realized by business units or regions when they share activities or transfer capabilities and competencies from one part of the group to another. Consider, for example, a food products company subsidiary that sells more than one product from the company's total range of products.

3. *Global brand recognition*: The benefit gained from having a brand that is recognized everywhere globally—Disney provides a good example.

4. *Global customer satisfaction*: Global customers who demand the same product, service, and quality at all locations worldwide. For example, Hyatt customers expect to receive the same service level at all its hotels worldwide.

5. *Reduced labor and other input costs*: Lower input costs can be realized by choosing and switching to manufacturers and assemblers with lower labor costs. An example is computer assembly in Southeast Asia from imported parts where labor costs are lower.

6. *Recovery of R&D and other costs by spreading these costs over a large number of countries:* Pharmaceutical research and trials cost billions of dollars. Selling the resulting drugs worldwide means a greater number of countries that can contribute to defraying such costs.

7. *Extending product lifecycles by entering emerging markets:* Consider, for example, selling low-end laptops in developing countries.

8. *Diversification of risk:* By doing business in multiple countries, companies can diversify their exposure to international conflict, national disasters, and currency risk.

9. *Pre-empting competitive pressures:* By engaging competitors abroad, a company may prevent foreign competitors from entering the local market or reducing their domestic market effectiveness.[3]

Costs of a Global Strategy

Global strategies can be costly—even to the point where the costs exceed the benefits:

1. *Lack of responsiveness to local needs and preferences:* Adaptation is costly, but an insufficient adaptation level can be even more costly when local customers refuse to compromise on their individual tastes. When this occurs, a company incurs increased costs due to adaptation, but does not realize its market penetration objectives.

2. *Transportation and logistics costs*: If a company manufactures in one country but sells in many others, it must transport finished products. The costs for some heavy products, like tractors, may exceed the savings from economies of scale realized from the centralized production in one country.

3. *Economies of scale benefits can be difficult to obtain in practice*: Building or renovating manufacturing facilities abroad takes time, money, and patience. If local competitors are still using old plant and equipment and have lower labor costs, economies of scale may be elusive for a long time.

4. *Communications costs will be higher:* When a company standardizes its products and services, it needs to communicate carefully the *what and why* to every country in which it participates. It also needs to monitor and control the results of the decision to standardize. Such communications are delicate, time-consuming, and expensive. What is more, the success or failure of these efforts often depends on local managers' decisions who may have their agendas and interests.

5. _Management coordination costs:_ Senior executives working with a global strategy need to visit the different countries where they participate or wish to participate. Foreign managers and workers often need to be consulted, issues need to be explored and discussed, and local variations in tax and legal issues need to be addressed.

6. _Barriers to trade:_ Taxes and other restrictions on goods and services set by national governments can cause delays and increase costs.

7. _Other costs imposed by national governments to protect their home industries:_ Sometimes, countries engage in protectionist policies such as imposing special taxes or restrictions on shareholdings.[4]

Strategy and Business Models

Every company has a _business model_—a blueprint of how it does business—defined by its core strategy, although it may not always be explicitly articulated. This model most likely evolved as the company rose to prominence in its primary markets and reflects key choices about what value it provides to whom, how, and at what price and cost. As shown in Exhibit 6.2, a business model describes who its customers are, how it

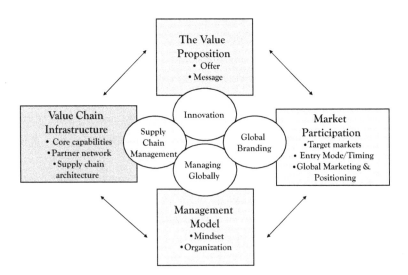

Exhibit 6.2 Four components of a business model

reaches them and communicates to them (*market participation*); what a company offers its customers (*the value proposition*); with what resources, activities, and partners it creates its offerings (*value chain infrastructure*); and finally, how it organizes, finances, and manages its operations (*management model*).

A company's *value proposition* comprises the core of its business model; it includes everything it offers to its customers in a specific market or segment. This includes the company's bundles of products and services and how it differentiates itself from its competitors. Therefore, a value proposition consists of the full range of tangible and intangible benefits a company provides to its customers and other stakeholders.

The *market participation* dimension of a business model has three components:

1. What specific markets or segments a company chooses to serve, domestically or abroad;
2. What methods of distribution it uses to reach its customers; and
3. How it promotes and advertises its value proposition to its target customers.

The *business model's value chain infrastructure dimension* deals with such questions: What key internal resources and capabilities have the company created to support the chosen value proposition and target markets? What partner network has it chosen to support the business model? How are these activities organized into an overall, coherent value creation and delivery model?

The *management* submodel summarizes a company's choices about a suitable organizational structure, financial structure, and management policies. Typically, organization and management are closely linked. In companies that are organized primarily around a line of products, division management is often highly centralized. By contrast, companies operating with a more geographic organizational structure usually are managed on a more decentralized basis.

It used to be that each industry could be characterized by a single dominant business model. Competitive advantage was won mainly through better execution, more efficient processes, lean organizations, and product innovation. While execution and product innovation still matter, they are no longer sufficient today.

Companies are now operating in industries that are characterized by multiple and coexisting business models. Competitive advantage is increasingly achieved through focused and innovative business models. Consider the airline, music, telecom, or banking industries. In each one, different business models compete against each other. There are traditional flag carriers in the airline industry, low-cost airlines, business class-only airlines, and fractional private jet ownership companies. Each business model is based on a different approach to achieving a competitive advantage.

Southwest Airlines' business model offers customers an alternative to traveling by car, bus, or train, by giving them a no-frills flight enhanced through complementary services. Southwest's business model differs from those of other major U.S. airlines on several dimensions. It provides more than low fares, point-to-point connections, highly rated customer service, and the use of a standardized fleet of aircraft. A key differentiating factor is the way Southwest treats its employees—providing profit-sharing and empowerment programs. Southwest also creates a fun experience onboard and in the terminal with relaxed behavior by the cabin crew and ground staff. Not surprisingly, Southwest's demonstrably successful business model has spawned numerous imitators worldwide, including Ryanair, EasyJet, JetBlue, and Air Arabia.

Capital One provides an example of why it is useful to focus on a company's overall business model rather than individual components such as products, markets, or suppliers. Capital One is a Fortune 500 company that provides financial services such as credit cards and loans to consumers, small businesses, and commercial clients. The company operates mainly in the United States, Canada, and the UK. Unlike rival banks, the company has very few branches and much lower real estate costs. Instead, it relies primarily on technology. Its approach is rooted in an information-based strategy that combines marketing with extensive data analysis of customer needs and risk profiles. For example, the company uses internal and external information in its lending practices in addition to the FICO score, which gives it an edge over its competition.[5]

> *Each business model embodies a different approach to achieving a competitive advantage. Describing a company's strategy in terms of its business model allows explicit consideration of the logic or architecture of each component and its relationship to others as a set of design choices that can be changed. Thus, thinking holistically about every component of the business model—and systematically challenging orthodoxies within these components—significantly extends the scope for innovation and improves the chances of building a sustainable competitive advantage.*

Global Strategy as Business Model Change

When a company decides to expand into foreign markets or change its global footprint, for example, by moving from an international to a multinational or global posture, it must take its business model apart and consider the impact of such a global strategic change on every component of the model. For example, concerning its value proposition, a company must decide whether and how to change its product(s) and support services. What is more, to what extent and how it standardizes or further adapts its product(s) and support services is intimately linked to the choice of what markets the company wishes to expand into and why. Next, the company must decide whether its market positioning needs to be changed, which value-adding activities to keep in-house, which to outsource, and which to relocate to other parts of the world—and so on. Finally, decisions need to be made about organizing and managing these efforts on a global basis. Together, these decisions define a company's global strategy on a continuum from a truly global orientation to a more local one. *Therefore, crafting a global strategy is about deciding how a company should change or adapt its core (domestic) business model to achieve a competitive advantage as it globalizes its operations or changes its global footprint.*

Exhibit 6.3 shows how the adaptation, aggregation, arbitrage (AAA) framework relates to the definition of global strategy as business model change. At each strategic transition in a company's foreign footprint, all business model components need to be re-evaluated using the AAA framework to maintain or enhance its global competitive advantage.

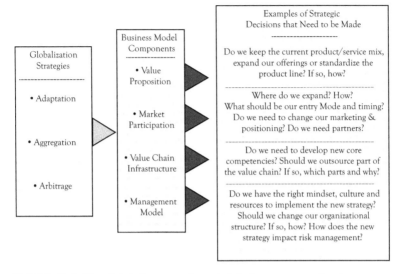

Exhibit 6.3 The AAA framework and global strategy as business model change

Linking competitive strategy analysis to business model design requires segmenting the market, creating a value proposition for each segment, deciding how to create and deliver that value, and determining how to prevent the business model or strategy from undermined through imitation by competitors or disintermediation by customers. This is important because *a particular business model's value, unless constantly maintained, nourished, and improved, erodes with time.* At any given point in time, a company competes with a particular mix of resources. Some of the company's assets and capabilities are better than those of its rivals; others are inferior; the superior assets and capabilities are the source of positional advantages. Whatever competitive advantage the firm possesses, it must expect that ongoing change in the strategic environment and competitive moves by rival firms continuously erode it. Thus, competitive strategy has a dual purpose: (1) slowing down the erosion process by protecting current sources of advantage against the actions of competitors and (2) investing in and nurturing new capabilities that are key to creating the next position of competitive advantage. The creation and maintenance of advantage is, therefore, a continuous process.

Mini-Case 6.1: Zara's Unique Business Model— Driven by Supply Chain Capabilities[6]

Zara SA is the largest company in the Inditex group, the world's largest apparel retailer. The Spanish company specializes in fast fashion, and products include clothing, accessories, shoes, swimwear, beauty, and perfumes. In 2019, Zara was ranked as the *46th most valuable brand* in the world by *Forbes*.

The company's core target market is women 24 to 35 years old. It reaches this market by locating its stores in town centers and places with high concentrations of women in this age range. Short production runs deliberately create a scarcity of given designs, which generates a sense of urgency and a reason for consumers to buy while supplies last. Consequently, Zara does not have much excess inventory and does not need to mark down its clothing items.

Zara competes with a global business model driven by supply chain capabilities that few, if any, competitors can match. Its manufacturing and distribution are centralized—to effect economies of scale and speed. Its supply chain is organized around a huge, highly automated distribution center called *The Cube*—64,500 square meters (five million square feet) with highly automated monorail links to 11 Zara-owned clothing factories within 16 kilometers (10 miles) radius of the Cube (see Exhibit 6.4). All raw materials pass through the Cube on their way to the clothing factories, and all finished goods pass through on their way out to the stores. The Zara factories are connected to the Cube by underground tunnels with high-speed monorails to move cut fabric to the factories for dyeing and assembly into clothing items. The monorail system then returns finished products to the Cube for shipment to stores.

Zara buys large quantities of only a few fabric types and does garment design, cutting, and dyeing in-house. This way, fabric manufacturers can make quick deliveries of bulk quantities of fabric directly to Zara's Cube. The company purchases raw fabric from suppliers in Italy, Spain, Portugal, and Greece.

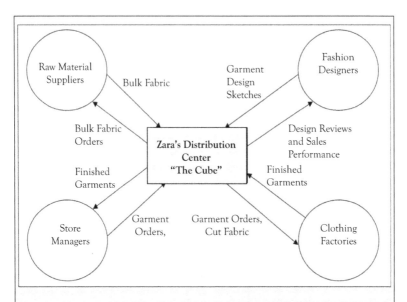

Exhibit 6.4 Zara's global distribution center **The Cube**

With its flexible and agile business model, Zara can change its clothing designs on average every two weeks, whereas competitors can only change their designs every two to three months. It carries about 11,000 different items per year in thousands of stores worldwide compared to competitors that carry 2,000 to 4,000 items per year. Zara's highly responsive supply chain is central to its business success. Its factories can quickly increase and decrease production rates, so there is less inventory in the supply chain and less need to finance that inventory with working capital. They do only 50 to 60 percent of their manufacturing in advance versus the 80 to 90 percent done by competitors. Zara does not need to place big bets on yearly fashion trends. They can make many smaller bets on short-term trends that are easier to call correctly.

Zara can deliver garments to stores worldwide in just a few days. It uses trucks to deliver to stores in Europe and air freight to ship to other markets. Zara can afford the increased shipping cost because it does not need to do much discounting and does not advertise extensively. Making the supply chain the core of its business model has changed a very traditional industry. And, because supply chains are composed of people, processes, and technology, even the latest and greatest technology is not a competitive advantage all by itself. People must be well trained, and processes must be put in place to enable people to apply their training and technology to the best effect.

Global Strategy From a Capabilities Perspective

A complementary, resource-based view of global strategy focuses on (1) building a platform of capabilities collected from the resources, experiences, and innovations of units operating in multiple locations; (2) transplanting those capabilities wherever appropriate; and (3) then systematically upgrading and renewing them ahead of the competition. This framework has three elements—*exploiting, renewing,* and *enhancing* core capabilities.[7]

Exploiting existing capabilities. The easiest way for a company to gain an advantage in foreign markets is by exploiting capabilities first developed at home. A good example is provided by IKEA, which successfully transferred its conception of low-cost, modular furniture with a Nordic design. The exploitation of capabilities can also occur through the acquisition of companies abroad. NH Hotels created one of Europe's largest business hotel chains by transferring core capabilities it developed in its home market to other European markets.

Identifying which capabilities can be transferred abroad and where they are best replicated involves applying the so-called RAT test. RAT stands for *relevant, appropriable, and transferable.* The RAT test consists of asking three questions:

1. Are the capabilities developed in the home market *relevant* to customers in the target market? Do they create value for the customer?

2. If used in a foreign target market, would these capabilities be *appropriable*? In other words, are there sufficient barriers to imitation and innovation that prevent competitors from matching these capabilities or finding alternative solutions? Are the necessary

value chain partners present in the target market and willing to cooperate?

3. Are the capabilities *transferable*? Can the firm deploy its capabilities effectively in the target foreign location without sacrificing value creation at home?

Creating new capabilities. Companies sometimes expand internationally to gain access to strategic assets or to develop new capabilities. In these cases, the key issue is whether the new additions will enhance the company's capabilities and global competitive position. Developing new capabilities can sometimes be achieved by making a single strategic move, such as acquiring a foreign company with a particular technology. At other times, the development of new capabilities occurs incrementally, as the company learns from dealing with the challenges presented by another country's competitive environment.

The *CAT* test is useful for evaluating opportunities for enhancing current sources of competitive advantage through assets and new capabilities developed in foreign markets. The CAT test helps explore whether new capabilities will be *complementary, appropriable, and transferable,* revealing the potential of the new assets and capabilities to enhance existing advantages[8]. The CAT test is comprised of three questions:

1. Are the new assets and capabilities that the company wants to develop or acquire in the new market *complementary* to the existing capabilities that constitute the base of the company's competitive advantage?

2. Are the new assets *appropriable*? Can the company appropriate enough of the value of these new capabilities, or will other companies extract the value of the capabilities or resources that they supply?

3. Are the new assets *transferable*? Can the company effectively bring them back from the source location and integrate them into its capability set without sacrificing its value?

Enhancing capabilities: the RAT–CAT cycle. As shown in Exhibit 6.5, enhancing capabilities involves exploiting RAT in another target country.

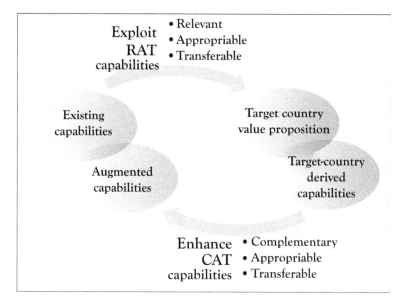

Exhibit 6.5 The RAT–CAT cycle

Then, after the company adds to its capabilities by competing in the new market, it can enhance its overall capabilities. To do so, it must identify those newly acquired capabilities that are CAT and transfer them to all or part of the rest of the corporation.

As a company goes through successive RAT–CAT cycles, it gains leverage from an increasingly rich and diverse capability set. This leverage includes the benefits of scale and arbitrage across locations. As it grows, a company becomes less dependent on the specific home-grown capabilities that made its initial international expansion possible. And, as the firm increases its geographic scope, it is increasingly likely to become a truly transnational company, capable of creating value by leveraging new technologies and market intelligence across the globe.

Exhibit 6.6 summarizes the conceptualization of global strategy from a capability perspective. It identifies—at each stage of capability development—the primary strategic objective, conditions that must be met for capability development to occur, which companies this approach is most suitable for, and how the process is best managed.

STAGE	EXPLOIT	ENHANCE	RENEW
Strategic objective	Leverage existing capabilities in new markets.	Develop complementary capabilities that can increase the power of existing capabilities.	Create a virtuous cycle that allows the company to renew its capabilities—and through them gain a stronger competitive advantage.
Boundary conditions	Existing capabilities should be relevant, appropriable and transferable to the new market.	Newfound capabilities should be complementary to the existing set and be appropriable and transferable.	New capabilities should have the potential to shake up the status quo and set off a new round of upgrading of capabilities.
Best for	Companies that are internationalizing by entering new markets	Companies that have entered a number of markets but are still building their overall competitive advantage	Companies that are at an advanced stage of global strategy development
Organizational architecture	Led from the company headquarters	Increasing importance of subsidiaries and stronger relationship between headquarters and subsidiaries	Distributed network
Nature and direction of the relationship between headquarters and subsidiaries	From the center to the subsidiaries	Subsidiaries gain in importance. They need to understand the existing sources of advantage to succeed locally and work with headquarters to integrate newfound capabilities into a global core capability.	Bidirectional
Sustainability	Short- term	Medium- term	Long- term
Test	RAT Test	CAT Test	RAT + CAT Tests
Challenges	Identify markets where existing advantages are relevant.	Identify assets and capabilities that can complement the existing core sources of advantage.	Maintain the continuous reinvention cycle.

Exhibit 6.6 Global strategy from a capabilities perspective

Formulating a Global Strategy

There are many parallels between the process of crafting a domestic strategy and developing a global strategy. Each can be organized around three key questions: *Where are we now?*, *Where do we wish to go?*, and *How do we get there?* Each question defines a part of the process and suggests different types of analyses and evaluations. It also shows that the components of a strategic analysis overlap and that feedback loops are an integral part of the process.

As depicted in Exhibit 6.7, the *Where are we now?* part of the process is concerned with assessing the business's current state or the company as a whole. It begins with revisiting such fundamental issues as the company's mission, what management's current long-term vision for the firm is, and who its principal stakeholders are. At this stage, a second element is a detailed evaluation of the company's current performance, such as its current market share, financial and competitive condition. A third component comprises a detailed analysis of pertinent trends in the broader sociopolitical, economic, legal, and technological environment, and opportunities and threats in the industry or country environment. Finally, a detailed assessment of the company's competitiveness and other resources is appropriate at this stage. The answers allow the company to

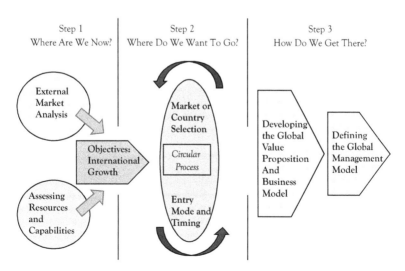

Exhibit 6.7 Three-step model for global strategy formulation

revisit its international objectives. The revised objectives should address three important questions:

1. What is the company's rationale for international expansion?
2. What levels of profitability and risk is the company willing to accept over what timeframe?
3. What level of commitment for the new direction is needed from top management, the board of directors, and major stakeholders?

The *Where do we wish to go?* question is designed to generate and explore strategic alternatives based on the answers obtained to the first question. In a global context, the principal issues are whether to concentrate on growth in a few markets abroad or adopt a wider market focus and what entry modes to consider. As shown in Exhibit 6.7, the target market and entry mode decisions are closely related because the choice of one often influences decisions about the other. For instance, the best *method of entering* a country might be to acquire a company. But, the acquisition may be expensive and risky, so the company may prefer to *select another country*. These two topics are explored in greater detail in Chapter 7.

The *How do we get there?* component of the process is focused on how to achieve the desired objectives. Key issues include developing a clear value proposition, the formulation of a global positioning and branding strategy, deciding whether to go it alone or partner with another company in the value creation process, and how to manage the business internationally. These questions are explored in Chapters 8 through 11.

One of the most important issues to be addressed when considering the *How do we get there?* dimension of the strategy formulation process is how to bridge the *capability gap* between the firm's current organizational skills and capabilities and those needed to achieve the stated strategic intent. It deals with the *strategic alignment* of *core competencies with target market needs* and identifying *key success factors* associated with successfully implementing the chosen strategy. The end product is a detailed set of initiatives for implementing the chosen strategy and exercising strategic discipline and control.

Mission, Vision, and Global Strategy

Mission and *vision* statements play an important role in strategy development. They articulate the fundamentals of a company's identity and define its purpose for existence, provide an understanding of its business directions, and provide means to create and weigh various strategic plans and alternatives.

When a business plans a global expansion, it is important for the top management team and board of directors to commit to basic goals and philosophies that will shape its strategic posture. The company mission is the document that states this fundamental purpose, which sets the firm apart from other businesses of its type and identifies the scope of its operations in product and market terms. The company mission is a broadly framed but enduring statement of a firm's intent. It embodies the firm's strategic decision-makers' business philosophy, implies the image the firm seeks to project, reflects the firm's self-concept, and indicates the firm's principal product or service areas, and the primary customer needs the firm will satisfy. In short, it describes the firm's product, market, and technological areas of emphasis, and it does so in a way that reflects the values and priorities of the firm's strategic decision making. Characteristically, it is a statement of attitude, outlook, and orientation, not of measurable targets.[9]

The mission statement is a message designed to include all stakeholders' expectations concerning the company's performance over the long run. The executives and board who prepare and periodically update the mission statement provide a unifying purpose for the company that will serve as a basis for strategic objective setting and decision making. In general terms, the mission statement addresses the following questions:[10]

- Why is this company expanding globally?
- What are our economic goals for the expansion?
- What is our operating philosophy in terms of quality, company image, and self-concept?
- What are our core competencies and competitive advantages, and are they sustainable?

- What do our customers do, and where can we assist?
- How do we view our responsibilities to stockholders, employees, communities, supply chain members, and competitors? What is our commitment to ESG (environmental, social, and governance)?

Elements of a Mission

The mission includes several fundamental elements, including the following:

1. The products and services of the business can provide benefits at least equal to its price.
2. The products and services can satisfy customer needs in specific market segments, currently not being met adequately.
3. Our production technology provides products and services that are cost- and quality-competitive.
4. With hard work and the support of others, the business can grow profitably.
5. Our management philosophy will result in a favorable public image. It will provide financial and psychological rewards for those willing to invest their labor and money in helping the business succeed.
6. The business's self-concept can be communicated and adopted by employees, investors, and our supply chain.

Following are the mission statements of Microsoft and Coca Cola:

Microsoft. "At Microsoft, our mission is to enable people and businesses throughout the world to realize their full potential. We consider our mission statement a commitment to our customers. We deliver on that commitment by striving to create technology that is accessible to everyone—of all ages and abilities. Microsoft is one of the industry leaders in accessibility innovation and in building products that are safer and easier to use."[11]

Coca Cola. "To refresh the world in mind, body, and spirit, to inspire moments of optimism and happiness through our brands and actions, and to create value and make a difference."[12]

Companies increasingly adopt formal statements of corporate values as the core of a mission statement, and senior executives now routinely identify ethical behavior, honesty, integrity, and social concerns as top issues on their companies' agendas. A good example is provided by Merck: At Merck,

> corporate conduct is inseparable from the conduct of individual employees in the performance of their work. Every Merck employee is responsible for adhering to business practices that are in accordance with the letter and spirit of the applicable laws and with ethical principles that reflect the highest standards of corporate and individual behavior

and at Merck,

> we are committed to the highest standards of ethics and integrity. We are responsible to our customers, to Merck employees and their families, to the environments we inhabit, and to the societies we serve worldwide. In discharging our responsibilities, we do not take professional or ethical shortcuts. Our interactions with all segments of society must reflect the high standards we profess.

To create a global *vision*, a company must carefully define what globalization means for its particular businesses. This depends on the industry, the products or services, and the requirements for global success. For Coca-Cola, it meant duplicating a substantial part of its value creation process—from product formulation to marketing and delivery—throughout the world. Intel's global competitive advantage is based on attaining technological leadership and preferred component supplier status globally. A mid-size company may mean setting up a host of small foreign subsidiaries and forging numerous alliances. For others, it may mean something entirely different. Thus, although it is tempting to think of global strategy in universal terms, globalization is company and industry-specific issue. It forces a company to rethink its strategic intent, global architecture, core competencies, and current product and service mix. For many companies, the outcome demands dramatic changes in how they do business—with whom, how, and why.

Therefore, a vision statement represents senior management's long-range goals for the company—a description of what competitive position it wants to attain over a given time and what core competencies it must acquire to get there. As such, it summarizes a company's broad strategic focus for the future. Most successful companies focus on relatively few activities and do them extremely well. Domino's is successful precisely because it sticks to pizza, H&R Block because it concentrates on tax preparation, and Microsoft because it focuses on software. This suggests that effective strategy development is as much about deciding *what not to do as it is about choosing activities on which to focus.* The second lesson is that most successful companies achieved their leadership position by adopting a vision far greater than their resource base and competencies would allow. To become the market leader, a focus on competition drivers is not enough; a vision that paints *a new future* is required.

With such a mindset, gaps between capabilities and goals become challenges rather than constraints, and the goal of winning can sustain a sense of urgency over a long period. Consider Amazon's vision statement: "Our vision is to be the earth's most consumer centric company; to build a place where people can come to find and discover anything they might want to buy online." It shows that a vision statement should provide both strategic guidance and motivational focus. A good vision should be clear but not so constraining that it inhibits initiative, meets all stakeholders' legitimate interests and values, and can be implemented.

Toward Sustainable Global Business Models[13]

As noted in Chapter 4, corporations are making significant progress in addressing sustainability. Most large companies now have a statement of social purpose, are signatories to the UN Global Compact, support Sustainable Development Goals, and report progress against quantitative metrics.

The acceptance of sustainability as a key component in strategy development reflects a major shift in corporate focus over the last two decades from a shareholder to a stakeholder perspective. Companies are expected to optimize for social *and* business value and deliver financial returns expected by their owners, and at the same time, help society meet its most significant challenges.

Many, however, are still at the early stages of the evolution toward sustainable business model creation. Some have made small changes to their core business model or value drivers to respond to corporate social responsibility pressures. Others have focused on process improvements to achieve compliance with new laws or codes. A few have gone a step further and made incremental changes to their business model to meet market and investor pressures. While these changes are welcome, they are mostly reactive and still far removed from the ultimate goal—*business model and ecosystem innovation to co-optimize for business and societal benefits.*

To achieve the qualities of a sustainable company—resilience, durability, and the ability to create value for the business and society—a company's business model minimally should have the following properties[14]:

- It can be scaled effectively without diminishing returns or increasing risk.
- It enhances competitive advantage through differentiation.
- It creates an environmental and societal surplus.
- It redefines entire ecosystems while increasing sustainability and returns for all stakeholders within and outside the company.
- It illustrates and articulates corporate purpose in ways that enhance engagement with all stakeholders.

At a minimum, the development of truly sustainable business models requires:

- Creating new modes of differentiation
- Embedding societal value into products and services
- Reimagining business models for sustainability
- Managing to new measures of performance
- Reshaping business ecosystems to support these initiatives.

Developing a sustainable business model is complex and time-consuming, and therefore, costly. The process should be led by top management, staffed with experienced strategic planners, and involve executives from all business partners in the broader *ecosystem* supply chain. We identify six main steps:

1. Describe the current business model from an ecosystem perspective. This means laying out the complete supply chain, including the roles played by all value-creating partners and stakeholders.

2. Identify current and future trends and issues that can impact the business model's sustainability, stakeholder interests, and profitability.

3. Create a few contrasting *scenarios* to *stress test* the current business model. For example, ask what the likely impact would be of a doubling of current sales, an environmental disaster, political instability, more stringent legislation, consumer or investor activism, material shortages, or an unexpected competitive entrance.

4. The analysis performed in Step 3 identifies key stress points in the expanded value chain—whether in the company's direct supply chain or the broader ecosystem.

5. Systematically reimagine—incrementally—every element of the broader ecosystem value chain with a view to (1) incorporate societal and environmental value, (2) enhance sustainability, and (3) mitigate risk while enhancing profitability and value for all stakeholders.

6. Enlist value creation partners in planning for ecosystem improvements by assigning ownership and linking the planned changes to the value drivers for each part of the *expanded* business model.

The goal should be to *embed* sustainable business model innovation into every aspect of the company's strategic planning process.

Mini-Case 6.2: Sustainable Business Model Innovation at Interface[15]

Interface is a global manufacturer of modular carpet tiles. Interface has manufacturing operations spanning North America, Europe, and Asia-Pacific, with 3,250 employees and annual revenue of approximately one billion U.S. dollars. Interface has long been regarded as a radical and innovative company, particularly in sustainability, where it has been recognized as one of the global leaders for more than 10 years[16].

Interface's environmental program is called *Mission Zero*. The overall goal of Mission Zero was to eliminate all negative environmental impacts of the company by the year 2020. Today, Mission Zero and its reputation as a sustainability leader are among Interface's key market differentiators and resonate strongly with its primary customers.

Exhibit 6.8 describes the seven subgoals of Mission Zero. The company has publicly committed to the goals of Mission Zero, which are presented as *must-do* activities. The fulfillment of Mission Zero (or not) has potentially significant implications for the company's reputation and investment risk profile. As a priority objective for the company, Mission Zero represents a wide-ranging portfolio of innovation activities within the organization.

Mission Zero Goals	Description of Goals
1. Eliminate Waste	Eliminating waste in all forms – material waste, wasted time and wasted effort.
2. Benign Emissions	Eliminating waste streams that have negative or toxic effects on natural systems.
3. Renewable Energy	Reducing energy demand and substituting fossil fuels with renewable ones like solar, wind and biogas.
4. Closing the Loop	Redesigning processes and products so that all resources used can be recovered at end of life and reused, closing the technical or natural loop.
5. Resource Efficient Transportation	Transporting people and with minimal waste and emissions. This includes consideration of plant location, logistics and commuting.
6. Sensitizing Stakeholders	Creating a community within and around Interface that understands the functioning of natural systems and our impact on them.
7. Redesign Commerce	Redesigning commerce to focus on the delivery of service and value instead of material. Encouraging external organizations to create policies and market incentives.

Exhibit 6.8 Mission zero goals

In 1994 to 2014, significant progress was made toward Goals 1, 2, 3, and 5. Various innovation activities focused on cutting waste, reducing reliance on fossil-derived energy, and reducing greenhouse gas emissions. The methods employed to achieve these savings included modifying the operating paths of forklift trucks on the factory floor and designing novel processing techniques for reducing production waste during the carpet-cutting process, among many other innovations. Small-scale waste reduction and energy-saving innovations of this kind have been the source of the vast majority of the company's financial savings within Mission Zero. Collectively, they form the basis for the company's claim of a "cumulative total of $480m in savings and avoided costs since 1994." In 1997, Interface released its first *Sustainability Report*. It was among the first corporate sustainability reports of this kind ever produced.

An example of a more radical innovation was Interface's decision in 2014 to invest in a new anaerobic digestion (AD) project in the Netherlands. The AD project produced a renewable substitute for natural gas using waste from the food industry. Interface purchased the AD gas to offset its consumption of fossil gas, enabling it to declare the Netherlands factory *off the grid* in 2014, using 100 percent renewable energy sources. The remaining Mission Zero goals (4, 6, and 7) were approached through R&D activities and various standalone innovation projects, a few examples of which are described here. In 2001, the company developed a nondirectional carpet tile design with beneficial material-saving properties and strong esthetics. This innovation produced a shift toward nondirectional tiles in the wider carpet tile industry. In 2007, Interface made meaningful progress toward Goal 4 of Mission Zero when introducing the first products containing recycled nylon. Interface utilized a novel process developed in partnership with supplier Universal Fibers. In 2013, Interface unveiled *Net-Works*, a socially oriented recycling program, and one of the few innovation activities, which directly contributed to Goal 7 (and, to a lesser extent, Goals 1, 4, and 6).

The co-innovation team was responsible for identifying, assessing, prioritizing, and funding innovation projects at Interface. It was formed in 2011 by the company's senior leadership. The team's goal was to accelerate the company's progress toward its Mission Zero goals by promoting radical innovation. It formalized the innovation process to support and accelerate *collaborative breakthroughs* and *game-changing* ideas. Initially, the focus was on projects with strong economic and environmental aspects. However, the chief co-innovation officer placed a different priority on projects that could improve social sustainability.

The majority of innovation projects at Interface were driven by entrepreneurial activity rather than by managed approaches. Initiatives were proposed and delivered by project leaders who identified an opportunity to contribute to the Mission Zero goals. These project leaders acted as internal entrepreneurs, undertaking the necessary background work to define each project, use organizational slack, and seek financial approval. The company's relationship-based culture and high levels of autonomy made this kind of activity possible. Some employees' roles appeared to be entirely based on entrepreneurship. One such entrepreneur was the company's European Sustainability Director, who was adept at working across internal and external boundaries, identifying market opportunities, and using unused organizational resources.

Today, Interface is recognized as the pioneer of sustainable business practices in the carpet and flooring industry. Interface's public commitment to sustainability in the 1990s created a race in the flooring industry, which caused many other major companies such as Mohawk, Milliken, Desso, and Shaw to adopt similar stances on sustainability. Interface has played an active role in shaping the regulatory environment at the national policy level, ranging from CEO Anderson chairing the President's Council for Sustainable Development in 1999 to ongoing lobbying efforts in Europe to enforce greater penalties for landfill carpet waste.

CHAPTER 7

Target Market Selection and Entry Strategies

Introduction

Few companies can afford to enter all markets open to them. Even the world's largest companies, such as General Electric or Nestlé, must exercise strategic discipline in choosing the markets they serve. They must also decide when to enter them and weigh the relative advantages of a direct or indirect presence in different regions of the world. Small- and mid-size companies are often constrained to an indirect presence. For them, the key to gaining a global competitive advantage is creating a worldwide resource network through partnerships with suppliers, customers, and sometimes competitors. What is a good strategy for one company, however, might have little chance of succeeding for another.

Picking the most attractive foreign markets, the best time to enter them, selecting the right way to enter them, and choosing the right partners and investment level are difficult decisions, especially when they involve complex emerging markets such as China. Even the most successful global companies often sustain substantial losses on their overseas ventures, especially in the early years. As a result, occasionally, they have to scale back their foreign operations or even abandon entire countries or regions in the face of ill-timed strategic moves or fast-changing competitive circumstances. Walmart's costly exit from Germany provides a good example. Eight years after buying into the highly competitive German market, Walmart executives admitted they had been unable to attain the economies of scale needed in Germany to beat rivals' prices, prompting an early and expensive exit. In 2006, it sold its 85 stores there to rival Metro at a loss of one billion U.S. dollars.[1]

Finally, a global evaluation of market opportunities requires a multidimensional perspective. In many industries, we can distinguish between *must* markets—markets in which a company must compete to realize its global ambitions—and *nice-to-be-in* markets—markets in which participation is desirable but not critical. *Must* markets include those that are critical from a *volume* perspective, markets that define *technological leadership*, and markets in which key *competitive* battles are played out.

As noted in Chapter 6, decisions about target markets and entry modes are closely related and often made simultaneously. For example, if a company has an attractive opportunity to buy or partner with another firm abroad, this decision may dictate the next target market(s) to enter. Conversely, the choice of a target market can affect the choice of entry. If the chosen region has a major local company seeking a partnership, the entering company will enter into a joint venture or an alliance. Alternatively, if the local infrastructure is underdeveloped or nonexistent, a green filed start-up may be required.

Researching Foreign Markets

Researching foreign markets is more complex than doing domestic market research because:

1. It is often performed by commercial firms for a large number of countries
2. Access to information about foreign markets is more difficult, especially in poorly developed countries, and when data is protected with confidentiality clauses
3. Cultural and language differences between countries make research more complicated
4. Foreign market research can be costly and time-consuming
5. Difficulties occur in comparing results for individual countries, as the systems of collecting statistical data are different

The contemporary global economy is a complex system characterized by versatility and uncertainty. To mitigate the risk of making an incorrect decision *vis-à-vis* foreign markets, foreign market research has become an essential input to making global strategy decisions. Traditionally, foreign markets were only available to large companies, but foreign markets are increasingly entered by small- and medium-sized enterprises.

Primary Versus Secondary Research

There are two basic market research methods:

1. *Primary*—Where information is gathered directly from the market; observations and interviews are examples of such techniques.
2. *Secondary* (document-based)—The gathering of secondary data, that is, data previously collected and processed.

Compared to primary market research, secondary techniques have several advantages:

1. They enable research to be conducted relatively quickly
2. Their cost is usually lower than that of primary research
3. Interpretation of results is easier (by using conclusions from source materials)
4. Some issues can be researched only by using secondary methods (e.g., basic information about a country and its economy)

However, secondary research methods also have significant weaknesses:

1. They have a reduced scope as some issues cannot be investigated with secondary research, for example, opinions, attitudes, and feelings
2. Secondary research often provides too few detailed results
3. They must deal with a limited accuracy of available materials— existing data that has been processed with various goals in mind is not necessarily connected with the goals of the current research project, and hence, they may not fully meet its needs
4. There may be limited access to existing resources
5. Comparability of data coming from different sources may be limited

6. Their validity and credibility may be limited—often true of data describing the economic performance of less developed countries

Nevertheless, a secondary study is useful to analyze a market about which a company knows very little.

Country or Region Research

Country or region research provides information about a particular country's economy, demographics, culture, legal structure, and natural conditions. It describes the conditions a company is likely to face if it decides to enter the market. It demonstrates how the market operates, how it is organized, and the possibilities for companies from other countries to pursue commercial activities. Product research is usually performed separately.

Country or region research principally deals with five sets of factors: (1) *economic factors*, (2) *institutional contexts*, (3) a region's *competitive environment*, (4) *political and legal factors*, and (5) *cultural factors*.

Economic factors. Relevant economic factors include a country or region's *market size and growth rate, per capita income trends, and financing and banking rules and practices*. There is no shortage of country information for performing this kind of analysis. A wealth of country-level economic and demographic data is available from various sources, including governments, multinational organizations such as the United Nations or the World Bank, and consulting firms specializing in economic intelligence or risk assessment. However, while valuable from an overall investment perspective, such data often reveal little about the prospects for selling products or services in foreign markets to local partners and end-users or about the challenges associated with overcoming other elements of distance. Yet, many companies still use this information as their primary guide to market assessment simply because country market statistics are readily available. By contrast, real product market information is often difficult and costly to obtain.

Institutional contexts. Mapping a country or region's institutions is useful for gauging the degree of difficulty associated with entering and operating in a foreign nation:

1. A country's *political and social systems* affect its product, labor, and capital markets. For instance, in socialist societies like China, workers cannot form independent trade unions in the labor market, affecting wage levels. A country's social environment is also important. In South Africa, for example, the government's support for the transfer of assets to the historically disenfranchised native African community has affected the development of the capital market.

2. The more *open* a country's economy, the more likely it is that global intermediaries can freely operate there, which helps multinationals function more effectively. From a strategic perspective, however, openness can have drawbacks: a government that allows local companies to access the global capital market can neutralize one of the key advantages a foreign company has.

3. Even though developing countries have opened up their markets and grown rapidly during the past decade, multinational firms struggle to get reliable information about *product markets and consumers*. Market research and advertising often are less sophisticated and, because there are no well-developed consumer courts and advocacy groups in these countries, people can feel they are at the mercy of big companies.

4. The nature of *local labor* markets can be a key issue. Recruiting local managers and other skilled workers in developing countries can be difficult because local credentials can be hard to verify. There are relatively few search firms and recruiting agencies.

5. *Capital and financial* markets in developing countries often are underdeveloped. Reliable intermediaries like credit rating agencies, investment analysts, merchant bankers, or venture capital firms may not exist, making it hard for multinational companies to raise debt or equity capital locally to finance their operations.

Competitive environment. The number, size, and quality of competitive firms in a particular target market define a third set of factors that affect a company's ability to enter a new market and compete profitably. While country-level economic and demographic data is widely available for most regions of the world, competitive data is much harder to come by, especially when the principal players are subsidiaries of multinational corporations or government-owned enterprises. Consequently, competitive analysis in foreign countries, especially in emerging markets, is difficult and costly. Its findings do not always provide the level of insight needed to make good decisions.

Political and legal factors. Understanding the political risk involved is another critical element in a decision to enter a foreign nation. Opportunities for fast growth and attractive profits often occur in countries with suspect levels of political risk. A frequent concern of foreign direct investors is how a host government is likely to treat them during periods of political, social, or economic transition. *Stability* is desirable because it minimizes risk. Stability also provides investors with confidence that the country's regulatory environment will achieve expected economic returns.

To understand how stability in a foreign nation is achieved, strategists often place a country's openness along a simple continuum from closed to open, as shown in Exhibit 7.1. Closed countries maintain their stability by restricting the flow of money, goods, services, people, and information across their borders. Countries that tend toward this extreme include Cuba, Iran, and North Korea due to their isolationist policies to restrict their citizens' access to information and conflicting viewpoints. At the other extreme, many nations achieve their stability by allowing and encouraging exchanges among their business and public institutions,

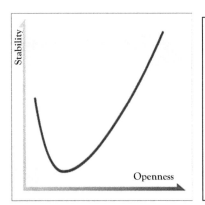

The J-curve is a useful approach for evaluating the relationship between stability and openness in a country. As depicted, each country moves along its J-curve, shifting with fluctuations in the economy. As a stable country becomes more open, it slides down the left side of the curve toward the dip in the J, the point of highest instability.

Exhibit 7.1 The J-curve on country stability and openness

and their citizens and those of other nations. Examples of open and stable countries include Australia, the European Union, Japan, and the United States.

A complicating factor in assessing risks in other countries is that there is a pervasive "the grass is always greener" effect that infects global strategic decision making in many globally inexperienced companies, which causes them to overestimate the attractiveness of foreign markets.[2] As noted earlier, *distance*, broadly defined, unless well understood and compensated for, can be a major impediment to global success: cultural differences can lead companies to overestimate the appeal of their products or the strength of their brands; administrative differences can slow expansion plans, reduce the ability to attract the right talent, and increase the cost of doing business; geographic distance influences the effectiveness of communication and coordination; and economic distance directly impacts revenues and costs.

Local laws can greatly affect a company's ability to do business. For example, Thailand has specific laws stating no foreign person or company can own more than 49 percent of a business, implying the need for a willingness to take on a Thai partner to do business there.

Sometimes, the only way to do business in a foreign country is to grant an expensive *permit or license* to another business in that country to manufacture and sell your product. Governments do this to make sure a larger percentage of income from sales stays in the home country. A good example is provided by licensing agreements. In the Netherlands, Pepsi provides Heineken with its formula or agrees to supply the cola syrup, and Heineken adds carbonated water, packages it in appropriate containers, and sells it. Pepsi cannot enter into a similar agreement with another firm to sell Pepsi in the Netherlands. Heineken cannot alter the product, nor can it duplicate other Pepsi products (such as Lays Potato Chips) without a separate agreement.[3]

Local *taxes and fees* can impact a company's profitability in a foreign country and affect its international marketing strategy. High tax rates on goods sold, like those charged in the United States, can make it hard for a business to profitable globally.

Tariffs have long been used to balance trade between countries and protect national companies from losing business to foreign competitors.

An example of this is China's 105.4 percent tariff on chicken that is shipped from the United States. *Currency risks* also can have a major impact on the bottom line, as can *investments and operational restrictions or quotas.*

Cultural factors. Cultural factors can make or break a global strategy. *Language*, specifically translation, has created problems for many companies. A great example is provided by Coca-Cola when it first entered China. The company phonetically translated its product's name into Ke-kou-ke-la. However, depending on the dialect, it meant "bite the wax tadpole" or "female horse stuffed with wax." No one at General Motors realized the translation for the name of their car, the "Nova," meant "it won't go" in South America. Gerber used the same packaging with the cute baby on it they had used in America for packaging its baby food in Africa. The company did not realize that because of the high illiteracy rate in Africa, it was common for food packaging to display a picture of the contents inside. These types of mistakes are humorous to an outsider but can spell financial disaster for a company.

Entering international markets can be very difficult for some companies because of their different *tastes and eating preferences.* McDonald's had to work on its image in India, where beef consumption is *off-limits*; the company successfully introduced vegetarian and regional choices to the menu selection. Similarly, many international fast-food chains such as Kentucky Fried Chicken, Wendy's, and McDonald's had to start offering menu selections with rice dishes to break into the Asian market.

Products and Services Market Research

Products and services market research can be conducted at different levels, such as an entire industry, a group of products, or just one product. For a firm considering establishing relationships abroad, products and services market research is often conducted together with country or region market research.

As shown in Exhibit 7.2, product and services market research covers six main areas: (1) *market trends*, (2) *competitive landscape*, (3) *distribution channels*, (4) *product trends*, (5) *consumer needs and preferences*, and (6) the *business environment.*

Market Trends What is the current size of the market? How much is the market expected to grow in volume terms?
Competitive Landscape How fragmented is the market ? Who are the competitors and what are their strengths and weaknesses? Are the majority of the products sold in this market imported or locally produced? Is there a high entry barrier?
Distribution Landscape What are the main distribution channels for my product in that country? How is this different from my local market? Which channels are expected to grow in the forecast period and how much growth is expected? How fragmented is the industry ?
Product Trends What are the differences between the products sold in this market and the ones sold in the domestic market? What are the price bands for my products? How do premium and mass products perform in the country? What are the packaging trends for my product in the country?
Consumer Trends How much do consumers spend in the product category? How important is digital marketing in that market? What are the consumers' preferences for my product? How big is my potential target population?
Business Environment How easy is it to do business in this country? What is the logistic landscape? What is the country's productivity?

Exhibit 7.2 Sample questions for products and services market research

Market trends. Estimates of the market's size typically focus on two scenarios: (1) current product sales and (2) potential demand with increased marketing. Analysis of commercial policy tools used in a foreign country is a vital component of the research. Rankings may help to acquire knowledge about manufacturers, exporters, and foreign investors.

Competitive landscape. Understanding local competition is crucial when deciding where and how to expand. A concentrated market will be hard to penetrate without making high investments in marketing and sales. Diversified industry competition makes entering the market somewhat easier and may require less investment. Questions that market research can help answer are: (1) How fragmented is the market?; (2) Who are the competitors, and what are their strengths and weaknesses?; (3) Are the majority of the products sold in this market imported or locally produced?; (4) Is there a high entry barrier?

Distribution channels. Distribution is key to understanding how a company can leverage its current business relations. Some questions to help a company understand the distribution landscape include: (1) What are the main distribution channels for the country's product?; (2) How is this different from the domestic market?; (3) Which channels are expected to grow in the forecast period, and how much growth is expected?; (4) How fragmented is the industry?

Product trends. By looking at product trends, a company learns what customers are buying locally. Key questions include: (1) What are the differences between the products sold in this market and the ones sold in the domestic market?, (2) What are the price bands for the product?, (3) How do premium and mass products perform in the country?, (4) What are the packaging trends for this product in the country?

Consumer trends. A key aspect of products and services research focuses on consumer behavior and attitudes in the chosen product market. Key questions include where purchases are made, how often, at what intervals, what is purchased, what product range is available, how brands are perceived, how consumers receive information about products, and so on. Research of attitudes that impact purchases covers a wide range of subjects, including attitudes potential customers have a manufacturer's country, firms and brands, products, packaging, prices, and distribution channels. This type of analysis aims to produce an actionable market segmentation, and ultimately, suggest the most attractive market segment(s). Key questions include: (1) How much do consumers spend in the product category? (2) How important is digital marketing in that market? (3) What are the consumers' preferences for the product? (4) How big is the potential target population?

Business environment. A key issue for any company considering foreign expansion is how much money and time it will take to start operations. Some key questions include: (1) How easy is it to do business in this country? (2) What is the logistic landscape? (3) What is the country's productivity?

Mini-Case 7.1: How Starbucks Brought Coffee to China—A Case Study of Market Research[4]

Starbucks' entry into emerging and developed markets is informed by careful market research. For example, the company conducted extensive market research to understand better the Chinese markets and how capitalism functions in the People's Republic of China (P.R.C.). China contains several distinct regionally based markets, a factor that makes market research crucial to launching new stores and franchises in China.

Starbucks articulated an entry strategy that addresses the dominant Chinese markets, designed to be compatible with Chinese culture. Instead of challenging the culture of drinking tea, Starbucks deliberately worked to bridge the gap between tea drinking and coffee drinking cultures by introducing beverages in the Chinese stores that included local tea-based ingredients.

Market research supported the development of Starbucks' competitive globalization strategy. The overarching goal was to create an aspirational brand. Prospective Starbucks customers in China could look forward to what Starbucks refers to as *The Third Place* experience.

The Starbucks experience conveys highly appealing status to those aspiring to Western standards or wishing to raise their standing in their own culture. Market research also indicated that brand consistency is important to Starbucks' customers. When Starbucks opens a new store in an emerging market like China, the best baristas are sent for the launch and to conduct training of the baristas who will carry on when once the launch has completed.

It is essential to understand the intellectual property rights laws and licensing issues when planning to enter an emerging market. Starbucks used intellectual protection laws to prevent its business model and brand from being illegally copied in China. Four years after opening its first café in China, Starbucks had registered all its major trademarks in China.

The organization and structure of Starbucks' global operations were also guided by market research. The organizational strategies employed by Starbucks were modeled after Starbucks' experiences in other emerging markets, recognizing that China is not one homogeneous market. The culture dominant in northern China differs radically from the culture in the eastern parts of China, as reflected in the differences in consumer spending. Purchasing power inland is considerably lower than the spending power in coastal cities.

The complexity of the Chinese markets led to regional partnerships to aid in Starbucks' plans for expansion in China; the partnerships provided consumer insight into Chinese tastes and preferences that helped Starbucks localize to the diverse markets.

Starbucks' competitive advantage is built on product, service, and brand attributes, many of which have been shown through market research to be important to Starbucks' customers. Western brands have an advantage over local Chinese brands because of a commonly accepted reputation for consistently higher-quality products and services. This factor establishes the Western brands as premium brands in the minds of consumers.

Entry Strategies—Modes and Timing

Selecting a *mode of entry* and *timing the entry* are key elements of the global strategy development process. They deal with questions such as: What is the best way for the company to enter a new market? Should we begin by establishing an export base or licensing the product to gain experience in a newly targeted country? Are there compelling reasons to make a bolder move, such as entering into an alliance, acquiring a local company, or even starting a new subsidiary?

As shown in Exhibit 7.3, entry mode and timing decisions typically call for the consideration of three types of factors: (1) industry-based considerations linked to the degree of competitiveness, (2) resource-based issues for the firm, and (3) various risk factors.

Escalating Commitment to Global Markets

To understand the risk–reward tradeoffs of different global entry strategies, executives must assess two critical dimensions of customer demand: customers' acceptance of standardized products and the rate of product innovation in the industry. As shown in Exhibit 7.4, markets

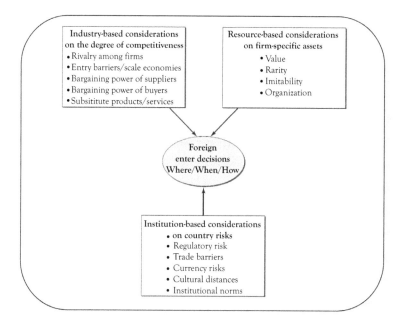

Exhibit 7.3 A model of foreign market entry

can be arrayed along a continuum from markets with standardized products to markets in which products must be customized for customers.
Standardized products include software, music CDs, and petrochemi-
cals, while food products, washing machines, and automobiles are good
examples of customized products.

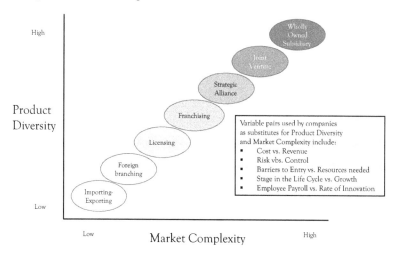

Exhibit 7.4 Escalating commitment to foreign markets

Exhibit 7.4 shows that the two dimensions can be combined to enable companies to simultaneously assess customer needs for both product standardization and the rate of product innovation. The examples listed demonstrate the model's usefulness in helping firms determine the degree of customization they must accept to become engaged in international or global operations.

It also highlights that the two dimensions of acceptance of standardization and innovation desired can be interchanged with other pairs of descriptive variables. These other variables add insights that give managers additional information on which to base their global entry decisions. Variable pairs used by companies include the cost of the strategy and level of revenues, barriers to entry and resources required, stage in the lifecycle and revenue growth, and employee payroll and rate of innovation.

However, foremost among the variable pairs that executives consider in choosing a strategy for moving toward globalization is the degree of complexity of the foreign market being considered and the diversity in a company's product line. *Complexity* is defined by the number of critical success factors a company must deal with to compete effectively against established competitors. In general, the higher the number of essential factors to consider, the more difficult formulating a successful global strategy is. *Diversity* refers to the number of products and services offered by the firm's business lines. Diversity is high when a company offers many product lines. Together, the complexity and diversity dimensions form a continuum of possible strategic choices.

Exporting–Importing

Different stages of globalization and investment require different combinations of corporate resources and capabilities. At the simplest and most popular level, a business becomes involved in the export–import activity. Sometimes referred to as drop shipping, importing material from the supplier or exporting a company's product or service to a foreign importer has a minimal effect on the required management orientation and activities or existing transformation processes or outcomes.

The niche market approach for a company that wants to export is to modify product performance characteristics to meet particular foreign demands. This process can be slow and tedious. However, several expansion techniques provide a U.S. firm with the know-how to exploit opportunities in the global environment. For example, it might adopt product innovations in countries with limited patent protection and utilize nonequity contractual arrangements with a foreign partner to produce rapid product innovation.

Foreign Branching

A foreign branch is a company unit that operates in a foreign market. Designed as a strategic business unit (SBU), it is usually directly responsible for a major share of the operational duties, for example, marketing, physical distribution, and customer service. The branch may also have the legal latitude to provide the company with opportunities not available within the boundaries of the United States. A foreign branch is frequently staffed by host country talent, including locals in middle and upper-level management positions.

GRUMA, S.A.B. de C.V. is one of the world's leading tortilla and corn flour producers. It excels with a global strategy centered on foreign branching. With leading brands in 89 countries, GRUMA has production or research and development (R&D) operations in the United States, Mexico, Central America, Europe, Asia, and Oceania. Headquartered in San Pedro Garza García, Mexico, GRUMA has approximately 21,000 employees and 73 plants, and net sales globally of four billion U.S. dollars a year.

Foreign Licensing

A higher level of global investment involves foreign licensing, contract manufacturing, or technology transfer but requires little change in management or operation. The relationship between domestic and foreign operations usually is contractual. It might have an arm's length quality. The domestic operation monitors the use of its license or technology transfer but is unlikely to be engaged in day-to-day operations, unless a consulting contract was also negotiated.

Licensing involves transferring some industrial property right from the licensor to a licensee in a foreign country. Most licenses include patents, trademarks, or technical know-how granted to the licensee for a specified time in return for royalty payments and avoiding tariffs or import quotas. Another licensing option is to contract the manufacturing of its product line to a foreign company to exploit local comparative advantages in technology, materials, or labor. Service and franchise-based firms have long engaged in licensing arrangements with foreign partners to enter new markets with standardized products that can benefit from marketing economies. Examples of companies engaged in licensing include Anheuser-Busch, Avis Budget Group, Coca-Cola, Hilton, Kentucky Fried Chicken, McDonald's, and Subway.

Another licensing strategy for firms is to contract the manufacturing of its product line to a foreign company to exploit local comparative advantages in technology, materials, or labor. Firms that use any of the licensing options can benefit from lowering the risk of entry into the foreign markets.

Franchising

Franchising is a particularly attractive option for global expansion because the franchising business model is transportable. For the franchisor, international franchising builds the brand much faster than other expansion models. Franchising allows a company to find partners in its target countries who know the language, infrastructure, local culture, and applicable laws. The key is finding a partner that shares the franchisor's values, vision, and goals.

For international franchisees, the benefits can be even greater. To effectively expand abroad, a franchise company should be well established with a number of proven units open in its home country. Important elements are training systems, ongoing support, and business and marketing systems that are already being successfully employed across the home country. Most of those systems are easily transported and adapted to another marketplace, saving the new international partner a great deal of time and money.

A solid international franchisee–franchisor partnership will allow both parties to recoup their investments more quickly than they could independently. Global partners almost always sign multiunit or area developer deals so that they should be able to expand more quickly in the target country with the support of the brand.

Mini-Case 7.2: Franchising Laws in India

Over the past 25 years, India has witnessed a sea change in its foreign investment[5.] Globalization, liberalization, and growing brand awareness have resulted in India becoming one of the largest and most attractive emerging markets. Geographically vast and culturally diverse, India offers a favorable franchising environment with a huge consumer market. The popularity of franchising as a business model in India is shown by its 1,200 franchise ventures, 300 international franchisors, growth in the range of 30 to 35 percent per annum, and projected 2030 sales of seven billion U.S. dollars.

Although India does not have franchise-specific legislation or regulation, numerous laws govern various aspects of franchising. The following are five of the most critical laws for franchisers in India to consider[6]:

- *Contract act.* The Indian Contract Act, 1872, governs the contractual relationship between the franchisor and the franchisee. A franchise agreement is enforceable under Indian law if it meets the criteria of a valid contract. However, care must be taken that the agreement does not contain any provision that makes it void or voidable.
- *Consumer protection and product liability.* The Consumer Protection Act, 1986, provides remedies to consumers in case of defects in products or deficiency in services making the manufacturers and service providers liable.
- *Competition law.* Given the globalization and liberalization of its economy, the focus has shifted from curbing monopolies to promoting healthy competition in India. Accordingly, the Competition Act, 2002, was enacted and is now in force in its entirety. The relevant provisions from the franchising perspective are those concerning anti-competitive agreements and abuse of dominant position.
- *Intellectual property rights (IPR) trademark protection*: India's IPR laws include the Trademark Act 1999, The Designs Act 2000, The Copyright Act 1957, The Patent Act 1970,

which protect the IPR of the franchisor and enforcement mechanism against infringement of the same.

- *Foreign exchange regulations.* The Foreign Exchange Management Act, 1999, and associated rules and regulations govern payments in foreign exchange. A franchise arrangement typically involves payments such as franchise fees, royalties for the use of trademarks and system, training expenses, and advertisement contributions are remitted to the foreign franchisor without any approvals. The issue of guarantees in favor of a foreign franchisor requires the Reserve Bank of India's approval.

Strategic Alliances

An intermediate level of global involvement occurs when a domestic company and a foreign company undertake a collaborative venture or project on a nearly equal basis. The two companies should have substantial resources to allocate to the project, including the bases for a competitively advantageous, distinctive, and profitable collaboration.

Cooperative strategies take many forms and are considered for many different reasons. However, the fundamental motivation is the corporation's ability to spread its investments over various options, each with a different risk profile. As shown in Exhibit 7.5, cooperative strategies can improve the economics of existing businesses or speed up or reduce risk in building new businesses. It also shows that strategic alliances become more attractive as globalization pressures increase, product development costs get higher, product lifecycles get shorter, or manufacturing cost increase. Essentially, the corporation is trading off the likelihood of a major payoff against the ability to optimize its investments by betting on multiple options.

Strategic alliances are limited-duration corporate *partnerships* in which partners contribute their skills and expertise to a joint project. For example, a manufacturing company might form a strategic alliance with a marketing firm known for its excellence in the narrow domain. The manufacturer might convince the marketer to be its only client

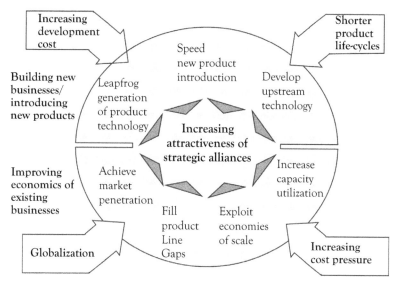

Exhibit 7.5 Alliances driven by economic factors

in the industry. In exchange, the manufacturer might promise to give the marketer all of its promotional business for the contract period. In other situations, a strategic alliance can enable competing companies to combine their distribution and marketing efforts to counter a much larger competitor's threats.

Key drivers behind cooperative strategies include the need for *risk-sharing*, the corporation's *funding limitations*, the *desire to gain market* and *technology access*[7]. *Risk sharing*. Most companies cannot afford *bet the company* moves to participate in all product markets of strategic interest. Whether a corporation is considering entry into a global market or investments in new technologies, the dominant logic dictates that companies prioritize their strategic interests and balance them according to risk.

Funding limitations. In the past, many companies created a sustainable advantage by establishing dominance in *all* of the business' value-creating activities. They attempted to build barriers to entry through cumulative investment and vertical integration that were hard to penetrate. However, as globalization accelerated and the technology race intensified, such a strategic posture became increasingly difficult to sustain. Going it alone is no longer practical in many industries. To compete globally, companies must incur immense fixed costs with a shorter payback period and a higher risk level.

Market access. Companies usually recognize the lack of knowledge, infrastructure, or critical relationships they need to distribute their products to new customers. Cooperative strategies can help them fill the gaps. For example, Hitachi has an alliance with Deere and Company in North America and with Fiat-Allis in Europe to distribute its hydraulic excavators. This arrangement makes sense because Hitachi's product line is too narrow to justify a separate distribution network.

Technology access. A large number of products rely on so many different technologies that few companies can afford to remain at the forefront of all of them. Carmakers increasingly rely on advances in electronics; application software developers depend on Microsoft's new features in its next-generation operating platform. Advertising agencies need more and more sophisticated tracking data to formulate schedules for clients. At the same time, the pace at which technology is spreading globally is increasing, making time an even more critical variable in developing and sustaining competitive advantage. As a result, it is increasingly difficult for any R&D unit to develop the technological advantage needed to independently disrupt the marketplace. Therefore, partnering with technologically compatible companies to achieve the prerequisite level of excellence is often essential. The implementation of such strategies, in turn, increases the speed at which technology diffuses around the world.

In industries in which competitive dynamics and sources of advantage are changing quickly or remain unclear, executives should be prepared to work in an unstable environment and function well under uncertainty. One specific benefit of a strategic alliance is the potential for accelerated speed-to-market. Partnering represents a more agile approach that enables companies to access external capabilities quickly, test growth strategies, and refine their investment priorities iteratively.

Other reasons to pursue a cooperative strategy include a lack of particular *management skills,* an *inability to add* value in-house, and a *lack of acquisition opportunities* because of size, geographical, or ownership restrictions. Recent prominent alliances include those by *Spotify* and *Uber*, and *Apple* and *Mastercard* (Apple Pay).

Extracting Value From Partnerships[8]

While strategic alliances are an important tool to drive growth and deliver needed capabilities, they come with their own challenges and risks. By one estimate, 40 percent of alliances fail to comprehensively address the commercial, strategic, operational, cultural, and technical leading practices required for complete success.[9]

Not all companies fully understand the leading practices that can foster a strategic alliance's success or have the necessary management structures to implement them. To successfully execute alliances and realize their potential value, companies need a robust alliance management capability that provides appropriate strategic alignment, due diligence, and operational excellence.

A strong alliance management capability requires a clear vision, defined growth pathways, and the development of an effective partnership with strong due diligence and effective negotiation. The process consists of three major steps:

1. *The company should define its principal strategic objectives and determine if external partnerships can enable that strategy.* This requires close alignment among corporate strategy, business development, and functional leadership to assess needed capabilities and agree on strategic decision factors. A common potential pitfall is a mismatch between the company's business strategy and alliance strategy. This occurs when the alliance strategy is not clearly articulated or developed without business unit leadership involvement.

2. *Assessing the suitability of potential partners.* This requires due diligence, business case development, structuring, and negotiation. This analysis goes well beyond evaluating the technical nature and commercial return of the joint offering. It should also focus on the nature of the relationship established because the level of collaboration and interdependence is correlated with the level of risk, complexity, and potential value that may be expected.

3. *Management of the partnership on an ongoing basis.* Performance metrics should be established and guide the alliance design. Ongoing engagement from stakeholders with an appropriate level of decision-making authority is important to ensure that the alliance meets performance targets and delivers on the partners' collective vision. Finally, it is crucial to agree on terms governing the alliance's termination process to enhance each partner's agility.

Types of Alliances

There are numerous typologies of alliances. Two of the most useful ones distinguish between *horizontal and vertical* alliances or characterize alliances according to the amount of *equity* involved.

Horizontal versus vertical alliances. Horizontal strategic alliances involve businesses that are involved in the same business area. A good example is two competitors getting together to enhance their position in the marketplace and improve their market power relative to other business rivals. Typically, horizontal alliances target collaborations in joint activities. R&D cooperation between microelectronic firms is a type of horizontal strategic alliance. It should be noted that horizontal partnerships can be anti-competitive and potentially are subject to anti-trust law. Examples of global horizontal strategic partnerships include (1) the acquisition of Citroen shares by Peugeot to build a partnership called PSA and (2) the partnership between Sina Corp and Yahoo to offer online auction services in China.

A *vertical strategic alliance* collaborates between two or more firms along the value chain for manufacturing or marketing or distribution. Vertical strategic alliances are partnerships among businesses in different industries. Examples of vertical strategic alliances include the complex collaborations between auto manufacturers and their suppliers. An automaker builds a relationship with suppliers that supply services and goods in any business process along the vertical chain, reflecting the automaker's *make-versus-buy* decisions. For example, Caterpillar provides manufacturing services to Land Rover.

Equity versus nonequity alliances. A second typology characterizes alliances according to the amount of investment involved for one or

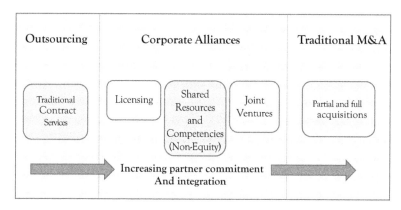

Exhibit 7.6 Equity versus nonequity alliances

both partners. As shown in Exhibit 7.6, three types are most prominent: (1) *nonequity* strategic alliances, (2) *equity* strategic alliances, and (3) *joint ventures.*

In a *nonequity* strategic alliance, companies agree to share resources without creating a separate entity or sharing equity. Nonequity alliances are more informal than a partnership involving equity and make up the majority of business alliances. One example is the partnership between Starbucks and Kroger: Starbucks has kiosks in many Kroger supermarkets.

In an *equity* strategic alliance, one company purchases equity in another business (partial acquisition), or each business purchases equity in the other (cross-equity transactions). A good example of an equity strategic alliance is Tesla's relationship with Panasonic. Their relationship began with a 30 million U.S. dollar investment from Panasonic to accelerate battery technology for electric vehicles and grew to include building a lithium-ion battery plant in Nevada.

A *joint venture* is a commercial company (child) created and operated to benefit co-owners (parents). Such a joint ownership company is maintained with shared resources and equity according to a binding agreement[10]. Whether it is formed for a specific purpose or an ongoing strategy, a joint venture has a clear objective, and profits are split between the two companies. Google provides a good example. In 2016, Google's parent company Alphabet announced a joint venture with GlaxoSmithKline to research treating diseases with electrical signals. The joint venture, Galvani

Bioelectronics, has continued to grow by bringing on more partners to build devices and further research in the emerging field of bioelectronics. A more detailed discussion of joint ventures is presented next.

Outsourcing

Outsourcing is defined by a vertical, nonequity strategic alliance that enables the outsourcer to gain a competitive advantage. Companies outsource primarily to cut costs, which is possible when contracting with a provider is less expensive than producing an input or performing a service internally. Strategic outsourcing can also be used to provide superior inputs from top industry providers. Examples of valuable inputs include increasing staffing flexibility, guaranteeing access to intellectual property or expertise, easing time constraints, and increasing cost control. These inputs can also accelerate production in most business functional areas. Examples include human resource management, supply chain management, accounting, and customer support.

The pace of change within many segments of global business encourages the use of outsourcing practices, particularly in the areas of the Internet and online-based digital technologies. India has become a global epicenter for leading information technology companies. These corporations include TCS, Infosys, Tech Mahindra, Wipro, HCL Technologies, LTI, Mindtree, Mphasis, Oracle Financial Services (IT counterpart of Oracle Corporation to the banking industry), and Rolta India.

Joint Ventures

Occasionally, two or more firms make equity investments in a new business because they believe that their different but compatible strengths will overcome their deficiencies and produce success in a particular competitive environment. In general, joint ventures are a grand strategy for companies to create a co-owned business that operates for their mutual benefit.

Certain countries mandate that foreign firms entering their markets do so on a joint ownership basis. India and Mexico are good examples. The rationale of these countries is that joint ventures minimize the threat of foreign domination and enhance their citizens' skills and employment and the growth and profits of local businesses.

Many strategic managers are wary of joint ventures, especially when they involve international arrangements. While they present opportunities with risks that can be shared, joint ventures limit the discretion, control, and profit potential of partners, while demanding managerial attention and other resources that might be targeted toward the firm's domestic activities. Nevertheless, increasing globalization in many industries requires considering large conglomerates' joint venture approach that needs global growth to remain viable.

A prime example of joint ventures' value is seen in their use by foreign firms in China.[11] In the early 2000s, China increased its foreign investment regulations to moderate its economic growth and ensure that Chinese businesses would not be at a competitive disadvantage when competing for domestic markets. The new restrictions require local companies to retain control of Chinese trademarks and brands, prevent foreign investors from buying a property that is not for their use, limit the size of foreign-owned retail chains, and restrict foreign investment in selected industries. With these increased regulations, investment in China through joint ventures with Chinese companies has become a principal strategy for foreign investors.

There is also a major social barrier that impedes the joint venture aspirations of foreign firms in China. As discussed in Mini-Case 7.3, guanxi is an essential capability for corporate success in China. Without a history of strong business relationships that developed over time, foreign companies have difficulty breaking into Chinese markets. One major challenge is that Chinese companies depend on business relationships for validation, support, and networking. Typically, a foreign firm lacks this important partner attribute. A Chinese host country partner can greatly facilitate the acceptance of a foreign investor and help minimize the costs of doing business in an unknown nation.

Typically, the foreign partner contributes to financing and technology, while the Chinese partner provides the land, physical facilities, workers, local connections, and knowledge of the country. In a wholly owned venture, the foreign company is forced to acquire the land, build the workspace, and hire and train the employees, all of which are especially expensive propositions in a country where the foreign company lacks guanxi. Additionally, because China restricts direct foreign investment in the life insurance, energy, construction of transportation facilities, higher education, and health care industries, asset or equity joint ventures are sometimes the only options for foreign firms.

Foreign partners in equity joint ventures benefit from the improved ease of entry into Chinese markets, tax incentives, motivational and competitive advantages of a long-term mutual commitment, and access to its Chinese partner's resources. Successful joint ventures have been created between Chinese and foreign corporations in the media, construction, oil refinery, national railroad transportation system (China) industries.

Additional opportunities arose in China's special economic zones, in which foreign firms operate businesses with Chinese joint venture partners. The foreign companies receive tax incentives in corporate tax rates that are lower than the standard 30 percent. For example, in the Shanghai Pudong New Area, a 15 percent tax rate was applied to income generated by nine Chinese joint venture partners.

China's admission to the World Trade Organization (WTO) has spurred the number of international joint ventures. Under the conditions of its membership, China expanded the list of industries that permit foreign investment. Foreign investors that participate with Chinese partners in joint ventures are permitted to hold an increased share of joint ventures in several major industries: banks (up to 20 percent), investment funds (33 percent), life insurance (50 percent), and telecommunications (25 percent).

Mini-Case 7.3: Guanxi Is an Essential Capability for Corporate Success in China

Guanxi is the network of relationships a person cultivates through exchanging gifts and favors to attain mutual benefits.[12] It is based on friendship and affection and on a reciprocal obligation to respond to requests for assistance. People who share a guanxi network are committed to one another by an unwritten code. Disregarding this commitment can destroy a business executive's prestige and social reputation. Guanxi networks bind millions of Chinese firms into social and business webs, largely dictating their success. In China, enterprises are built on long-lasting links with the political party, administrative leaders, and executives in other companies. Through connections with people who are empowered to make decisions, Chinese executives obtain vital information and assistance.

Because guanxi is based on reciprocity, executives implicitly accept an obligation to *return a favor* in the unspecified future whenever they benefit from the guanxi network. Thus, developing and expanding guanxi is a form of social investment that enriches the executive's current resources and future potential.

Personal relationships are the quintessential basis for all business transactions in China. People do business only with those they know and trust. Negotiations are undertaken more obliquely than in the West, often focusing on long-term goals, rather than specific current objectives. Negotiators take longer to gather information about the other party and evaluate the trustworthiness of a potential partner. Business relationships are designed to enhance guanxi and thereby lead to other opportunities. Chinese executives believe in the long-term benefits of guanxi and are committed to investing time and resources to cultivating it. The ability to initiate and maintain social contacts in the Chinese culture is one of the essential traits that expatriates can develop. While Westerners' business communications emphasize exchanging facts and information, the Chinese use communication primarily to enhance guanxi.

Strategic, Organizational, and Cultural Fit

The success of strategic alliances and joint ventures depends on the *strategic, organizational, capabilities, and cultural fit* between the partners (Exhibit 7.7). Two factors comprise *strategic fit*: (1) the congruence of partners' objectives and (2) the complementarity of the companies' resources and capabilities. *Organizational* fit is defined by factors such as (1) structural differences (centralized versus decentralized forms of organization); (2) the similarity of systems and processes including the importance of formal systems, the sophistication of financial controls, the complementary of IT systems, and commitment to teamwork; and (3) the compatibility of reward systems and opportunities for career mobility. *Capabilities*

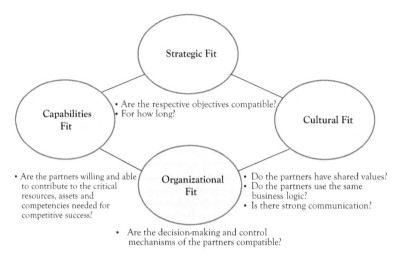

Exhibit 7.7 Strategic, organizational, capabilities, and cultural fit

fit is concerned with each partner's willingness to contribute to critical resources, assets, and core competencies needed for competitive success. Finally, *cultural fit* covers such issues as (1) the compatibility of the top management team's decision-making processes, (2) the similarity of leadership styles and corporate cultures, and (3) the quality of managerial communications between partners.

Wholly Owned Subsidiary

There are many ways for a company to expand its business operations in a new market, particularly in an emerging market like Vietnam. One of these is called FDI, or foreign direct investment, which means a company invests overseas by either setting up a subsidiary, acquiring shares of a foreign company, or a merger or joint venture.

FDI gives multinational companies an opportunity to expand their businesses beyond their low-growth or stable home market to new foreign markets. To become successful at FDI, foreign companies must identify secular trends in their target markets and whether their product lines can match the demanding new market.

FDI is the most complex global strategy because foreign assets can grow to a significant portion of a conglomerate's total assets. At this level of commitment, the firm becomes a global enterprise with global production, sales, finance, and control approaches. A conglomerate might, for example, decide to create a quasi-independent, wholly owned subsidiary in a country outside the United States. It could replicate a successful business model domestically; it could spinoff a unit that possessed new patents that would be better positioned closer to mass production facilities, or it could select among other promising strategic options. At this ultimate stage of global commitment, the conglomerate would be committed to providing necessary support for the entire range of resources that the subsidiary would need to launch, grow, and maintain a successful business. The conglomerate might commit to providing ongoing financial support, business insight, and guidance for the subsidiary's foreseeable future.

The parent company typically insists on full ownership to maintain control and managerial efficiency. Policy decisions about local product lines, expansion, profits, and dividends typically remain with the parent company's senior managers. Foreign subsidiaries can be started either from the ground up or by acquiring established firms in the host country. The parent firm can benefit significantly if the acquired company has complementary product lines or an established distribution or service network.

Timing of Entry[13]

Selecting the right target market and the right mode of entry are critical, but so is the *timing* of entry. Conceptually, the timing of entry is related to the resources and competencies of the firm. Firms' ability to assess market signals and opportunities is another key factor in explaining the entry timing decision. The decision to enter will depend on how fast market growth is anticipated and the relative presence of competitors in the market. Finally, the attractiveness of the host country and the level of risk are important determinants of the timing of entry because a country with significant growth prospects and a low-risk environment is more likely to attract foreign firms to enter early.

Timing of Entry and Firm Performance

Research on the effects of entry timing on company performance is inconclusive. Several studies suggest a positive correlation between early entry and performance, commonly referred to as a *first-mover advantage*. Advantages cited include (1) a lack of competition, (2) the ability to achieve a strong market position, (3) the early establishment of relationships with local stakeholders, (4) the opportunity to construct barriers for later entrants, and (5) the chance to monopolize the market. However, others maintain that, by entering early, pioneers are in a *disadvantaged* position and realize a lower rate of return on investment than later entrants. The reasons given for an *early-mover disadvantage* center around the higher level of risk associated with an early entry due to a lack of knowledge, resources, human capital, and experience. In other words, pioneers cannot recoup their investment in markets that require firms to *kick start* the new market. When that happens, a *fast follower* can benefit from the market development funded by the pioneer and leapfrog into earlier profitability, taking advantage of a first-mover disadvantage. Samsung provides a good example of a fast-follower company. Samsung did not invent the mobile phone—Motorola is the inventor—but Samsung perfected the technology. Samsung is a classic fast follower: it is attuned to what competitors are doing and what other companies are bringing to market first. Every time Apple launches a new product, Samsung brings out its version a year or so later—think of the touchscreen phone, the tablet, and the smartwatch.[14]

There are two conditions under which a first-mover advantage is real. The first is when a scarce resource in the market limits the number of early entrants that can compete. For example, when a foreign company is required to obtain one of a limited number of government permits or licenses to sell its products, a first-mover may have an advantage. Second, if the first mover can lock up a scarce resource in such a way that it creates a barrier to entry for potential competitors, a first-mover advantage may exist. An example is provided by the exclusive or preferred access to a distribution network or key resource.

PART III
Global Strategic Management

CHAPTER 8

Globalizing the Value Proposition

Introduction

Some managers seem to think that what works in their home country will work just as well in another part of the world. They take the same product, the same advertising campaign, even the same brand name and packaging, and expect instant success. In many cases, the result is failure. Consider the following classic examples. Coca-Cola had to withdraw its two-liter bottle in Spain after discovering that few Spaniards owned refrigerators with large enough compartments to accommodate it. General Foods squandered millions trying to introduce packaged cake mixes to Japanese consumers. The company failed to note that only 3 percent of Japanese homes were equipped with ovens. General Foods' Tang initially failed in France because it was positioned as a substitute for orange juice at breakfast. The French drink little orange juice and almost none at breakfast.

These failures occur because the assumption that one approach works everywhere fails to consider the complex mosaic of differences between countries and cultures. Marketing a standardized product with the same positioning and communications strategy worldwide—the purest form of *aggregation*—has considerable attraction because of its cost-effectiveness and simplicity. It is also extremely dangerous, however. Assuming that foreign customers will respond positively to an existing product can lead to costly failure.

With a few exceptions, the idea of an identical, fully standardized global value proposition is a myth, and few industries are truly global. How to adapt a value proposition most effectively, therefore, is a key strategic issue.

Value Proposition Adaptation Decisions

Value proposition adaptation deals with product quality and appearance to materials, processing, production equipment, packaging, and style. A product may have to be adapted to meet the physical, social, or regulatory requirements of a new market. It may have to be modified to operate effectively in country-specific geographic and climatic conditions. Or, it may be redesigned or repackaged to meet the diverse buyer preferences or standard of living conditions. A product's size and packaging may also have to be changed to facilitate shipment or to conform to differences in engineering or design standards in a foreign country. Other dimensions of value proposition adaptation include changes in the brand name, color, size, taste, design, style, features, materials, warranties, after-sales service, technological sophistication, and performance.

The need for some changes, such as accommodating different electricity requirements, will be obvious. Others may require an in-depth analysis of societal customs and cultures, the local economy, the technological sophistication of people living in the country, customers' purchasing power, and purchasing behavior. The legal, economic, political, technological, and climatic requirements of a country's market may also dictate some level of localization or adaptation.

While tariff barriers (tariffs, duties, and quotas) are still prevalent, other *nontariff* barriers such as *product standards* often present greater challenges. Take regulations for food additives. Many of the U.S. so-called *generally recognized as safe* (GRAS) additives are banned in foreign countries. For example, brominated vegetable oil (BVO)—a popular additive in sports drinks and citrus-flavored sodas—is illegal in Europe and Japan, and some U.S.-based companies have voluntarily removed it. The original patent on BVO was for use as a flame retardant, and its side-effects include depression, hallucinations, memory loss, and seizures. Also, consider the drug Ractopamine. Livestock farmers in the United States use the drug to make their animals more muscular and lower the meat's fat content. However, it has been linked to heart problems in humans.

As a consequence, the drug is banned in Europe and about 160 other countries.[1] In marketing abroad, documentation is important not only for the amount of additive but also its source, and often additives must be listed on the label of ingredients. As a result, product labeling and packaging must often be adapted to comply with another country's legal and environmental requirements.

Many kinds of equipment must be engineered in the *metric system* for integration with other pieces of equipment or compliance with a given country's standards. The United States is virtually alone in its adherence to a nonmetric system. U.S. firms that compete successfully globally have found metric measurement to be an important detail in selling to overseas customers. Ford, for example, was one of the first automakers to convert to the metric system. The St. Regis Lumber Mill provides another example in Montana. This company has benefited from its ability to saw rough-dimensioned lumber to Asian metric specifications. The 50 × 100 mm boards they produce are destined to be concrete form supports in China. Other boards with 50 × 150 mm dimensions are cut further into smaller-dimensioned lumber in China for furniture parts, molding, and other components.

Many products must be adapted to local *geographic and climatic* conditions. Factors such as topography, humidity, and energy costs can affect a product's performance or even define its use in a foreign market. Hot, dusty climates of countries in the Middle East and other emerging markets have forced automakers to fit vehicles with different types of filters and clutch systems than those used in North America, Japan, and European countries. Even shampoo and cosmetic product manufacturers must reformulate their products to make them more suited for people living in hot, humid climates.

The availability and performance of a suitable *commercial infrastructure* may necessitate the adaptation or localization of products. For example, a company may decide not to market its frozen food items in countries where retailers do not have adequate freezer space. Instead, it may choose to develop dehydrated products for such markets. Package size, the material used in packaging, before and after-sale service, and warranties may have to be adapted depending on the scope and level of service provided by the distribution structure in the country markets targeted. If postsale servicing facilities are absent or poor, companies may need to offer simpler, more robust products to reduce the need for maintenance and repairs.

Differences in *buyer preferences* also are a major driver behind value proposition adaptation. For example, a product's sensory impact, such as taste or visual impression, may be critical. Japanese consumers' desire for beautiful packaging has led many U.S. companies to redesign cartons and packages specifically for this market. To increase the affordability of mass-marketed consumer products in lesser developed countries, makers of products such as razor blades, cigarettes, chewing gum, ballpoint pens, and candy bars repackage them in smaller single units.

Expectations about *product guarantees* can vary from country to country. Strong warranties may be required to break into a new market, especially if the company is an unknown supplier. In other instances, warranties similar to those in the home country market may not be expected.

As a general rule, *packaging design* should be based on customer needs. For industrial products, the packaging is primarily functional and should consider storage, transportation, protection, preservation, reuse, and so on. For consumer products, packaging has additional functionality and should be protective, informative, and appealing. It should also conform to local legal requirements and buying habits—American consumers tend to shop less frequently than Europeans, so larger sizes are more popular in the United States.

In analyzing adaptation requirements, careful attention must also be given to *cultural differences* between the target customers in the country of origin and those in the host country. Cultural considerations and customs can influence branding, labeling, and package considerations. Certain colors used on labels and packages may be found unattractive or offensive. Red, for example, stands for good luck and fortune in China and parts of Africa, but suggests aggression, danger, or warning in Europe, America, and Australia and New Zealand, masculinity in parts of Europe, mourning (dark red) in the Ivory Coast, and death in Turkey.

A country's *standard of living* and the *target market's purchasing power* can also determine whether a company needs to adapt its value proposition. The level of income, the level of education, and the availability of energy are all factors that help predict the acceptance of a product in a foreign market. In countries with a lower purchasing power level, a manufacturer may opt to offer less sophisticated product models or obsolete products in developed nations.

When potential customers have limited purchasing power, companies may need to develop an entirely new product designed to address the market opportunity at a price point within reach of a potential target market. Conversely, companies in lesser developed countries that have achieved local success may find it necessary to adopt an *up-market strategy* whereby the product may have to be designed to meet world-class standards.

Mini-Case 8.1: How McDonald's Adapts Around the World[2]

In terms of revenue, McDonald's is the biggest restaurant chain in the world. It has almost 40,000 restaurants in over 100 countries, serves over 70 million consumers each day, employs more than two million people, and has revenues approaching 25 billion U.S. dollars. While its main menu offerings consist of hamburgers and fries, the fast-food chain serves other items, including milkshakes, soft drinks, desserts, breakfast fare, products made with chicken, and wraps. McDonald's also serves fruits, smoothies, fish items, and salads to counteract its main menu offerings' perceived unhealthiness.

The key factors for McDonald's success in different countries are standardization, adaptation, and innovation.

Standardization. The company's core offering around the world has identical food products such as *McFlurry, McNuggets, McChicken, Happy Meal,* or *Filet-O-Fish.* The plan provides the company with a strong image. The core strategy saves time and money for McDonald's as it helps realize economies of scale.

Adaptation and innovation. Adaptation enables the company to have a wider reach worldwide. Around the core menu, McDonald's adapts its offerings and business plans for each culture. By doing so, it enlarges its customer base and shows it respects differences between cultures. *China* is a big market for McDonald's with 2,700 outlets. It uses meat from chicken thighs rather than chicken breasts in its chicken burgers because of local preferences. Aside from the regular sauces such as *Honey Mustard, Sweet and Sour,* and *BBQ, McDonald's China's Chicken McNuggets* also have a *Chili Garlic Sauce.* The company also added soups like *Corn Soup* and *Vegetable and Seafood Soup.* In *Germany,* McDonald's combines *Nürnberger* sausages with beef in its burgers and serves beer. As the majority of the population in *Indonesia* is Muslim, McDonald's replaced pork with fish. In *India,* McDonald's replaced beef with chicken. The *Maharaja Mac* is the local version of the standard Big Mac. To attract vegetarian consumers, McDonald's in India offers a *Masala Grilled Veggie Burger, McAloo Tikki,* and *McVeggie.* One of McDonald's India's feature items is the *McCurry Pan,* a baked menu item with curried vegetables. In *Morocco,* pita bread sandwiches are available. The outlets also use traditional spices such as coriander and cumin. *Japanese* cuisine is very different from the rest of the world. In the initial stage, McDonald's in Japan retained the core U.S. menu. But slowly, it replaced and added menu items to cater to Japanese preferences. The company introduced *Green Tea ice cream, a Rice Burger, Seaweed Shaker, and Teriyaki Burger.* The Japanese McDonald's franchise also added shrimp burgers, shrimp nuggets, milkshakes flavored with green tea, and breakfast meal with hotdogs, mustard, ketchup, and relish. The *McRaclette* is only served in McDonald's outlets in *Switzerland.* It is a beef sandwich with raclette cheese, unique raclette sauce, onions, and gherkin pickles. McDonald's has unique locations worldwide and utilizes architecture native to the region and modern architectural designs to further differentiate itself.

Adaptation or Aggregation: The Value Proposition Globalization Matrix

A useful construct for analyzing the need to adapt the product or service and message (positioning) dimensions is the *value proposition globalization matrix.* As shown in Exhibit 8.1, the matrix shows four options: (1) a pure aggregation approach—also referred to as a *global mix* strategy—under which both the product and the message are the same, (2) a *global product* strategy characterized by a similar product or service (aggregation) but different positioning (message adaptation) around the world,

	The Offer (Product or Service)	
	Same	Different
Same	Global "Mix"	Global Message
Different	Global Offer	Global Change

(The Message (Brand) labels rows: Same, Different)

Exhibit 8.1 The value proposition globalization matrix

(3) a *global message* strategy under which the product offer might be different in various parts of the world (adaptation), but the message is the same (aggregation), and (4) a *global change* strategy under which both the product and the message are adapted to local needs and preferences.

Global mix or pure aggregation strategies are rare because only a few industries are truly global in all respects. They apply (1) when a product's usage patterns and brand potential are homogeneous on a global scale, (2) when scale and scope cost advantages substantially outweigh the benefits of partial or full adaptation, and (3) when the competitive environment permits a standardized approach to secure a long-term, sustainable advantage. The best examples are found in industrial product categories, such as basic electronic components, certain commodity markets, and luxury goods.

Global product strategies are feasible when the same product or service can be positioned differently in different parts of the world. There are several reasons for considering differential positioning in different parts of the world. When fixed costs associated with the offer are high, when key core benefits are identical, and when there are natural market boundaries, adapting the message for stronger local advantage is tempting. Automobile manufacturers often use this approach. Although such strategies increase local promotional budgets, they give country managers a degree of flexibility in positioning the product or service for maximum local advantage. The primary disadvantage of this type of strategy is that it could be difficult to sustain or even dangerous in the long term as customers become increasingly global in their outlook and confused by the different messages in different parts of the world.

Global message strategies use the same message worldwide but allow for local adaptation of the product. For example, McDonald's is positioned virtually identically worldwide, but it serves vegetarian food in India and wine in France. The primary motivation behind this type of strategy is the enormous power behind a global brand. As with global product strategies, however, global message strategies can be risky in the long run; global customers might not find elsewhere what they expect and regularly experience at home.

Global change strategies define a *best fit* approach and are by far the most common. As we have seen, for most products, some form of adaptation of both the product or service and the message is necessary. Differences in a product's usage patterns, benefits sought, brand image, competitive structures, distribution channels, and governmental and other regulations all dictate some form of local adaptation. Corporate factors also play a role. Companies that have achieved a global reach through acquisition, for example, often prefer to leverage local brand names, distribution systems, and suppliers rather than embark on a risky global one-size-fits-all approach. As the markets they serve and the company become more global, selective standardization of the message and the offer can become more attractive.

Combining Aggregation and Adaptation: Global Product and Service Platforms

One way to mitigate the tradeoff between creating global efficiencies and adapting to local requirements and preferences is to design a global product and communication platform adapted efficiently to different markets (see Exhibit 8.2). A product or service logic starts with the core product—usually developed for the firm's domestic market. As the company expands its footprint abroad it may have to adapt the product to

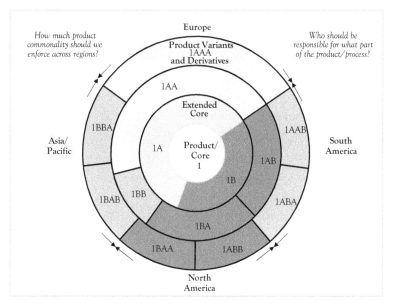

Exhibit 8.2 Developing a global product or service logic: is our strategy built around **platforms** *and* **derivatives?**

different markets and/or add suppliers to serve different regions. The most efficient way to accomplish this is to create "variants" or "derivatives" from the original core product. Such a modularized approach to global product design has become particularly popular in the automobile industry. One of the first *world car platforms* was introduced by Ford in 1981. The Escort was assembled simultaneously in three countries—the United States, Germany, and the UK—with parts produced in 10 countries. The U.S. and European models were distinctly different. Still, they shared standardized engines, transmissions, and ancillary systems for heating, air conditioning, wheels, and seats, thereby saving the company millions of dollars in engineering and development costs.

Combining Adaptation and Arbitrage—Global Product Development[3]

Globalization pressures have changed the practice of product development (PD) in many industries in recent years. Rather than using a centralized or local, cross-functional model, companies have moved to a global Internet-based collaboration model in which skilled development teams worldwide collaborate to develop new products. Today, a majority of global corporations have engineering and development operations outside of their home region. China and India offer particularly attractive opportunities; Microsoft, Cisco, and Intel all have made major investments there.

The old model was based on the premise that the colocation of cross-functional teams to facilitate close collaboration among engineering, marketing, manufacturing, and supply chain functions was critical to effective product development. Colocated PD teams were thought to be more effective at working together on a whole range of activities from understanding market and customer needs to conceptual and detailed design, testing, analysis, prototyping, manufacturing engineering, and technical product support or engineering. Such colocated concurrent practices were thought to result in better product designs, faster time to market, and lower-cost production. They were generally located in corporate research and development centers, which maintained linkages to manufacturing sites and sales offices worldwide.

Today, best practice emphasizes a highly distributed, networked, and digitally supported development process. The resulting global product development process combines centralized functions with regionally distributed engineering and other development functions. It often involves outsourced engineering work as well as captive offshore engineering. A distributed model's benefits include greater engineering efficiency (through the utilization of *lower-cost* resources), *access to technical expertise* internationally, more *global input to product design,* and greater *strategic flexibility*.

Combining Aggregation, Adaptation, and Arbitrage— Global Innovation[4]

Most international companies have global supply chains and product development processes, but a smaller number has developed effective global innovation capabilities. A core competency in global innovation— the ability to leverage new ideas worldwide—has become a major source of global competitive advantage. General Electric (GE) is a good example of a company committed to global innovation. GE recently formed a partnership with Quirky, a crowdsourced innovation platform where designers and engineers build the most promising innovations upvoted by the Quirky community. When it needed to lighten a jet engine bracket by 30 percent, GE turned to GrabCad, the largest online community of designers and engineers. After reviewing submissions from 56 countries, GE chose an engineer from Indonesia who was able to reduce the weight by 84 percent—proof that global innovation initiatives are alive and well.[5]

Firms committed to global innovation have learned that the principal constraint on innovation *performance* is knowledge. Therefore, accessing a diverse set of sources of knowledge is a key challenge and critical to successful differentiation. Companies whose knowledge pool is the same as that of their competitors likely will develop uninspired *me too* products; access to a diversity of knowledge allows a company to move beyond incremental innovation to attention-grabbing designs and breakthrough solutions.

There is an interesting relationship between *geography* and *knowledge* diversity.[6] Some of America's strongest international rivals, including Japan, South Korea, and many European countries, have made significant investments in national cluster initiatives and made innovation the main focus of their economic policies.[7]

France, for example, has a 1.5 billion euro program called Pôles de Compétitivité that is focused on creating, supporting, and encouraging the growth of innovation clusters throughout the country.[8] In fact, 26 of 31 European Union countries have cluster initiative programs in place.[9] Japan also has large investments in two cluster programs called the Knowledge Cluster Initiative and the Industrial Cluster Program. South Korea has made innovation clusters the central focus of its industrial policy. Numerous other European and Asian countries, especially China, have launched national programs dedicated explicitly to promoting specific regional innovation clusters.

Sometimes, innovation is spurred by local challenges. In Finland, for example, the high cost of installing and maintaining fixed telephone lines in isolated places created rapid advances in radiotelephony. In Germany, cultural and political factors have encouraged a strong *green movement*, which has created a distinctive market and technical knowledge in recycling and renewable energy. Just-in-time production systems were pioneered in part because of high land costs there.

Recognition of the role of geography in innovation has prompted many companies to think more globally about their innovation process. For example, pharmaceutical companies such as Novartis AG and GlaxoSmithKline Plc now tap knowledge far beyond traditional chemistry and therapeutics, including biotechnology and genetics. Much of this new knowledge comes from sources other than the companies' traditional R&D laboratories in Basel, New Jersey, California, Tel Aviv, Cuba, or Singapore. For these companies, the globalization of innovation processes is no longer optional; it has become imperative. A side benefit of global innovation is cost reduction. Consider, for example, how companies are now leveraging software programmers in Bangalore, India; aerospace technologists in Russia; or chipset designers in China to cut their innovation processes' costs.

To fully benefit from global innovation, companies must do three things: (1) *prospect*: find the relevant pockets of knowledge from around the world, (2) *assess*: decide on the optimal *footprint* for a particular innovation, and (3) *mobilize*: use cost-effective mechanisms to move distant knowledge without degrading it.[10]

Prospecting, that is, finding valuable new pockets of knowledge to speed up innovation, may well be the most challenging task. The process involves knowing what to look for and where and how to tap into a promising source. A good example is provided by the electric car industry and the search for new battery technologies. Before electric cars can become more widespread, several technological hurdles must be cleared, including the distance drivers can go before having to recharge the car's battery and the life of the battery itself. At present, the range runs from around 100 miles on the low end up to 200+ miles in newer models, and most warranties run out after 150,000 miles or eight years.[11] A recent announcement by Chinese company Contemporary Amperex Technology Co. Ltd. (CATL) may change all that. The company stated it has new battery technology that lasts up to 1.2 million miles (2 million kilometers) and 16 years—and that it is ready to manufacture the batteries on demand.[12]

Assessing new sources of innovation, that is, incorporating new knowledge into and optimizing an existing innovation network, is the second important challenge companies seeking to globalize their innovation strategy must meet. Consider a semiconductor manufacturer that is developing a new chipset for mobile phones. It could access technical and market knowledge from Silicon Valley, Austin, Hinschu, Seoul, Bangalore,

Haifa, Helsinki, or Grenoble but probably should restrict its choices to just some of those sites. Every time a company adds a source of knowledge into the innovation process, it might improve its chances of developing a novel product, but it also increases costs. However, determining an optimal innovation footprint is more complicated because the direct and indirect cost relationships are far more imprecise.

Mobilizing the footprint, that is, integrating knowledge from different sources into a format from which new products or technologies can emerge, is the third challenge. To accomplish this, companies must bring the various pieces of (technical) knowledge together that are scattered around the world and provide a suitable organizational form for innovation efforts to flourish. More importantly, they have to add the more complex, contextual (market) knowledge to integrate the different pieces into an overall innovation blueprint.

Mini-Case 8.2: P&G's Success in Trickle-Up Innovation—Vicks Cough Syrup With Honey[13]

Trickle-up refers to a strategy of creating products for consumers in emerging markets and then repackaging them for developed-world customers. While many affluent consumers in the United States and Western Europe can afford the latest and greatest in everything, there still is a sizable segment of budget-minded consumers in these markets. An over-the-counter medicine from Vicks that has become popular in the West is not new. Vicks Cough Syrup with Honey is a product that Vicks' parent Procter and Gamble initially created for lower-income consumers in Mexico and then *trickled up* to more affluent markets.

Developing and marketing a new product for each nation or ethnic group can take years. Trickle-up innovation can reduce this time significantly, which explains its appeal. P&G needed to do little more in each rollout than adjust for each nation's health regulations.

For companies looking to speed up the development and launch of product offerings while dealing with shrinking budgets and cash-strapped consumers, P&G's experience with its Honey Cough line shows how an international product portfolio can be tapped quickly and cheaply.

P&G is not the only multinational company using this strategy. Other practitioners of trickle-up innovation include GE and Nestle. A dual-slice computed tomography imaging system called HI Speed Dual was the first computed tomography (CT) system that the health care arm of GE Healthcare made in India and the first high-end CT imaging system that anyone had made in the country. GE Healthcare had previously imported the system for Indian customers. By manufacturing it in Bangalore, GE Healthcare cut the price by 10 percent, reduced an 8- to 10-week waiting period, and boosted sales.[14] The product is now used in the United States and other Western countries. Nestlé offers inexpensive instant noodles in India and Pakistan under its Maggi brand. The line includes dried noodles that are engineered to taste as if they were fried, while they have a whole-wheat flavor that is popular in South Asia.

The Globalization of Services—The Next Frontier[15]

While importing and exporting physical products is a big part of going global, the fastest growing global expansion sectors are digital products and data flow. There is now more economic value created in global digitization and the flow of data and information than in the global trade of goods. Additionally, the globalization and digitization of products, processes, labor pools, communications, and services have converged. The primary way data, information, commerce, and communication flow online is through global platforms and marketplaces. Many such platforms have transformed how global business is conducted and how global knowledge is shared. Examples of platforms and marketplaces shaping international trade include:

1. *Data—communication—marketing platforms. Data* sites that enable international trade and globalization include search engines such as Google, knowledge bases such as Wikipedia, and social media sites such as Facebook, LinkedIn, Pinterest, and Instagram. *Communication* platforms make it easier to communicate worldwide through companies such as WeChat and Skype. *Digital*

marketing uses platforms and marketplaces to reach customers in new ways.

2. *Manufacturing and trade marketplaces.* The search for manufacturing sites and new supply chains has never been more accessible. The most prominent company in this space is Alibaba, but it is getting more competition from TradeKey.com, GlobalSources.com, and many others. E-commerce and digital trade distribution leaders include Amazon, Tencent, eBay, JD.com, Alibaba, and Baidu.

3. *Knowledge base platforms.* Knowledge about almost any topic is increasingly available online. Key sites for knowledge include Wikipedia, Quora, Globig.co, and various other niches.

4. *Services marketplaces.* Services comprise one of the more diverse categories consisting of a large number of niche industries. Prominent sites include Lawyers.com, Realtor.com, Home Advisor, Airbnb, Uber, and Globig.com.

5. *Labor marketplaces.* Finding employees worldwide to do *jobs* with specific skills is the focus of Upwork, 99Designs, Freelancer.com, and Mturk.com.

6. *Funding marketplaces.* Even finding investors and funding for companies is available online by using crowdfunding sites like Kickstarter. Potential investors can be identified through sites such as AngelList.

Digitization also makes it easier for people to travel and move around. People can rent properties on Airbnb and VRBO.com, travel with Expedia, TripAdvisor, and obtain transportation via Uber, Lyft, and others. While there is a lot of opportunity for companies in the increasingly digital and global economy, there are also challenges to be aware of:

1. *Data security.* Probably, the single biggest challenge is keeping data secure. Data breaches are all too common; companies should expect they will be hacked and prepare for that eventuality. Global companies have learned that governments have different requirements around notifications and expectations for mitigation.

2. *Intellectual property.* Copyrights, trademarks, patents, URLs, and social media names are important considerations in a global

business context. Companies need to be prepared and diligent about registering and protecting a firm's assets. Countries are not consistent in registering, recognizing, and enforcing laws on any of these aspects of intellectual property. As a consequence, counterfeits and IP theft is still on the rise.

3. *Protectionism.* With global competition, governments want to protect their economies by encouraging others to do business in and with their country. Ways of doing this include signing trade agreements and enacting protectionist legislation.

4. *Data privacy.* Each country has a different perspective on what data is private and how companies can use that data. Companies often do not realize that they are subject to data privacy laws in other countries when collecting data and selling it to customers from those countries.

5. *Global talent.* Developing a top-notch management team, and attracting the skills needed to compete globally takes careful planning. First, companies need to evaluate what skills they already have and may need in the next 3 to 5 years. Next, they need to identify the gaps to develop and hire the skills needed. Important skillsets include specific country knowledge and experience, language skills, global cultural awareness, expertise in international manufacturing and supply chain management, and international marketing and sales experience.

The challenges related to applying the principles of adaptation, aggregation, and arbitrage to the globalization of services—economic, technical, and cultural—are formidable. Even powerhouse Amazon had to retrench significantly in the Chinese market.

Mini-Case 8.3: Why Platform Companies Scale Easier Than Product Firms[16]

Many people think Amazon started as an online bookstore and then expanded into other e-commerce vertical markets. In reality, it began by building a core platform with distinct capabilities and features such as user authentication, order management, pricing, clearing, and content recommendation. These capabilities are enabled by sophisticated machine learning technology that took years to build and scale and require ongoing development and refinement. Amazon subsequently leveraged these capabilities by creating distinct *business-to-consumer* (B2C) or *business-to-business* (B2B) products, which allows its customers—whether they are individual consumers buying books or independent booksellers—to adopt some or all of these products. Using a platform-first approach enabled Amazon to scale its business in an initial vertical market (books) and subsequently build products in adjacent vertical markets such as music, film, and clothing. All of its products and services—its bookstore, streaming service, the third-party marketplace, and Web services—are dependent on that underlying platform.

Platform-first companies often are successful where product-first companies fail, as exemplified by the Amazon Kindle e-reader. Although the Kindle was not the first such product on the market, it rapidly became the most popular one after its launch in 2007. After the iPhone and iPad were introduced, the Kindle—like all e-readers—instantly became obsolete. However, even though Kindle product sales dropped off, the application continued to thrive, in part because it leverages Amazon's powerful platform, which in turn allowed Amazon to become dominant in global book distribution.

A major benefit of platform-first companies is that they create partners' opportunities to build complementary products and services. Amazon was able to move its Kindle application to the iPhone because the iPhone's underlying technology platform is designed to encourage such co-innovation.

Apple's development of iOS provides another example. Because iOS was based on its mature and widely adopted Macintosh desktop platform, developers could quickly adapt earlier applications and build new ones for the mobile platform. As a result, Apple inherited a wide-ranging ecosystem of partners and competitors, all building products and marketplaces that used iOS. Today, Apple sells music and streaming services on the iPhone, but so do Amazon, Netflix, Spotify, Hulu, and Pandora.

Platform companies are also important players in the B2B space. Salesforce, a pioneer in the software-as-a-service space, saves its enterprise customers the cost of constructing and maintaining their core computing infrastructure. Its marketplace, AppExchanger, offers other companies an opportunity to use the Salesforce platform to develop their products adjacent to Salesforce. The company even developed its programming language, Apex, which enables third parties to write and run programs on its shared architecture. Though most of its products and partners are not familiar to consumers, the Salesforce ecosystem is a major customer relations management (CRM) asset to millions of sales and marketing professionals.

CHAPTER 9

Global Positioning and Branding

Introduction

Global brands—brands whose positioning, advertising strategy, personality, look, and feel are the same in most respects from one country to another—have become increasingly popular. Even though most global brands are not identical from one country to another—Visa changes its logo in some countries—companies whose brands have become more global reap clear benefits.

Companies such as IBM, American Express, and Apple realize significant economies of scale through global branding. The cost of creating a single, global advertising campaign is much lower than that of developing separate campaigns for different markets around the world, especially if a single agency is used.

Benefits of Global Branding

An effective global branding strategy helps to:

1. *Maintain consistency*. Although brand campaigns may need to change in some countries to suit a new target audience's needs, consistency is still crucial in a global campaign. A brand's *integrity* is defined as how consumers perceive a company or brand through its products, image, and reputation. And, while every customer experience may not meet or exceed the brand promise, when a brand loses integrity, its meaning and value to consumers are diminished. A consistent commitment to the company's values shows the integrity that makes the brand valuable anywhere in the world.

2. *Foster positive relationships.* A positive reputation across geographical boundaries helps a brand grow by creating a positive image for the company.

3. *Deliver value.* No matter where a company goes in the world, it needs to deliver value to its stakeholders, that is, it needs to know its unique value and selling proposition and how it addresses the needs of target customers in different parts of the world.

Risks of Global Branding

Global branding is not without risks; however:

1. *Targeted economies of scale may not materialize.* Sometimes, it is cheaper and more effective for companies to create ads locally than to import ads and then adapt them for each market. What is more, cultural differences may make it difficult to create a truly global campaign.[1]

2. *Designing a global brand strategy is difficult.* Designing a good brand strategy for one country is challenging. Creating one that can be applied worldwide is even more difficult. A great deal of information must be gathered; designers must be extremely creative, and they need to anticipate a host of challenges in execution.

3. *Global brands cannot be imposed on all markets.* A brand's image may not be the same throughout the world. For example, Honda means quality and reliability in the United States. In Japan, where quality is taken for granted for most cars, Honda represents speed, youth, and energy. In Britain, where Ford is number one, the company positioned its Galaxy minivan as the luxurious *nonvan* to appeal to soccer moms and executives. In Germany, where Volkswagen is number one, Ford positions the Galaxy as *the clever alternative*.

Global Branding Versus Global Positioning

As shown in Exhibit 9.1, the key difference between global branding and positioning is that branding involves creating a unique image of the company's product through brand logos, taglines, and advertising

Branding vs Positioning	
Branding is the process of creating a unique image of the company's product in the mind of the customer, through brand logos, tagline and advertising strategies.	Positioning is the process of acquiring a space in the mind of the customer among competitor brands
Nature	
Branding is a standalone concept that is indirectly affected by competition.	Positioning is conducted relative to the competitors.
Intangible Asset Value	
Branding strategies directly increase the intangible asset value.	Positioning strategies indirectly increase the intangible asset value by strengthening the brand.

Exhibit 9.1 Global branding versus global positioning

strategies, whereas positioning refers to acquiring space in the mind of the customer among competitor brands. Both global branding and position-ing are important elements in formulating a foreign expansion strategy due to differences in competition and cultures in each country entered. How successfully a company can position itself and brand the products worldwide directly affects its profitability and long-term survival.

Carefully adhering to a particular global positioning is both aggregation and adaptation; it creates uniformity in different world markets. It also defines target segments as the company enters new countries or regions. Consider Diageo's decision, the British beer-and-spirits company, to maintain its premium pricing strategy wherever it does business, even when it enters a new market. By projecting a premium positioning for brands such as Johnnie Walker Black, Smirnoff vodka, Captain Morgan rum, Tanqueray gin, and Guinness stout, it identifies loyal consumers who will pay for its well-known products.

Similarly, to maintain consistency, Johnson and Johnson (J&J) will not sacrifice premium pricing for its well-known brands. It believes that its popular Band-Aid adhesive bandages are superior to competitors' products, and a premium price is a way to signal that. However, J&J must allow for some improvisation as it expands worldwide, especially into less-developed countries. For instance, it might sell a four-pack of Band-Aids instead of the larger box it markets in the developed world or a sample-sized bottle of baby shampoo instead of a full-sized one.

Global Brand Structures

Multinational companies typically operate with one of three brand structures: (1) a *corporate-dominant*, (2) a *product-dominant*, or (3) a *hybrid* structure. Corporate-dominant brand structures are most common among firms with a small range of products or little market diversity, such as Shell, Toyota, or Nike. By contrast, product-dominant brand structures are often used by companies such as industrial conglomerate Akzo Nobel that have multiple national or local brands. Procter and Gamble has similarly expanded internationally by leveraging their *power* brands. The most commonly used brand structure is a hybrid—think of Toyota Corolla cars or Cadbury Dairy Milk chocolate—consisting of a mix of global (corporate), regional, and national product-level brands or different structures for different product divisions.

In many companies, *global* branding evolves as they enter new countries or expand their product offerings within an existing country. Typically, such expansion decisions are made incrementally and often on a country-by-country, product division, or product line basis without explicitly considering their implications for the global brand portfolio's overall balance. As their global market presence evolves, companies must pay closer attention to the consistency of their branding decisions across national markets and formulate an effective overall global brand strategy. In addition, they must decide (1) how to manage brands that bridge different geographic markets and product lines, (2) who should have custody of international brands, (3) who is responsible for coordinating branding decisions across different national or regional markets, and (4) who decides about the use of a particular brand name on other products or services.

A coherent set of principles is needed to guide the effective use of brands in the global marketplace. These principles must define the company's *brand architecture*, that is, provide guidance to decide which brands should *lead* at what levels in the organization and how the use of brands is coordinated across product lines and markets.

Determinants of a Global Brand Structure

A brand portfolio structure typically reflects a company's past management decisions and the competitive realities the brand faces in the marketplace. Some companies, such as Procter and Gamble and Coca-Cola, expanded primarily by taking domestic *power* brands to international markets. As they seek to expand further, they must decide whether to extend their power brands further or develop brands geared to specific regional or national preferences and integrate the latter into their overall brand strategy.

Others, such as Nestle and Unilever, grew primarily by acquisition. Consequently, they mainly relied on country-centered strategies to build or acquire a mix of national and international brands. Their challenge is to decide how much harmonization of brands across countries is optimal and how to achieve it. Streamlining of brands is particularly important in markets outside the United States, which often are fragmented, have small-scale distribution, and lack the potential or size to warrant the use of heavy mass media advertising needed to develop strong brands.

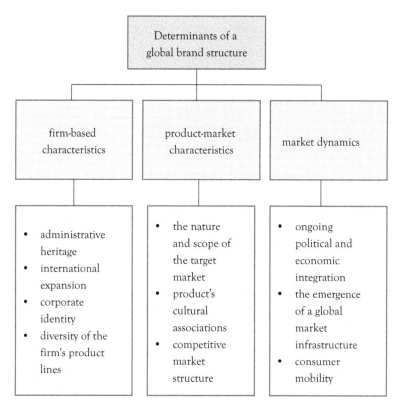

Exhibit 9.2 Determinants of a global brand structure

As shown in Exhibit 9.2, a company's international brand structure is shaped by three sets of factors: *(1) firm-based characteristics, (2) product-market characteristics, and (3) underlying market dynamics.*[2]

Firm-based characteristics. Firm-based characteristics reflect the full array of past management decisions. First, a company's *administrative heritage*—and its organizational structure—defines the template for its brand structure. Second, a firm's *international expansion strategy*—acquisition or organic growth—affects how its brand structure evolves. In particular, strategic alliances to expand a firm's operations' geographic scope often result in a *melding* of the partners' brand strategies. Third and fourth, the importance of *corporate identity* and the *diversity of the firm's product lines and product divisions* also are determinants of the range and number of brands.

Knowledge of a company's *administrative heritage* is key to understanding its global brand structure.[3] A firm that historically has operated on a highly decentralized basis in which country managers have substantial autonomy and control over the strategy and day-to-day operations is likely to have a substantial number of local brands. In some cases, the same product may be sold under different brand names in different countries. Alternatively, a product may be sold under the same brand name but have a different positioning or formulation in different countries.

Firms with a centralized organizational structure and global product divisions, such as Panasonic or Siemens, are more likely to have global brands. In such companies, product lines are typically standardized worldwide, with minor variations in styling and features for local country markets.

Firms that *expand internationally* by acquiring local companies often inherit local brands. If these brands have high local recognition or a strong customer or distributor franchise, they will normally retain the brand. Retaining a local brand is particularly attractive if the brand does not occupy a similar positioning to another brand currently owned by the firm.

Expansion is often accompanied by diversification. Nestle grew mostly by acquiring companies in various product markets, mostly in the food and beverage segment. These acquisitions included well-known global brands such as Perrier and San Pellegrino (mineral water), confectionery companies such as Rowntree and Perugina, pet food companies such as Spillers and Alpo, and grocery companies such as Buitoni, Crosse and Blackwell, and Herta. The resulting proliferation of brands created the need to consolidate and integrate company branding structures.[4]

Firms that have expanded predominantly by taking strong domestic, so-called *power* brands abroad primarily use product-level brand strategies. For example, Procter and Gamble has rolled out several of its personal product brands, such as Camay and Pampers, into international markets. Taking strong domestic brands abroad appears most effective when customer interests and desired product attributes are similar worldwide, and brand image is important to consumers.

The relative importance placed by the firm on its *corporate identity* also affects brand structure. Companies such as General Electric (GE) and Apple place considerable emphasis on corporate identity. In the case of GE Appliances, "Good Things, For Life" reinforces the company's corporate reputation for turning innovative ideas into leading products and services. Equally, Apple uses its apple logo to project a strong innovator's image in the personal computer market. Increasingly, companies use their corporate identity to reassure customers and distributors that the company is reliable and stands behind their products. As a result, even companies with highly diverse product lines—such as Samsung—rely on the corporate brand name (and logo) to project an image of reliability.

The *diversity or, conversely, the interrelatedness of the product businesses* in which the firm is involved is another relevant firm-based determinant of its brand structure. Firms involved in closely related product lines or businesses that share a common technology or rely on similar core competencies often emphasize corporate brands. 3M Corporation, for example, is involved in a wide array of product businesses worldwide, ranging from displays and optics to health care products to cleaners to abrasives and adhesives. All rely heavily on engineering skills and have a reputation for being cutting-edge. The use of 3M provides reassurance and reinforces the firm's reputation for competency and reliable products worldwide.

Product-market drivers. Three product-market factors play an important role in brand architecture: the *nature and scope of the target market*, the *product's cultural associations*, and the *competitive market structure*.[5]

When companies target a *global market segment* with relatively homogeneous needs and preferences worldwide, global branding is an effective approach to establishing a distinctive global identity. Luxury brands such as Godiva, Moet and Chandon, and Louis Vuitton and brands such as DeBeers, Benneton, and L'Oréal target the same market segment worldwide and benefit from their appeal to a global consumer group. Sometimes, it is more effective to segment international markets by region and target regional segments with similar interests and purchase behavior, such as Euro-consumers. Macro-segmentation provides cost efficiencies when customer segments are readily accessible through targeted regional media and distribution channels.

A critical factor influencing brand structure is how the *product or service is associated with a particular culture.* A cultural association is indicated when strong and deeply held local preferences for specific products are an integral part of a culture (think of bratwurst, soccer teams). The stronger the cultural association, the less likely global product brands will thrive; instead, local branding may be needed.

A third product market driver of a company's brand structure is its *competitive market structure*—the relative strength of local (national) versus global competitors in a given product market. If markets are fully integrated, and the same companies compete in these markets worldwide, as, in aerospace, global branding helps create a competitive differentiation on a global basis. When strong local, national, or regional competitors and global competitors are present in a given national or regional market, using a multitier branding structure, including global corporate or product brands and local brands, is desirable. For example, Coca-Cola has introduced several local and regional brands that target specific market tastes worldwide beyond promoting its power brands.

Market dynamics. Finally, while the firm's history and the product markets in which it operates shape its brand structure, market dynamics— *ongoing political and economic integration, the emergence of a global market infrastructure, and consumer mobility*—shape and continually change the brand's global context.[6]

Increasing *political and economic integration* in many parts of the world has been a key factor in the growth of global branding. As countries remove tariff and nontariff barriers, and as people and information move more easily across borders, the business climate has become more favorable to the marketing of international brands. In such situations, firms are less frequently required to modify products to meet local requirements or develop specific variants for local markets and increase market standardized products with the same brand name in multiple country markets. In many cases, the harmonization of product regulation across borders has further facilitated global branding growth.

The growth of a global *market infrastructure* is also a major factor in the spread of international brands. Global and regional media provide economical and effective vehicles for advertising international brands. Global media also helped by developing an awareness of these brands and their associated lifestyles in other countries.

The globalization of retailing has made it easier to develop international manufacturer brands. As retailers move across borders, they provide an effective channel for international brands, but at the same time, increase their power. Consequently, manufacturers must develop strong brands with an international appeal to negotiate their shelf position more effectively and introduce new products.

A final factor shaping the context for international branding is increased *consumer mobility*. Growing international travel and the movement of customers across national boundaries provides exposure to brands in different countries. Awareness of the availability and high visibility of an international brand in multiple countries enhances its value to consumers and reassures its strength and reliability. Familiarity with new and diverse products and the lifestyles and cultures that they represent also generate a greater receptivity to products of foreign origin. All these factors help create a climate more favorable to international brands.

Mini-Case 9.1: Global Branding in the Pharmaceutical Industry.

In Paris, stomach ulcers are treated with Mopral; in Chicago, it is called Prilosec. These two products are, in fact, the same drug. Prilosec is the U.S. brand of AstraZeneca's omeprazole; Mopral is its French counterpart. Unlike manufacturers of consumer goods, the pharmaceutical industry traditionally has been wary of creating big, international brands. But, that has changed in recent years. Think of Celebrex for arthritis pain, the antidiabetic agent Avandia, and the anticoagulant Plavix.

It is somewhat surprising that pharmaceutical companies did not consider global branding sooner because a drug works for everybody in the same way in every country. While the industry has become global from a technological and geopolitical perspective, few pharmaceutical companies have successfully globally integrated their marketing practices. Increasingly, companies want to avoid any brand inconsistencies while maximizing exposure. Another globalizing force is the growing standardization of the regulatory environment. The creation of the European Medical Evaluations Agency, which approves drugs for all the members of the European Union, provides a good example. Japan has also adopted a new approval system to facilitate the entry of Western products.

Increased use of direct-to-consumer (DTC) advertising worldwide is another key factor favoring global branding practices. When doctors and health care professionals were the primary targets for pharmaceutical marketing, consumer-targeted branding was unnecessary. Today, companies are preparing for the spread of DTC beyond the United States. The introduction of global branding anticipates the transition to a more consumer-driven market.

The pressure to cut or contain costs is perhaps the most powerful driver behind the pharmaceutical industry's shift to global branding. Mega mergers were important in containing the costs of research and development (R&D) and finding pipeline products. The big companies still need around five new blockbuster products every year to grow and be profitable. Global branding reduces marketing costs and produces a much faster and higher product rollout.

Local market conditions such as reimbursement policies may still override the benefits of global strategies and therefore inhibit the globalization of brands. Significant cost savings may, therefore, be slow in coming. Even with a centralized, global brand, most companies will likely use local agencies for their marketing campaigns.

Use of Country-of-Origin Effects in Global Branding[7]

Many beer brands invoke their country of origin. Guinness comes from Ireland, Heineken and Amstel are Dutch, and Budweiser is a truly American brand. Using the country of origin as part of the brand equity is free, so companies can avoid building an image from scratch over decades. For a long time, Foster's used a kangaroo in its advertisements, while Lapin Kulta, from Lapland in Finland, relies heavily on its unusual origin in its marketing. Images of Finland's stark landscapes adorn communications material and bottle labels.

Swiss watchmakers leverage the value of their *Swiss made* brand. The Federation of the Swiss Watch Industry actively polices all uses of the term and has strict guidelines on how it may be used on clocks and watches. Similarly, the French leverage their reputation for good wine, cooking, and fashion, and the Italians portray themselves as the masters of style.

German firms have been particularly effective at leveraging country effects. Of Interbrand's Top 100 Global Brands in 2019, 10 were German brands—five automobile brands (BMW, Porche, Mercedes-Benz, Volkswagen, and Audi) as well as brands in technology (SAP and Siemens), clothing (Adidas), financial services (Allianz), and cosmetics (Nivea). Germany was second only to the United States in the number of brands making the Top 100 list.

Assigning Custody for Key Strategic Brands

Global brand management is key to ensuring that a company's brands retain their integrity, visibility, and value. An important dimension of global brand management is brand custody—appointing a brand champion responsible for approving brand extensions and monitoring brand positioning worldwide.

One option is to negotiate the coordination of specific brand positions between corporate headquarters and country managers. Firms often use this option with strong country managers who operate in product markets where brands historically were tailored to local market characteristics.

A more proactive approach calls for appointing a brand champion responsible for building and managing a brand worldwide. The job includes monitoring the consistency of the brand positioning in international markets and authorizing brand extensions to other products or other product businesses. The brand champion can be a senior manager at corporate headquarters, a country manager, or a product development group. It is critical that the brand champion report directly to top management and have clear authority to sanction and refuse brand extensions to other product lines and product businesses to maintain the integrity of the brand.

A third option is to centralize control of brands within a global product division. This approach is likely to be most effective when the business is focused on a specific global market segment or when new products or brands are introduced. Central control of brands is easier when there is a high level of consistency in market characteristics across countries, and when the company's administrative heritage has only a limited history of strong country management.

Brand Globalization: Pitfalls to Avoid[8]

When brands are extended to new national markets, they invariably have to compete with local market leaders and regional brands firmly entrenched with that market's institutions and infrastructures. And, as the number of markets that brands enter increases, they are vulnerable to attack from multiple competitors on multiple fronts. Formulating strategies that fit different markets and outcompete rivals can be highly challenging.

The growing interest among companies to extend leading brands into Asian markets, especially China and India, demonstrates the *challenges of brand globalization*. When Google refused to be censored by the Chinese government, it was forced out of the Chinese market. Such a challenge not only diverted Google's resources from effectively competing against Yahoo!, Baidu.com, and Bing.com, but it also reduced Google's competitive flexibility in strategically dealing with new competition points.

As a company's number of brands grows, either in their home market or in multiple foreign markets, effectively managing the brand portfolio becomes more difficult. What is more, as brands enter new segments, new industries, or start to represent a growing number of product variants, variety and chaos are added to the brand portfolio. Each new addition to the brand portfolio creates a new challenge for brand managers: effectively align the corporate brand's overall value proposition with those of all other brands in the portfolio. Such scenarios become even more complicated when coordination and consolidation among all the different markets are not tightly implemented.

Brands such as Toyota, Honda, Procter and Gamble (P&G), Unilever, Canon, Nikon, Harley-Davidson, Creative Technologies, Samsung, and many others have long faced the challenges of crafting their product variants demands on varied segments. Factors such as locally accepted price points, market-specific positioning, and the brand variant's relative position in a given market increase the complexity of managing a global brand portfolio.

A key challenge faced by companies trying to globalize their brands is *maintaining a brand's identity, while at the same time, customizing the brand message.* Usually referred to as *glocalization,* the process of optimally combining the global aspects of a brand's characteristics with the local aspects of a brand's positioning and value delivery can be highly challenging. Companies have to be cautious to ensure that the extent to which they *glocalize* their brands does not erode the brand's positioning and identity in the most important home markets. As brands are extended to more foreign markets, the process of ensuring brand consistency gets more complicated.

Benefits of Corporate Branding[9]

Corporations are increasingly becoming aware of the enhanced value that global branding strategies can provide. A strong *corporate* branding strategy can add significant value. Corporate branding helps a corporation and its management implement its long-term vision, create unique positions in the company's marketplace and its brands, and signaling a commitment to a broader set of stakeholder issues. Therefore, an effective corporate branding strategy enables a company to leverage its tangible and nontangible assets and promote excellence throughout the corporation. To be effective, corporate branding requires a high level of personal attention and commitment from the CEO and senior management. Examples of effective corporate brands include Microsoft, Intel, Singapore Airlines,

Disney, CNN, Samsung, and Mercedes. Global financial companies such as HSBC and Citibank have acquired many companies across the globe in recent years. They adopted them fully under their international corporate brands with great success and within a relatively short timeframe. All these companies understand that a well-executed corporate branding strategy can confer significant benefits:

1. *The corporate brand as the face of the company.* A strong corporate brand acts as the face of the company and portrays what it wants to do and what it wants to be known for in the marketplace. In other words, a corporate brand encapsulates its vision, values, personality, positioning, and image, among many other dimensions. HSBC employs the same slogan, "The world's local bank," around the world, thereby allowing the corporation to portray itself as a *bridge between cultures.*

2. *Simplicity.* An effective corporate branding strategy creates simplicity by adopting the top of the brand's folio as the corporation's ultimate identity. P&G is widely known for its multibrand strategy. Yet, the corporate name P&G encapsulates all of its activities. Depending on the business strategy and the potential need for multiple brands, a corporate brand can help management focus on its core vision and values. Once established, it facilitates revisiting other brands' definition in the corporations' portfolio and creating new brand identities.

3. *Cost savings.* A corporate branding strategy is often more cost-effective than multibrand architecture. Specifically, corporate branding produces efficiencies in marketing and advertising spending as the corporate brand replaces budgets for individual product marketing efforts. Even a combined corporate and product branding strategy can enable managers to reduce costs and exploit synergies from a new and more focused brand architecture. For example, the Apple brand has established a very strong position as a design-driven and innovative company offering many products and services.

Global Brand Value[10]

Successful global brands are highly valuable. As shown in Exhibit 9.3, a strong global brand (1) shapes consumer preferences, (2) facilitates global innovation, (3) provides economies of scale, (4) promotes marketing benefits, and (5) creates organizational benefits.

Interbrand, an international brand consulting firm, has developed a method for *valuing global brands*. It looks at factors such as a brand's financial strength, the importance of the brand in driving consumer selection, and the likelihood of generating ongoing revenue by the brand. A *brand value* score is a financial representation of a business's earnings resulting from the demand created for its products and services through the strength of its brand.

Each year, Interbrand compiles a list of publicly held global brands for analysis based on five criteria: (1) there must be substantial publicly

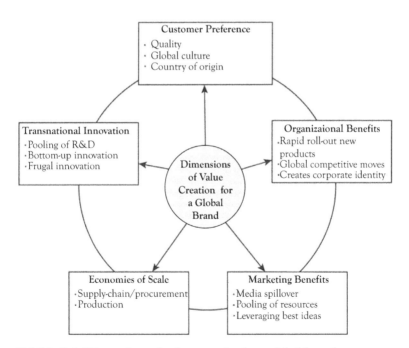

Exhibit 9.3 Dimensions of value creation by a global brand

available financial data for the brand; (2) one-third of the brand's revenues must come from outside its country of origin; (3) the brand must be positioned to play a significant role in the consumers' purchase decision; (4) the economic value added (EVA) must be positive, showing that there is revenue above the company's operating and financing costs; and (5) the brand must have a broad public profile and awareness.

To determine a brand's *brand value*, the company looks at the *financial health* of the business and brand, the *brand's role in creating demand*, and the *future strength of the brand* as an asset to the business.

Financial analysis is used to measure economic profit or the company's overall financial return to its investors. Economic profit is the after-tax operating profit of the brand, minus a charge for the capital used to generate the brand's revenue and margins.

Brand analysis. Brand analysis is concerned with measuring the portion of the purchase decision attributable to the brand instead of other factors (e.g., purchase drivers such as price, convenience, or product features). The role of brand index (RBI) quantifies this measurement. RBI scores for best global brands are derived, depending on the brand, from three types of evaluations: commissioned market research, benchmarking against the role of brand scores from client projects with brands in the same industry, or expert panel assessment.

Brand strength score. Brand strength measures the ability of the brand to create loyalty and, therefore, sustainable demand and profit into the future. Brand strength analysis is based on an evaluation across four internal (clarity, commitment, governance, and responsiveness) and six external factors (authenticity, relevance, differentiation, consistency, presence, and engagement). Performance in each of these areas is judged relative to other industry brands and relative to other world-class brands. The brand strength analysis delivers a snapshot of the brand's strengths and weaknesses and is used to generate a road map of activities to grow the brand's strength and value into the future.

The Number 1 global brand on Interbrand's 2019 list is *Apple*. *Google* is second, *Amazon* ranks third, *Microsoft* comes in fourth, and *Coca-Cola* is fifth. Rounding out the top 10 are *Samsung* (6), *Toyota* (7), *Mercedes Benz* (8), *McDonald's* (9), and *Disney* (10).

Mini-Case 9.2: Uniqlo: The Strategy Behind the Global Japanese Fast Fashion Retail Brand.[11]

Uniqlo was virtually unknown 10 years ago to anyone outside of Japan. Today, Uniqlo is a global brand with associations of quality, affordability, and fashion. Despite having to compete against other bigger fashion retailers like *ZARA (Inditex)*, H&M, Gap, and *Forever21*, Uniqlo has managed to grow at an astounding pace.

Uniqlo is a wholly owned subsidiary of Fast Retailing Company Limited and is known for providing high-quality, private-label casual wear at low prices. The brand has grown to more than 2,196 stores in 21 countries across Asia, Europe, and the United States in just a matter of 21 years. It is the biggest apparel chain in Asia, with over 800 retail stores in Japan alone. Fast retailing's market capitalization is over 57.7 billion U.S. dollars, and the company employs more than 52,000 people globally. According to Forbes, Uniqlo has a brand value of 8.6 billion U.S. dollars and is 84th on the World's Most Valuable Brands list.

The Uniqlo brand strategy. Uniqlo's brand message summarizes a clear vision: "Uniqlo is a modern Japanese company that inspires the world to dress casual." Uniqlo's unique corporate strategy is to ignore fashion. Instead of following fast-fashion trends like its competitors, the company positions its clothing as simple, essential, yet universal. The Uniqlo brand offers unique functional performance and uses in-house fabric and design. The company distinguishes itself from its price-driven competitors by branding its signature innovations with names like HeatTech, LifeWear, and AIRism. Key brand success factors for Uniqlo include:

1. *A delivery system supporting a clear brand promise.* Uniqlo successfully defines a clear brand promise to provide high-quality, performance-enhanced, universal, basic casual wear at affordable prices. The company has created a strong delivery system to deliver on its brand promise with in-house product planning, design, manufacturing, and distribution, which creates efficiency and focuses on core products in a limited range of fabrics.

2. *Product development and an efficient supply chain.* While Zara has built the world's largest apparel business based on rapidly responding to fast-changing fashion trends, Uniqlo has taken the opposite approach, planning the production of its wardrobe essentials up to a year in advance.

3. *Company culture and visionary leadership.* In 2018, Tadashi Yanai was ranked number 35 on the list of the best-performing CEOs in the world by Harvard Business Review. Since 2000, he has provided a 700 percent return for shareholders, and the market capitalization of Uniqlo has increased by 39 billion U.S. dollars. The company's culture is inclusive. The company's values and goals are embedded in its processes and performance measures and shared by employees worldwide. Company financials are completely transparent to employees and sales and charted and posted daily.

4. *High dedication to innovation.* One of Uniqlo's signature innovations is HeatTech, a fabric developed with Toray Industries (a Japanese chemical company) that turns moisture into heat and has air pockets in the fabric to retain that heat.

5. *Uniqlo brand architecture.* Uniqlo caters apparel to mainly three customer segments: women, men, and kids and babies. The brand is divided into five sub-brands separated by style but sold in the same Uniqlo store, within which Uniqlo showcases its different collections: outerwear, tops, bottoms, inner wear, home wear, and accessories.

6. *Uniqlo brand communication strategy.* Uniqlo communicates its brand position and values through its unique in-store environment, celebrity brand ambassadors (called Uniqlo Global Ambassadors), and digital marketing with designers and brand campaigns.

7. *Uniqlo's approach to global sustainability.* The brand strongly signals the belief that the company's value is intrinsically linked to the value it brings to society as a whole. Its corporate statement "*Changing clothes. Changing conventional wisdom. Change the world.*" reflects its goal to help transform society and enhance its stakeholders' environment and lives.

CHAPTER 10

Globalizing the Value Creation Infrastructure

Introduction

The term *value chain* refers to how companies procure raw materials, add value to them through production and other processes to create a finished product, and then sell the finished product to consumers. A *supply chain* represents the steps it takes to get the product or service to the customer.[1] Put differently, while a supply chain involves all parties in fulfilling a customer request, a value chain is a set of interrelated activities a company uses to create a competitive advantage.

The two concepts are closely related. In a global competitive environment, individual companies no longer compete as autonomous entities, but as supply chain networks. Instead of brand versus brand or company versus company, it increasingly is suppliers–brand–company versus suppliers–brand–company. In this new competitive environment, a single business's success increasingly depends on a management's ability to integrate the company's intricate network of business relationships. Supply chain management (SCM) offers the opportunity to capture synergies produced by intra- and intercompany integration and management.

The Dimensions of Global Value Creation

Globalizing a company's value creation infrastructure—from the procurement of raw materials and components to manufacturing and research and development (R&D) to distribution and customer service—has three primary dimensions: (1) *deciding which activities to perform in-house and which ones to outsource, to whom and where*; (2) *developing the right partnerships to support a company's globalization efforts*; and (3) *implementing a suitable SCM model* for integrating them into a cost-effective, seamless value-creating network.

Deciding which activities to perform in-house and which ones to outsource, to whom and where. *Outsourcing* is about moving internal operations to a third party. It can come in the form of selling a physical plant to a supplier, buying back goods or services, or shifting an entire business division to a third party and again buying the service back. The basic philosophy is to move transactional activities to others to give a company the capacity to focus on its core competencies. Unlike outsourcing, *offshoring* is primarily a geographic activity. Offshoring takes advantage of cost differentials by relocating factories from costly countries to cheaper economies. Think of industries such as clothing and electronics. Offshoring does not only relate to the production of physical goods but also services. The Indian information technology (IT) industry, for instance, has flourished because of offshoring by technological companies in the West.

Which activities should be kept in-house and which ones can effectively be outsourced depends on a host of factors, most prominently the company's core strategy. In principle, every functional or value-adding activity, from research to manufacturing to customer service, is a candidate for outsourcing. However, few companies differentiated by their operational excellence would consider outsourcing activities critical to their supply chain's efficacy. Similarly, companies operating with a focus on customer relations should be reluctant to outsource customer service-related functions, while leading innovation-focused companies should nurture their capacity to develop new products and technologies. That is why, Toyota made continuous investments in its production system as it expanded abroad. Similarly, Procter and Gamble strengthened its world-class innovation and marketing capabilities, and Walmart continued to refine its SCM capabilities as it globalized.

Firms tend to concentrate their investments in global value chain activities that contribute directly to their competitive advantage, while, at the same time, helping the company retain the right amount of strategic flexibility. Making such decisions is a formidable challenge; capabilities that may seem unrelated at first glance can turn out to be critical for creating an essential advantage when they are combined. For example, consider the case of a leading consumer packaged goods company that leveraged strong capabilities in sales. Its smaller brands showed up on retailers' shelves far more regularly than comparable brands from competitors. It was also known for its short-term R&D in rapidly bringing product variations to the market. These capabilities are worth investing in separately, but together they add up to a substantial advantage over competitors, especially in introducing new products.

Developing the Right Partnerships to Support a Company's Globalization Efforts

Formulating cooperative strategies—*joint ventures, strategic alliances, and other partnering* arrangements—complements outsourcing. For many corporations, cooperative strategies produce the benefits of internal development and acquisition while avoiding the drawbacks of both. Selecting the most appropriate arrangement involves analyzing the nature of the opportunity, the mutual strategic interests in the cooperative venture, and the prior experience with joint ventures of both partners. The essential question is: How can we structure this opportunity to maximize the benefit(s) to both parties?

In a strategic partnership, the partners remain independent, share the benefits, risks, and control over joint actions, and commit to making ongoing investments in strategic areas. Most often, they are established when companies need to acquire new capabilities within their existing business. Strategic partnerships can take the form of minority equity investments, joint ventures, or nontraditional contracts such as joint R&D, long-term sourcing, shared distribution or services.

Key challenges in structuring strategic partnerships include isolating proprietary knowledge, processing multiple knowledge flows, creating adaptive governance, and operating global virtual teams. If these challenges are not resolved, the partnership is likely to fail.

Exhibit 10.1 shows the most commonly cited factors for the success or failure of a strategic partnership. Key reasons include the importance of matching the two parties' objectives and values, the balance of the benefits and costs accruing to each, and an effective governance structure.[2]

To mitigate these factors and find the right partner, companies should use various approaches to search for potential partnerships, including consulting members of their current ecosystem such as suppliers, research partners, and industry organizations.

Strategic Partnerships	
Reasons for Success	**Reasons for Failure**
• Win-win for both sides • Alignment of relevant stakeholders • Value match • Complementary skill sets • Clear Communications • Strong, shared governance	• Competing Agendas • Value Mismatch • Objectives not aligned • Lack of communication • Lack of trust • Win-lose situation • Lack of Governance • Mis-alignment of stakeholders

Exhibit 10.1 Reasons for success or failure in strategic partnerships

Implementing a suitable SCM model. Top-performing *supply chains* have three distinct qualities. First, they are *agile* enough to react readily to sudden changes in demand or supply. Second, they can *adapt* over time as market structures and environmental conditions change. And third, they are designed to *align* all members of the supply chain network to optimize performance.[3] These characteristics—agility, adaptability, and alignment—are possible only when partners promote knowledge flow between supply chain nodes. Knowledge flow creates value by making the supply chain more transparent and allowing better answers to customer needs. Deep knowledge about customers and the overall market, as opposed to just information from order points, provides other benefits, including a better understanding of market trends, resulting in better planning and product development.[4]

Agility—the ability to respond quickly and cost-effectively to unexpected change—is critical because, in most industries, both demand and supply fluctuate more rapidly and widely than they used to. The best companies use agile supply chains to differentiate themselves from rivals. As discussed earlier in Mini-Case 6.1, Zara has become one of Europe's most profitable apparel brands by building agility into every link of its supply chains. As soon as designers spot new trends, they create sketches and order fabrics. That gives them a head start over competitors because of the long lead times required by fabric suppliers. However, the company approves designs and initiates manufacturing only after it gets feedback from its stores. This policy ensures that Zara makes products that meet consumer tastes and reduces the number of items they must sell at a discount. Combined with a highly efficient distribution system, these features have produced annual revenue growth above 20 percent since the late 1990s.

Adaptability has two components. *Resiliency* has become more critical because unexpected shocks to supply chains have become more frequent in recent years. The terrorist attack in New York in 2001, the dockworkers' strike in California in 2002, the SARS epidemic in Asia in 2003, and more recently, the COVID-19 coronavirus pandemic, for instance, have disrupted many companies' global supply chains. To make global supply chains more robust, increasing agility and resilience is key. To achieve this, building *flexibility* into the supply chain structure, processes, and management is critical.[5] Flexibility creates the capacity to manage risk or even gain an advantage from disruptions.

Alignment of all the firms' interests in the supply chain is important because every supply chain partner firm—whether a supplier, an assembler, a distributor, or a retailer—will focus on its interests. If any company's interests differ from those of the other partners in the supply chain, its actions will not maximize the chain's performance.

One approach to aligning the different partners' interests is to redefine the terms of their relationships so that firms share risks, costs, and rewards equitably. Another involves using intermediaries, for example, when financial institutions buy components from suppliers at hubs and resell them to manufacturers. Everyone benefits because the intermediaries' financing costs are lower than the vendors' costs. Although such an arrangement requires trust and commitment to suppliers, financial intermediaries, and manufacturers, it is a powerful way to align companies' interests in supply chains.

A prerequisite to creating alignment is the availability of information. All the companies in a supply chain should have equal access to forecasts, sales data, and plans. Next, partner roles and responsibilities must be carefully defined to minimize the scope of conflict. Finally, companies must align incentives so that when companies seek to maximize returns, they also maximize the supply chain's performance.

Best-in-class supply chains have several characteristics that define their success and set them apart[6]. These characteristics include a proactive use of big data, highly optimized inventory management, flexibility, and speed with order fulfillment, customization with process implementation, energy sustainability, and compliance.

Global Supply Chain Strategy and Implementation

Formulating and implementing a global supply chain strategy implies translating a chosen global strategy and value creation architecture into a set of decisions about how to source, deliver, store and protect goods in collaboration with partners in the supply chain.

The starting point for a global supply chain strategy is its value proposition, the nature of its competition, and the perception of value from the customer's perspective. Customers in different countries or regions have different requirements and perceptions of value. Therefore, aligning the needs and preferences of local customers to the supply chain set up is important. Such an alignment can result in low touch, cost-efficient supply chains for *bronze* customers and responsive, high service supply chains for *platinum* customers that value service.

Internal and external branding of the chosen global supply chain strategy is important as well—a well-documented and articulated logistics strategy creates internal engagement from stakeholders in different regions on the future ambition and links a company's corporate strategy with its global supply chain strategy. A clear strategy helps avoid mistakes like being too cost-focused when the business requires a responsive supply chain characterized by flexibility, innovation, and short pipelines.

Global supply chain network design focuses on creating an optimal footprint in terms of the number, mission, location, and size of distribution centers, manufacturing plants, and suppliers. Global supply chain network design aims to determine which plant or region should produce which product and determines which warehouse or region should fulfill a certain customer's demand.[7]

Why Use Outsourcing or Offshoring?

Outsourcing and offshoring of component manufacturing and support services can offer significant strategic and financial advantages, including *lower costs, greater flexibility, enhanced expertise, greater discipline,* and *the freedom to focus on core business activities*:

Lower costs. Offshoring typically offers significant infrastructure and labor cost advantages over traditional outsourcing. Also, many offshoring providers have established very large-scale operations not economically possible for domestic providers.

Greater flexibility. Using an outside supplier can sometimes add flexibility to a company, allowing it to adjust the scale and scope of production rapidly at low cost. As the Japanese keiretsu and Korean chaebol conglomerates have shown, networks of organizations can often adjust to demand more easily than fully integrated organizations.

Enhanced expertise. Some suppliers may have proprietary access to technology or other intellectual property advantages that a firm cannot access by itself. Such new technology can improve operational reliability, productivity, efficiency, or long-term total costs and production. The significant scale of today's offshore manufacturers, in particular, allows them to invest in technology that may be cost-prohibitive for domestic providers.

Greater discipline. The separation of purchasers and providers can assist with transparency and accountability to identify the true costs and benefits of certain activities. It can enable transactions under market-based contracts where the focus is on output, not input. What is more, competition among suppliers creates choice for purchasers and stimulates innovative work practices.

Focus on core activities. The ability to focus frees up resources internally to concentrate on those activities where the company has a distinctive capability and the scale, experience, or differentiation to yield economic benefits. In other words, focus allows a company to concentrate on creating a *relative* advantage to maximize total value and allow others to produce supportive goods and services.

Traditionally, outsourcing has been regarded as a black or white decision. More recently, brand owners are reviewing a hybrid model in which the brand owner remains in control of an operation but leverages a third party for specific value or expertise.

While outsourcing is primarily concerned with the scale and ability to provide services at a more competitive cost, offshoring is mainly driven by the dramatic wage-cost differentials between developed and developing nations. However, cost should not be the only consideration in making offshoring decisions. Other relevant factors include the quality and reliability of process improvements, the environment, and infrastructure. Political stability and the economic and legal environment should also be considered. In reality, even very significant labor cost differentials between countries cannot be the sole driver of offshoring decisions. Companies need to be assured of quality and reliability in the services they are outsourcing.

The Growth in Knowledge-Based Outsourcing

Over the last few decades, companies have outsourced many activities, including manufacturing, back-office functions, information technology (IT) services, and customer support. More recently, the focus has shifted to more knowledge-intensive areas, such as product development, R&D, engineering, and analytical services. Pharmaceutical companies today depend on a steady pipeline of new products from R&D. The competitive pressures on these firms to bring out new products at an ever-growing pace are increasing and, with it, are the pressures on the R&D function.

While the growth in knowledge-based outsourcing is driven mainly by cost, growing shortages of talent in home markets also play a role. In addition, standard business processes and IT services are increasingly becoming *commoditized*, depressing margins on such activities for outsourcers. This development has encouraged service providers to switch to other activities for which profits are potentially greater—including *innovation services*, such as new product development (NPD), R&D, and engineering. Simultaneously, providers of standardized services recognize that they need to focus on efficiency and seamless client integration if they wish to stay competitive. By contrast, innovation-related services, including everything from prototype design to credit analysis, are more complex and client-specific, and therefore more likely to command a premium.

For companies considering knowledge-based outsourcing, the lack of standardization means that partner vetting is key, and that they may need to invest in captive or near-captive operations that can be sufficiently customized. That may imply turning to smaller providers that can better meet special requirements. Contracting with multiple small service providers in different parts of the world is challenging. Outsourcing knowledge-intensive activities involve a new level of organizational complexity. Additionally, outsourcing key activities such as prototype design and engineering support is fraught with risk and has potentially significant downsides.

Companies that successfully manage knowledge-based outsourcing often use collaborative management models that share responsibilities, risks, and rewards, thereby enabling both sides to reach their objectives. Under a *co-management* approach, outsourcers treat contractors as valued collaborators even though competitors may employ the same company.

Mini-Case 10.1: BP Plc's Global Business Services Center in Pune, India[8]

The British oil company, BP Plc, announced plans in 2017 to create a new center for its global business services (GBS) operations in the western city of Pune. The BP led and operated center, which will provide business processing and advanced analytics capabilities in support of BP businesses worldwide, will begin operations in January 2021. It will support every part of BP, from customer service and vendor payments to financial accounting and control. The center will allow the company to provide innovative solutions as it taps into India's diverse and skilled workforce, expands its footprint there, and develops low-carbon businesses around the world.

With its many investments in India and employing around 7,500 people in the oil, gas, lubricants, and petrochemical businesses, BP is one of the largest international energy companies in India. It has a 30 percent interest in gas blocks of Reliance Industries. Besides owning a 49 percent stake in Reliance Industries' fuel retail venture, BP also has a 50:50 joint venture with Mukesh Ambani firm, called India Gas Solutions Pvt Ltd, for sourcing and marketing gas in India.

Risks Associated With Outsourcing and Offshoring

Outsourcing and offshoring can have significant benefits but also carry risks. Some risks, such as potentially higher offshoring costs due to the eroding value of the U.S. dollar, can be anticipated and addressed through contracts by employing financial hedging strategies. Others, however, are more difficult to manage.

Functions that can *interrupt* the flow of products to customers are the riskiest to outsource. For example, delegating control of the distribution process to an online retailer creates a risk that customers will not receive goods promptly. Another example is the risk associated with outsourcing call center responsibilities, resulting in negative customer reactions, higher product returns, lower repurchases, or complaints that could endanger its reputation.

A second risky type of activity to outsource concerns the relationship between a company and its employees. Outsourcing the human resources function, for example, can affect employee hiring quality. The outsourcing of payroll and benefits processing can result in information breaches that generate identity theft issues and resultant legal issues.

Finally, outsourcing software design can threaten innovation. By contrast, support functions such as accounts payable and maintenance are less risky to outsource because they have few direct links to customers or internal organizational processes.

Overall, risks associated with outsourcing typically fall into four general categories: *loss of control, loss of innovation, loss of organizational trust, and higher-than-expected transaction costs.*

Loss of control. Managers often complain about the loss of control over their process technologies and quality standards when specific processes or services are outsourced. When tasks previously performed by company personnel are given to outsiders over whom the firm has little or no control, quality may suffer, production schedules may be disrupted, or contractual disagreements may develop. Airbag failures in the automobile industry provide a recent example. Japanese airbag manufacturer Takata has recalled more than seven million vehicles affected by an airbag that may deploy incorrectly if the vehicle is involved in a collision. The list of manufacturers subject to the recall includes BMW, Chrysler, Dodge, Ford,

Honda, Infiniti, and Nissan. Instead of making the airbags themselves, these manufacturers decided to outsource and have another company make parts cheaper. They may have been able to save on parts cost, but the recall requires them to replace the affected airbags for consumers at no charge.

Control issues can be aggravated by geographic distance, particularly when the vendor is offshore. Monitoring performance and productivity can be challenging, and coordination and communication may be difficult. The inability to engage in face-to-face discussions and explore problems in detail can cripple a project's flow. Depending on where the outsourced work is performed, there can be critical cultural or language-related differences between the outsourcing company and the vendor. Such differences can have important customer implications. For example, if customer call centers are outsourced, how an agent answers, interprets, and reacts to customer questions or complaints may be influenced by the local culture and language.

Loss of innovation. Companies focused on innovation need to recruit and hire highly qualified individuals, provide them with the right incentives, and appraise their performance for positive long-run impact. When support services such as IT, software development, or materials management are outsourced, innovation may be hampered. Moreover, when external providers are hired to cut costs, gain flexibility, or adjust to market fluctuations, long-standing work patterns are interrupted, which may negatively affect the company's morale.

Loss of organizational trust. Outsourcing, especially of services, sometimes is perceived as a breach in the employer–employee relationship. Employees may wonder which group or what function will be the next to be outsourced. Workers displaced into an outsourced organization often feel conflicted about who they work for—the new external service contractor or the client company they previously employed.

Higher-than-expected transaction costs. Some costs and benefits related to outsourcing are easily identified and quantified because the accounting system captures them. Other costs and benefits are important but not tracked by the accounting system; such factors cannot be ignored simply because they are difficult to obtain or require the use of estimates. A prime example of the make-or-buy decision is the cost of outsourcing risk.

There are many other factors to consider in selecting the right level of participation in the value chain and choosing the best location for key value-added activities. The presence of supporting industrial activity, the nature and location of the demand for the product, and industry rivalry all should be considered. Also, issues such as tax consequences, the ability to repatriate profits, currency and political risk, the ability to manage and coordinate in different locations, and synergies with other elements of the company's overall strategy should be considered.

New Global Manufacturing Trends

A 2019 survey by the Bank of America's Global Research Unit of over 3,000 companies revealed that a growing number of firms in 12 global product sectors are considering shifting at least a portion of their supply chains away from current locations. Specifically, companies in more than 80 percent of global sectors in North America and the Asia Pacific region (excluding China) have either implemented or discussed plans to shift at least a portion of their supply chains from current locations, while 90 percent of global sectors in Europe are doing the same.[9]

Reducing their dependence on China is the principal motivation for many companies. While the ongoing trade war and national security are key concerns for executives, China's rising wages, stricter environmental norms, complex regulatory framework, and government focus to transform the country into a high-skill service-oriented economy also inform their plans.

Significantly, companies are inclined to move their supply chains either back to their home countries or region or closer to the markets where their products are bought. North American companies in almost half of the global sectors plan to relocate portions of their supply chains back into the region; South East Asia is the other popular destination for these companies. In Europe, firms in 8 of 12 sectors plan to shift their supply chains closer to their markets. Similarly, in the Asia Pacific region (excluding China), companies in all but two sectors either already have moved or are planning to move their supply chains back within their national borders or their primary markets. A key finding is that South East Asia is emerging as one of the biggest beneficiaries of the realignment of supply chains as companies consider the region as a viable alternative to China.

The reshoring of manufacturing facilities—mainly to North America—is likely to have far-reaching, lasting effects on the United States and global economy. It can boost long-term growth potential because manufacturing industries have the highest multiplier effects on the economy through productivity enhancement, R&D, and jobs. However, about half of the global sectors will experience moderate to high margin compression when they relocate onshore.

Global Supply Chains and Sustainability

As noted in Chapter 4, the direct relationship between a company's performance—especially in financial markets—and its record on Environmental, social and corporate governance (ESG) issues has been proven essential to corporate success. A growing scientific consensus regarding the need for big improvements and pressures from governments, business leaders, and consumers have made sustainability a key issue in global supply chain network design.

The challenges for companies are formidable. For example, the Paris Agreement of 2015 aims to reduce global greenhouse gas emissions enough to prevent the planet from warming by more than 2 degrees Celsius. To get there, McKinsey estimates that to achieve the Paris target while, at the same time growing sales at 5 percent a year, consumer product companies will have to lower their carbon intensity—the amount of greenhouse gas emitted per unit of output—by more than 90 percent by 2050.[10]

A high-functioning global supply chain—the worldwide ecosystem of organizations, including energy providers, involved in making and distributing goods—allows a consumer company to manage two types of sustainability-related risks. The first type of risk has to do with the *sustainability impact of providing goods and services to customers*. According to McKinsey, a typical consumer company's global supply chain creates far greater social and environmental costs than its operations. Collectively, such businesses account for more than 80 percent of greenhouse gas emissions and more than 90 percent of the impact on air, land, water, biodiversity, and geological resources.[11] Consumer product companies are, therefore, focusing on reducing those costs significantly by redesigning their supply chains.

The second type of risk is the *impact of sustainability issues on consumer companies' global supply chains.* Drought can reduce the output of the agricultural sector. For example, Unilever estimates that it loses some 300 million euros per year as worsening water scarcity and declining agricultural productivity led to higher food costs.[12]

Working with suppliers to manage these risks can be difficult. Global supply ecosystems have grown so large and complex that companies may not deal directly with all the firms in their supply chains. Primary suppliers routinely subcontract parts of large orders to other firms or rely on purchasing agents to place orders with other firms. Companies may not know how sustainability issues impact their supply chains and where the biggest impact is likely to occur in such situations. In a survey by The Sustainability Consortium (TSC), a nonprofit organization dedicated to improving consumer products' sustainability, less than one-fifth of the 1,700 respondents said they have a comprehensive view of their supply chains' sustainability performance.[13]

To understand the impact of sustainability issues in their supply chain, companies must take three steps: (1) *identify critical issues along the entire supply chain*, (2) *link supply chain sustainability goals to the global sustainability agenda*, and (3) *assist supply chain partners with managing impact.*

Identify critical issues along the entire supply chain. To understand the impact of various sustainability issues, companies must evaluate how natural and human resources are employed at every step of the supply chain or direct operations. Companies must also consider environmental, social, and economic issues. The enormous variety of consumer products being produced worldwide implies that these issues can differ significantly from one product to another. For example, manufacturing liquid crystal displays (LCDs) causes the emission of fluorinated greenhouse gases, while coffee plantations often hire underage workers to cultivate and harvest coffee beans.

Several organizations offer measurement frameworks and instruments that can help companies find the most critical sustainability issues in their supply chains:

- TSC has created a set of performance indicators and a reporting system that highlights sustainability hot spots for more than 110 consumer product categories, covering 80 to 90 percent of the impact of consumer products.
- The World Wildlife Fund (WWF) monitors more than 50 performance indicators for measuring supply chain risks associated with the production of a range of commodities, as well as the likelihood and severity of those risks.
- The Sustainability Accounting Standards Board (SASB) has developed standards that help public companies across 10 sectors, including consumer goods, to give investors material information about corporate sustainability performance along the value chain.
- The Carbon Disclosure Project (CDP)—an international nonprofit organization based in the UK, Germany, and the United States—and the Global Reporting Initiative have created standards and metrics for comparing different types of sustainability impact.

Link supply chain sustainability goals to the global sustainability agenda. Increasingly, companies are using scientific recommendations for bringing sustainability impact under specific thresholds. The Intergovernmental Panel on Climate Change, for example, a scientific body established by the United Nations, has defined global targets for reducing greenhouse gas emissions. Based on these recommendations, CDP and WWF calculated that the consumer-staple and consumer-discretionary sectors in the United States could cut their greenhouse gas emissions by 16 to 17 percent and 35 to 44 percent, respectively, to comply with global reduction targets between 2010 and 2020.[14]

General Mills uses this approach to set an emissions-reduction goal for its entire global value chain. The goal reflects an internationally agreed-upon target of reducing emissions by more than half by 2050. To reach its goal, the company encourages its agricultural suppliers to follow sustainable practices. It also has promised to obtain 100 percent of 10 priority ingredients from sustainable sources by no later than 2020. Some suppliers have set sustainability targets of their own, ahead of receiving mandates from their customers. For example, Cargill committed to creating a transparent, traceable, and sustainable palm oil supply chain by 2020.

Assist suppliers with managing impact. The purchasing power of consumer companies and retailers gives them significant influence over their suppliers' business practices. A growing number of companies are using that influence to get their suppliers to reduce their sustainability impact. Membership CDP's supply chain program is rising but still stands at a little over 100 companies. The number of suppliers participating in the program has increased to more than 5,000. This supply chain collaboration has eliminated more than 3.5 million tons of carbon emissions, with suppliers saving an average of 1.3 million U.S. dollars per emissions-reduction initiative.[15]

A growing number of companies go beyond disseminating codes of conduct, performing audits, and fielding questionnaires to help suppliers design and implement sustainability programs. For example, in collaboration with the Environmental Defense Fund, Campbell Soup Company offers farmers technologies, guidelines, and products to help them optimize their fertilizer use and improve soil conservation.[16]

Online tools have increased companies' ability to assist large numbers of suppliers. Walmart has helped its Chinese suppliers to reduce their energy consumption by an average of 10 percent using digital technology. Unilever collects and shares data on whether farmers in its supply chain are using sustainable practices. It's goal was to procure 100 percent of its agricultural content from sustainable sources by 2020.

Beyond monitoring suppliers' global sustainability performance and holding them accountable for it, companies have started offering their suppliers' incentives to improve sustainability performance. Levi Strauss, for example, in cooperation with the International Finance Corporation, established a 500 million U.S. dollars Global Trade Supplier Finance program to provide low-interest short-term financing to those suppliers that rate high on Levi's sustainability scorecard for suppliers.[17]

Because supply chains overlap in many consumer sectors, companies have recognized the benefit of working together to involve their supplier networks in sustainability efforts. For example, the Consumer Goods Forum (CGF), a global network of more than 400 retailers, manufacturers, and other companies, have made a collective commitment to achieve zero net deforestation by 2020. CGF members are pursuing that goal through the responsible sourcing of four key commodities: beef, palm oil, pulp and paper, and soy.

CHAPTER 11

Globalizing the Management Model

Introduction

The careful globalization of a company's management model is critical to unlocking the potential for global competitive advantage. However, globalizing a company's management model can be ruinous if conditions are not right or the process for doing so is flawed. Key questions include: When and to what extent should a company globalize its decision-making processes and its organizational and control structure? What are some of the key implementation challenges? How does a company get started?

Challenges in Globalizing the Management Model

Globalizing a company's management model is difficult. As firms expand into more countries and extend the lifecycles of existing products by bringing them into emerging markets, costs can often be reduced through global sourcing and better asset utilization. But, capturing such profit opportunities is hard because every opportunity for increased globalization has a cost and carries a danger of actually reducing profit. For example, a company's customer focus may be diluted if excessive standardization alienates key customer segments and causes market share to fall. Similarly, a wrong globalization move can make innovation slow down and cause price competition to sharpen.

Well-defined organizational structures can both help execute current strategies and be an obstacle to growth. On the one hand, they establish the roles and norms that enable large companies to get things done. Therefore, when growth plans call for doing things that are entirely new such as expanding abroad or adding products, companies must examine existing organizational structures to see if they are flexible enough to support the new initiatives.

Business processes define another area that companies need to consider carefully when they go global. Companies must assess which of their processes can *travel* to different cultures and scale across borders. Failure to do so can impede the successful implementation of an international move and create morale problems among managers and employees alike. Other organizational factors, such as the rigidity of organizational structures, a lack of scalability, or shortcomings in capabilities or skill sets, can also represent formidable challenges in implementing a global management model.[1]

The best executives in a global company often are the country managers who are protective of *their* markets and value delivery networks. But, globalization shrinks their power. Some rise to senior positions within the organization by taking extra global responsibilities; some leave. Many fight the globalization process, making it tough for the CEO. Sometimes, they win, and the CEO loses. Overcoming organizational resistance, therefore, is the key to success.

Finally, even the best global companies struggle to adapt to the shift of economic activity from Europe and North America to emerging economies in Asia, Africa, and Latin America. There is evidence that some high-performing global companies score lower than more locally oriented ones on key dimensions such as creating a shared vision, building relationships with local companies and governments, and implementing their strategies effectively.[2]

Corporate Strategy: Key to Globalizing a Management Model

Corporate strategy is defined as the set of choices diversified and multinational companies used to create and capture value across the business. The choices are largely driven by how business units or countries or regions work together and use corporate resources and capabilities.

The matrix depicted in Exhibit 11.1 shows four distinct logics underlying corporate strategy. The Business Unit/Region-Business Unit/Region Linkage (shown on the horizontal axis) represents how dependent the business units or regions are on creating and capturing value. The vertical axis—the Corporate/Business Unit/Region Linkage—shows

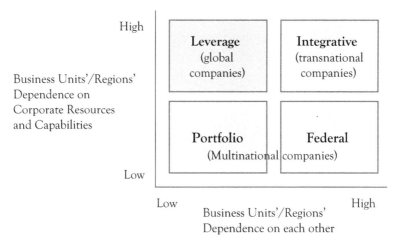

Exhibit 11.1 Linking corporate and global strategy

the dependence of business units or regions on corporate resources and capabilities to capture or create value.[3]

The matrix suggests four distinct ways to think about corporate strategy in a global setting:

- *Portfolio logic:* A portfolio logic is used by *multidomestic* companies and applicable when business units or regions can operate independently of corporate and each other. Under a portfolio logic:
  - ○ The role of corporate strategy is to decide which businesses or regions to enter or exit and how to allocate corporate resources.
  - ○ Business units or countries or regions have considerable latitude in formulating their business strategy, that is, business units or regions are the primary decision makers about where and how to expand and to what extent to use *adaptation, aggregation, and arbitrage* principles.

  Unilever provides a good example of a company operating this way.
- *Leverage logic:* A leverage logic is used by *global* companies whose business units or regions rely heavily on the corporate brand, a core technology, or other common expertise. With this logic:

- ○ Corporate decides how to develop and leverage corporate resources and competencies and where to expand.
- ○ Business units or regions do not formulate standalone strategies because centrally applied *aggregation and arbitrage* principles are deemed more important than local *adaptation* decisions to competitive success.

Microsoft is a company that uses a leverage corporate strategy.

- *Federal logic:* As the name implies, a *federal* logic defines a loose configuration of business units or regions that share business leads and best practices but do not rely on a corporate parent's resources or capabilities. Sometimes found in *multidomestic* portfolio investment companies, under this logic:
  - ○ No explicit corporate strategy is discernable. The primary function of corporate is to coordinate and consolidate and report results.
  - ○ Business units or regions develop standalone business strategies and work together to share business leads and resources where appropriate.

Berkshire Hathaway provides an example of a federal corporate strategy.

- *Integrative logic:* An integrative logic is used by *transnational* companies and applicable when business units or regions rely heavily on each other and corporate resources and competitive success capabilities. Under an integrative corporate strategy:
  - ○ Key global strategy decisions such as which businesses or regions to enter, how resources are developed and allocated, and how business units or regions should work together are made centrally
  - ○ Business unit or regional strategy is about supporting the corporate strategy.

IBM and P&G are examples of companies that use an integrative corporate strategy.

The Importance of the Global Finance Function

The role of the finance function in major corporations has changed significantly in recent years. Globalization has presented CFOs with new challenges well beyond traditional functions such as cost control, operating budgets, and internal audits. Globalization often means setting up subsidiaries abroad, which implies the finance function has to deal with currency risks, taxation challenges, and country risks (see Exhibit 11.2). Creating a set of balanced reward and incentive systems for managers worldwide is a second problem that needs to be addressed.[4]

At the same time, globalization has created new opportunities for the finance function to create value. The addition of subsidiaries abroad has created new internal markets for capital, which, in turn, allows companies to use arbitrage in international financial markets. Funds can be shifted from corporate headquarters to foreign subsidiaries and vice versa to take advantage of currency movements, differences in tax rates, or hedge against risks and thereby tailor a firm's capital structure and profit repatriation policies.

The global finance function's interdependence with other aspects of global strategy has also increased. In leveraging international arbitrage opportunities for competitive advantage, today's CFO must balance potential financial gains with the strategic opportunities and risks of a global operating environment. What may seem like a savvy financial move may undermine individual and organization momentum and motivation. For example, saddling a subsidiary with debt and thereby

Sources of Funds: Issues	Uses of Funds: Issues

• Cost
• Risk
  • Exposure to Interest Rate Risk
  • Exposure to Exchange Rate Risk
  • Exposure to Credit Risk
  • Exposure to Political Risk
  • Impact on Firm's Default Risk
  • Impact on Corporate Control
  • Impact on Ability to re-finance
• Application
  • Domestic vs. Foreign Capital
   Structure Decisions
	• Global Working Capital Management
	
	• Global Capital Budgeting
	
	• Global Risk Management
	  • Operating Hedging
	  • Financial Hedging
	
	• Global Portfolio Management
	  • Diversification
	  • Global Asset Allocation

Exhibit 11.2 Optimizing global financial strategy

depressing its profitability or aggressive profit repatriation may benefit the company as a whole but demotivate local managers and reduce their professional opportunities within or outside the company. Similarly, the existence of internal markets creates powerful opportunities for managing currency risk. However, those same moves can advantage or disadvantage local subsidiaries' financial prospects through cost or price differences. Therefore, it is no surprise that many companies require regional entities to hedge locally against currency risk and forego the opportunities a centralized approach may offer. Finally, capital budgeting on a global scale can improve investment decision making by adjusting hurdle rates to country risk levels.

Desai suggests an effective global finance function must:

1. Establish an appropriate geographic locus of decision making for the company. To prevent dilution of the company's global strategy, this may imply making suboptimal financial decisions.
2. Recruit and rotate financial managers in the same way marketing and other operating executives are employed to enhance global knowledge and promote coordination.
3. Ensure regional organizations understand which financial decisions and practices can be adapted to local conditions and which are standardized throughout the corporation and the rationale behind these choices.[5]

Attracting and Retaining a Global Talent Pool

Having the right global talent management practices can make or break a corporate globalization strategy. As reported by McKinsey and Company, there is a proven relationship between a firm's financial performance and its worldwide talent management practices.[6] In particular, three practices stand out:

1. Creating globally consistent talent-evaluation processes
2. Achieving cultural diversity in a global setting
3. Developing and managing global leaders

Practicing consistent talent evaluation means that employees around the world are evaluated on the same standards. Doing so facilitates transfers from one country transfers to another and helps create consistent career opportunities. Achieving cultural diversity helps bring about open-mindedness across cultures, while the development of global leadership is accomplished by rotating executives through different cultures, giving them international experience. Companies that do this best also tend to give managers incentives to share their employees with other units.

For the long-term success of any multinational company, a set of global leadership competencies is needed. Executives must evaluate the company's future leadership needs and then identify the skills needed for these roles. It will then be easier to determine potential candidates' abilities and the existing talent pool looks with the demand for upcoming global leaders. Many of the competency skills that are essential for global leaders are not ethnic or culturally based. Rather, they include leadership skills such as change management, critical thinking, problem-solving, collaboration, strategy development, and execution.

Ecosystem Management

Globalization has changed the *nature of collaboration* between companies. Consider car manufacturing. About 25 years ago, automakers either formed a joint venture or an alliance with another manufacturer to enter a new geographical market. Also, they maintained numerous fixed contractual relationships with part suppliers as part of the value creation process. While most car manufacturers still have those relationships, they also have become part of a much wider ecosystem across several industries and countries to make cars that are "connected, electric, and autonomous".[7] In this new climate of collaboration, carmakers act mainly as *orchestrators* whose primary role is to shape, organize, and manage the ecosystem by defining the strategy and selecting its participants.[8]

Ecosystems are often defined by more flexible deal structures, such as contractual relationships, platform partnerships, and minority shares in venture capital investments, rather than longer-term joint ventures or alliances. These new forms of collaboration allow the ecosystem to respond quickly to changing customer preferences, new technologies, emerging competitive threats, and regulatory changes. In addition, their relatively simple setup and dissolution allow companies to form new partnerships or exit existing ones quickly.

Mini-Case 11.1: Lego's Global Expansion Strategy— New Stores, Standardization and Simplification, and Less Reliance on Wholesale Partners[9]

Lego, the number 1 toymaker globally, reported its first drop in sales and profits in more than a decade in 2017. According to the family-owned Danish company, demand was weaker in established markets such as the United States and parts of Europe close to saturation.

In the previous five years, Lego had invested in significant growth. The company had tripled its workforce and vastly expanded the number of product lines it offered. Inventories in warehouses were growing because Lego had too many product lines, and there was not enough shelf space in toy stores to accommodate all competitors. As the toy trade is all about what is new, the company only had one solution: reduce prices at the risk of devaluing the brand.

The toymaker recognized the need to expand into markets that were still growing, such as China, but struggled to do so. The company was at a turning point and had to overhaul its global strategy. It eliminated 1,400 jobs—about 8 percent of its 18,200-person global workforce, drastically reduced its number of product lines, focused on reaching new markets with a simplified business model.

When establishing its new growth strategy, Lego set its sights on China, where it had already seen double-digit growth. It decided to put money into opening stores while shipping less product to retailers in the United States and Europe. Opening its third-largest global factory in Jiaxing positioned Lego to supply products for the Chinese market and other Asian markets, including Japan and South Korea.

Research showed that children in China play with Lego in much the same way as children of any nationality. This meant Lego would not have to develop new product lines specifically for Chinese or Asian markets and could take advantage of opportunities for standardization. However, it did innovate to combine physical and digital play to adapt to China's advanced digitization.

Lego's growth plans included adding stores in smaller cities in China to increase its reach. According to the company's website, it will have more than 140 stores across 35 cities in China by the end of 2020.

Financials for 2019 show steady progress with a 5 percent increase in global sales, including double-digit growth in China. The success comes despite counterfeiting issues, where other manufacturers have tried to imitate Lego's colorful blocks and branding. The Chinese authorities have been supportive in protecting the firm's intellectual property—Lego has won six cases against copy-cat companies.

The company's long-term growth strategy includes expanding into India, and it has committed to opening an office in Mumbai. The company also plans to open more than 70 Lego brand stores outside of China this year, including a flagship store in Amsterdam, The Netherlands.

Lego's expansion comes as America's malls are actively seeking new tenants, with store closures continuing to mount and on pace to set a new record by the end of 2020. Lego's expansion strategy is also a response to Target's recent announcement that it is teaming up with Walt Disney to open permanent Disney stores within some of its shops ahead of this holiday season.

In a 2019 interview, Lego's CEO Niels Christiansen stated:

"We are making these investments from a sound financial base to capture the opportunities being created by megatrends, such as digitalization and global demographic and economic shifts which are reshaping the industry. Being ahead of these trends will allow us to inspire future generations of children."[10]

Meanwhile, Lego is also investing heavily in e-commerce, ensuring it will not lose sales to online rivals like Amazon. In addition, Lego has pledged to use sustainable materials in its products and packaging by 2030.

Lessons Learned in Going Global

The research done in writing this book, along with the first author's experience in delivering a half dozen or more executive programs on global strategy held in the United States, Europe, and Asia over the last three years, suggests ten key observations about global expansion—most of which are illustrated in the preceding Lego mini-case:

(1) *A Global Presence Does Not Automatically Confer a Global Competitive Advantage*

No matter how attractive the growth opportunities, simply expanding overseas does not create a global competitive advantage. Rather, building a global presence dictates that companies must respond to the inevitable heterogeneity encountered in different overseas markets. Differences in language, culture, incomes, consumer preferences, and physical, financial, and regulatory infrastructures are just some of the factors to be considered. The right degree of adaptation can help companies gain market share, obtain pricing freedom, and getting a stronger competitive position.

Two major challenges associated with adapting a product, service, or entire business model to a particular country or region are keeping costs down and coordinating with other parts of the corporate structure. While an increased global presence does expand a company's scale of operations through a larger revenue and asset base, the larger footprint does not automatically confer a global competitive advantage. Whether a competitive advantage is achieved depends on how the company translates scale into economies of scale by spreading fixed costs, pooling purchasing, controlling regional expenses, and creating critical mass in marketing, research and development, and sourcing. Similarly, creating economies of scope can be an important source of competitive advantage, for example, by providing coordinated services to customers and global marketing across multiple target markets.

(2) *A Clear Statement of Vision and a Well-Defined Set of Global Decision-Making Processes are Key to Securing a Global Competitive Advantage*

In many global companies, top management's role has changed from its historical focus on strategy, structure, and systems to developing purpose and vision, processes, and people. This new philosophy reflects the growing importance of communicating a strong corporate purpose and vision in a diverse, globally competitive environment. Under this new model, middle and upper-middle managers behave more like business leaders and entrepreneurs than administrators or controllers. Companies must spend more time engaging middle management in developing a strategy to facilitate this role change. This process allows middle and upper-middle managers to contribute to global corporate plans and create a shared understanding and commitment to global business issues. The new philosophy calls for a company's development less through formal structures and more through effective management processes.

(3) *Successful Globalization is CEO-led, but Broad Buy-In is Key to Success.*

Shaping a global mindset starts at the top. After consulting with key internal and external stakeholders, the senior management team and the board of directors is responsible for finalizing a globalization agenda. An experienced board can help operating managers by providing a broader perspective and specific knowledge about new trends and changes in the environment. Senior managers have to communicate the company's new vision and long-term goals continually.

Periodically people from various divisions, regions, and countries will need to be assigned to joint projects. Ultimately, a global company will have to develop cross-border business teams to run all its operations worldwide.

(4) *Optimize Global Financial Strategy[11]*

Finance increasingly provides operational or companywide decision support in addition to meeting its critical responsibilities in governance and oversight. As companies and their clients become global and are served by more complex business structures, they tend to place a higher percentage of finance staff in business units or foreign countries.[12] When centralization is not appropriate, finance leaders must consider which service delivery model will best support their business. Some might choose to move toward shared services or a center of excellence; others might divide responsibilities between corporate and local finance teams. Ultimately, the *best* model for a given organization is one that balances finance's competing governance and guidance responsibilities given the available human and financial resources.[13]

Innovations in technology and management practice create new opportunities for the finance function to add value to a business. CFOs and their teams must be involved in counseling business units or regions on innovative approaches for creating value. The time has passed when the finance function could be limited to a focus on management reporting, budgeting and planning, and ad hoc analysis.

Although traditional quantitative competencies will always matter, finance professionals will need to become adept at shaping the economic value-creation agenda. At the corporate level, finance professionals must develop a deep understanding of strategic principles and create returns for customers, shareholders, and other stakeholders. They also must become more involved in managing stakeholders and processes outside of a formal hierarchy.

(5) *Develop a Global Perspective on Employee Selection and Career Planning*

Recruiting from diverse sources worldwide is important to the development of a global mindset. Multicultural top management improves the company's chances of recruiting and retaining high-potential candidates from various countries. Many companies now hire local managers and put them through intensive training programs. Microsoft, for example, routinely brings foreign talent to the United States for intensive training. Procter and Gamble runs local courses in several countries and then sends trainees to its headquarters in Cincinnati or large foreign subsidiaries for a significant period. After completing their training, they are expected to accept local management positions.

Similarly, a career path in a global company must include recurring local and global assignments. Typically, a high-potential candidate will start in a specific local function, such as marketing or finance. A successful track record in that function provides the candidate with greater credibility in the company and, equally important, the self-confidence to take the next step. This typically involves taking on more complex and demanding global tasks, often as part of a global team. With each new assignment, managers broaden their perspectives and establish informal networks of contact and relationships. In the past, international assignments were primarily demand-driven to transfer know-how and solve specific problems. Today, they are much more learning-oriented and focus on allowing the expatriate to understand and benefit from cultural differences and develop long-lasting networks and relationships.

To accomplish these goals, CEOs and chief human resource officers (CHROs) should work together to create a shared culture, cultivate new management, leadership, and career development models for younger leaders, employing a strategy of diversity and inclusion.

(6) *The More Global the Context, the Higher Performance Ambiguity*

The globalization of key business processes such as information technology (IT), purchasing, product design, and R&D is critical to global competitiveness. Decentralized, standalone local business processes are increasingly unsustainable in today's intense global competitive environment. In this regard, creating the right *metrics* is important. When all of a company's metrics are focused locally or regionally, locally or regionally inspired behaviors can be expected. Until a consistent set of global metrics is adopted, globalization is unlikely to take hold, much less succeed. Resistance to such global process initiatives runs deep, however. As many companies have learned, country managers will likely invoke everything from the 'not invented here' syndrome to respect local culture and business heritage to defend the status quo.

Top management should understand the impact of uncertainty on the workforce and accept that most people are not comfortable with ambiguity. Showing confidence and clarifying the company's purpose, strategic direction, values, and determining employee expectations throughout the firm can help alleviate this problem. Line managers play a significant role in providing this clarity. Leaders need to eliminate unnecessary red tape and empower line managers and employees to take the action they need to be agile and deliver through ambiguity.[14]

(7) *Respect Distance—Use the CAGE Framework*

The CAGE framework, discussed in Chapter 1, is useful to assess the cultural, administrative, geographic, and economic differences between the countries within an international strategy. Identifying these differences and categorizing them in these groups allows businesses to develop an effective international business strategy. It can be useful in making decisions about what to standardize and what to differentiate when adapting to local tastes and leveraging a global footprint.

(8) *Respect Different Cultures and Adapt Your Management Style*

The roles of leaders in the workplace vary in different countries and cultures. The leader's role and its importance can greatly impact the interactions and expectations within a team. For example, the importance of rank in a company's hierarchy is very common in Latin American and Asian cultures. In these cultures, leaders take a more dominant and clearly-defined role. Hierarchies and rank in Western cultures are comparatively less important. Relationships between managers and employees typically are much less formal, and leadership tends to be more collective and inclusive.

(9) *Shared Value Is Becoming Key to Global Success*

As noted in Chapter 4, integrating ESG factors into a global strategy is becoming more important to success. To achieve this, companies must plan for and address potential impacts of global megatrends—drivers that can fundamentally change business and society. These influences include the need to demonstrate ethical behavior and describe an organization's purpose to all stakeholders.

A continued focus on sustainability by some of the world's leading organizations is creating a forward-looking definition of sustainability. The new definition incorporates a redesign of strategy and operational processes that meet the market and society's changing needs and expectations to support long-term value.

(10) *Globalization Requires Flexibility and a Tolerance for Ambiguity*

Creating a flexible global organization is a multifaceted challenge. Globalization is driving a wholesale reinvention of organizational structure and management. The need for global scale and process efficiency is challenging corporate leaders to replace old models of centralized control and decentralized autonomy with new ones. Achieving the potential of global operations requires a mix of *soft* and *hard* approaches. Optimizing global processes requires cultural change management; proactive team- and relationship-building; and more traditional budgetary and accountability mechanisms, and metrics.

Notes

Chapter 1

1. https://ec.europa.eu/info/index_en
2. https://ec.europa.eu/info/index_en
3. https://ustr.gov/issue-areas/trade-organizations/association-southeast-asian-nations-asean/us-asean-10-trade-and-investmant-facts
4. (Broda, Greenfield and Weinstein 2006)
5. (Feenstra 2006)
6. (Ben Yahmed and Dougherty 2017)
7. (Grossmana and Rossi-Hansberg 2006)
8. (Syversen 2004)
9. (Lopez-Garcia 2015)
10. (McKinsey and Company 2019)
11. Ibid.
12. (McKinsey Growth Institute 2019)
13. https://tutorialspoint.com/blockchain/index.htm
14. (Iansiti and Lakhani 2017)
15. (Fan and Chiffelle 2018)
16. (Freund, Mulabdic and Ruta 2020)
17. (Martin 2018)
18. (Ghemawat 2007)
19. (Hamel and Prahalad 1985)
20. (A Bigger World 2008)
21. United Nations Conference on Trade and Development
22. (Yip 1992)
23. (Pearce and Robinson, Jr. 2015)
24. (Pettinger 2019)
25. Ibid.

Chapter 2

1. (de Kluyver 2010)
2. (Gupta, et al. 2008)
3. (de Kluyver 2010)
4. Lemonade's European Expansion begins in Germany
5. (de Kluyver 2010)

6. https://thcguardian.com/us-news/2018/mar/10/harley-davidson-tariffs-trump-motorcycles; https://timesofindia.indiatimes.com/business/india-business/harley-brand-stores-skip-metros-for-north-east/articleshow/63673938.cms
7. (Ghemawat 2007)
8. (Meenakshi February 26, 2018)
9. (Ghemawat 2017)
10. (Morschett, et al. 2015)
11. (Ricart, et al. 2004)
12. Ibid.
13. https://us.pg.com/structure-and-governance/corporate-structure/
14. (Helhoski 2020)
15. (Sofi 2020)
16. (Shu 2020)
17. (Edwards 2014)
18. (Kennedy 2020)
19. Ibid.
20. (Bartlett and Ghoshal 1989)
21. Ibid.
22. (Norwich University Online 2017)

Chapter 3

1. (Muller 2018)
2. (Van Agtmael 2007)
3. The main criteria used for classification are (1) per capita income level, (2) export diversification, and (3) degree of integration into the global financial system.
4. For 2018, low-income countries are those with GNI (gross net income) per capita of 1,005 U.S. dollars or less in 2016; lower middle-income economies are those with GNI per capita between 1,005 and 3,955 U.S. dollars; upper middle-income economies are those with GNI per capita between 3,956 and 12,235 U.S. dollars.
5. (Muller 2018)
6. (Cavusgil, Knight and Riesenberger 2012)
7. (Muller 2018)
8. (Cuervo-Cazurra and Dau July 5, 2008)
9. https://ec.europa.eu/knowledge4policy/foresight/topic/expanding-influence-east-south/emerging-market-developing-economies-growth-en
10. (IMF World Economic Outlook April 2018)
11. (Muller 2018)

12. (Aulakh and Kotabe 2008)
13. (Muller 2018)
14. (OECD Development Center 2018)
15. (Muller 2018)
16. (Khanna and Yafeh 2007)
17. https://multilingualexecutives.com/how-cultural-differences-impact-international-business/
18. (Prahalad and Hart 2002)
19. (Prahalad and Lieberthal 2003)
20. (Gunther May 2014)
21. Ibid
22. (Simanis June 2012)
23. http://grameen.com/
24. Ibid.
25. https://sab.co.za/
26. (Efrat, Ghadar and Peterson 2020)
27. (Coppola, Krick and Blohmke 2019)
28. (Maclean 2016)
29. https://multilingualexecutives.com/how-cultural-differences-impact-international-business
30. Stranded assets and scenarios, Smith School of Enterprise and the Environment, Oxford University, (January 2014), https://smithschool.ox.ac.uk/research/sustainablefinance/publications/Stranded-Assets-and-Scenarios-Discussion-Paper.pdf
31. Global trends in climate change litigation: 2019 snapshot, LSE, (July 2019), http://lse.ac.uk/GranthamInstitute/
32. (Fariborz 2006)
33. Ibid.
34. wp-content/uploads/2019/07/GRI_Global-trends-in-climate-change-litigation-2019-snapshot-2.pdf
35. (Bhagwaty n.d.)
36. (Daly 2007)

Chapter 4

1. (Kell August 13, 2014)
2. (ADEC Innovations, ESG Solutions n.d.)
3. (2018 Responsibility Highlights Report 2018)
4. (5by20 Coca-Cola 2020)
5. (Ford Sustainability Report 2018/19)
6. (Environmental Social and Governance Report 2018)

7. (VF Made for Change Report 2018)
8. (Temple-West 2019)
9. (Rajesh and Rajendran 2019)
10. (Henisz, Koller and Nuttall 2019)
11. (Randolph 2019)
12. (NextEra Energy assessed as having best -in-class preparedness, according to S&P Global Ratings' methodology for environmental, social and governance factors 2019)
13. (Wallens 2016)
14. (Parks, et al. 2020) and (Woetzel, et al. 2020)
15. (Norton 2020)
16. https://forbesindia.com/blog/climate-change/why-it-makes-business-sense-to-flatten-the-global-warming-curve/
17. (Hoti, McAleer and Pauwels 2005)
18. (Sudha 2015)
19. (Halkos and Sepetis 2007)
20. (Vasal 2009)
21. (Van Beurden and Gössling 2008); (Friede, Busch and Bassen 2015); (Ortas, et al. 2015) and (Duque-Grisales and Aguilera-Caracuel 2019)
22. (Cahan, et al. 2015); (Eccles and Serafeim 2013); (Fatemi, Fooladi and Tehranian 2015); (Filbeck, Gorman, and Zhao 2009); (Lo and Sheu 2007) and (Rodriguez-Fernandez 2016)
23. (Branco and Rodrigues 2008); (Brammer, Brooks and Pavelin 2006); (Lee, Faff and Langfeld-Smith 2009)
24. (Orlitzky, Schmidt and Rynes 2003); (Galema, Plantinga and Scholtens 2008); (Statman 2006) and (Horváthová 2010)
25. (Hamilton, Jo and Statman 1993)
26. (Kell July 31, 2018)
27. (KPMG Survey of Corporate Responsibility Reporting 2017)
28. (ESG information is now critical for investors 2019)
29. (Cohen 2019)
30. (Davis 2020)
31. (Henisz, Koller and Nuttall 2019)
32. (Holger 2019)
33. Ibid.
34. (Kyriakou 2020)
35. (Scaggs 2019)
36. (Tschopp 2003)
37. (Eccles and Klimenko 2019)
38. (Defining Materiality: What matters to reporters and investors 2015)
39. (Asset owner strategy guide: How to craft an investment strategy 2018)

40. (Driving ESG investing in Asia: The imperative for growth 2018)
41. (ESG integration in the Asia Pacific: Markets, practices, and data 2019)
42. Ibid.
43. (ESG and alpha in China 2020)
44. (KPIs for ESG: A guideline for the integration of ESG into financial analysis and corporate valuation 2009)
45. (Van Duuren, Plantinga and Scholtens 2016)
46. (ESG integration in Europe, the Middle East, and Africa: Markets, practices, and data 2019)
47. (ESG integration in the Asia Pacific: Markets, practices, and data 2019)

Chapter 5

1. We are extremely grateful to Dr. Richard B. Robinson, Jr. for his collaboration on major sections of this chapter. Prahalad and Hamel (May/June 1990).
2. https://bain.com/insights/management-tools-core-competences/ (accessed June 2020).
3. (Herbert 2000)
4. Ibid.
5. (Herbert 2000)
6. (McNulty October. 27, 2015)
7. https://strategy-business.com/blog/Leading-in-an-Increasingly-VUCA-World?gko=5b7fc
8. (Chesbrough 2006) and (Chesbrough 2006)
9. Adapted from - Openinnovation.eu, (accessed June 2020).
10. http://mixprize.org/hack/global-solutions-local-failure-overcomig-barriers-implementing-open-innovation/ (accessed June 2020).
11. Palzer (2018)

Chapter 6

1. (Lynch 2008)
2. Ibid.
3. Ibid.
4. Ibid.
5. (Berrada December 2015)
6. (Mhugos January 4, 2020)
7. (Lessard, Lucea, and Vives October 25, 2012)
8. Ibid.
9. (Pearce and David 1987)

10. (Pearce 1982)
11. https://mission-statement.com/microsoft/#:~:text=%20Some%20of%20 the%20components%20that%20emerge%20from,While%20doing%20 what%20it%20does%20best%2C...%20More%20
12. https://mission-statement.com/coca-cola/
13. (Young and Reeves March 2020)
14. Ibid.
15. (Luqmania, Leacha and Jesson 2017)

Chapter 7

1. (Zimmerman and Nelson July 29, 2006)
2. "A Practical Guide to Alliances: Leapfrogging the Learning Curve" (1993)
3. Los Angeles, CA: Booz Allen & Hamilton.
4. (De Vault October 2018)
5. 10 Most Profitable Franchise Businesses in India for 2020 (2020).
6. (Mehta 2012)
7. https://heineken.com
8. (Engelbrecht, et al. 2019)
9. Alliance Best Practice, Ltd.
10. Engelbrecht, et al., op. cit.
11. (Pearce and Hatfield 2002)
12. Extracted with permission from (Pearce and Robinson 2000).
13. (Green, Barclay and Ryans 1995)
14. (Birkinshaw and Brewis October 12, 2016)

Chapter 8

1. The Liberty Beacon (January 06, 2014)
2. https://mcdonalds.com; https://corporate.mcdonalds.com/corpmcd/about-us/around-the-world.html; and Bernadine Racoma (2019) How McDonalds Adapts Around the World, https://daytranslations.com/blog/how-mcdonalds-adapts-around-the-world/
3. Eppinger and Chitkara (Summer 2006)
4. Santos, Doz, and Williamson (Summer 2004)
5. Ariel (n.d.)
6. Sallet, Paisley and Masterman (September 2009)
7. Ezell (January 12, 2009)
8. WebTimesMedia (December 18, 2013)
9. Mills and others (2008)

10. Santos, et al. op. cit. p.
11. Ramirez (June 11, 2020)
12. Ibid.
13. Jana (March 31, 2009)
14. (Samuel 2015)
15. Corbin (January 16, 2017)
16. O'Kelley (March 22, 2017)

Chapter 9

1. (Aaker and Joachimsthaler November–December 1999)
2. (Kahn 2013)
3. (Bartlett and Ghoshal 1989)
4. (Douglas, Craig and Nijssen 2001)
5. Ibid, p. 103.
6. Ibid, p. 104.
7. (Silverstein 2008)
8. (Roll March 2014).
9. (Holt, Quelch and Taylor September 2004)
10. https://interbrand.com/best-brands/best-global-brands/methodology/ (accessed May 2020)
11. (Roll October 2019)

Chapter 10

1. https://investopedia.com/ask/answers/043015/what-difference-between-value-chain-and-supply-chain.asp, (accessed June 2020).
2. (Henderson, Dhanaraj and Avagyan with Perrinjaquet 2014)
3. (Myers and CheungJuly 2008)
4. (Lee October2004)
5. (BCI Global 2020)
6. (MSN June 1919, 2020)
7. (BofA Global Research 2020)
8. (Sheffi October2005)
9. (Kazemi 2019)
10. (Bové and Swartz November 11, 2016)
11. Ibid.
12. (NatWest September 4, 2020)
13. (The Sustainability Consortium 2016)

14. (World Wildlife Fund and CDP 2013)
15. (CDP 2016)
16. (Bové and Swartz November 11, 2016)
17. Ibid.

Chapter 11

1. (Dewhurst, Heywood and Rieckhof 2011)
2. (Dewhurst, Harris and Heywood 2011)
3. (Sull, et al. November 2017)
4. (Desai July–August 2008)
5. Ibid.
6. (Guthridge and Komm May 2008)
7. (Lang, von Szczepanski and Wurzer 2019)
8. Ibid.
9. (Starvish 2013)
10. Lego to open more than 140 stores in 35 Chinese cities (2019)
11. (Korn 2015)
12. (Gartner July 18, 2019)
13. Ibid.
14. (Eklund, Woodcock and Tam 2018)

References

10 Most Profitable Franchise Businesses in India for 2020. 2020. "TopFranchise. Com" January, 29. https://topfranchise.com/articles/10-most-profitable-franchise-businesses-in-india/

1993. *A Practical Guide to Alliances: Leapfrogging the Learning Curve.* Los Angeles, CA: Booz Allen & Hamilton.

2018 Environmental Social and Governance Report. 2018. https://jpmorganchase.com/corporate/Corporate-Responsibility/document/jpmc-cr-esg-report-2018.pdf

2018 Responsibility Highlights Report. 2018. "Amgen Inc.," p. 20. https://amgen.com/~/media/amgen/full/www-amgen-com/downloads/responsibility-report/amgen-2018-responsibility-highlights-report.ashx

5by20 Coca-Cola. 2020. https://coca-colacompany.com/shared-future/women-empowerment

A Bigger World. 2008. *The Economist*, Special Report.

Aaker, D., and E. Joachimsthaler. November-December 1999. "The Lure of Global Branding." *Harvard Business Review*, https://hbr.org/1999/11/the-lure-of-global-branding

ADEC Innovations, ESG Solutions. n.d. "What is ESG Investing?" https://esg.adec-innovations.com/about-us/faqs/what-is-esg-investing/

Alliance Best Practice, Ltd.

Ariel. n.d. "4 Examples of the Most Innovative Global Teams." https://arielgroup.com/4-examples-of-the-most-innovative-global-teams

Asset Owner Strategy Guide: How to Craft an Investment Strategy. 2018. "Principle for Responsible Investing (PRI)." https://unpri.org/asset-owners/investment-strategy

Aulakh, P., and M. Kotabe. 2008. "Institutional Changes and Organizational Transformation in Developing Economies." *Journal of International Management* 14, pp. 209–216.

Bartlett, C.A., and S. Ghoshal. 1989. *Managing Across Borders*. Boston: Harvard Business School Press.

BCI Global. 2020. "Supply Chain Strategy and Implementation." https://bciglobal.com/en/supply-chain-strategy-implementation Supply Chain Strategy & Implementation.

Ben Yahmed, S., and S. Dougherty. 2017. "Domestic Regulation, Import Penetration and Firm-level Productivity Growth." *Journal of International Trade & Economic Development* 26, no. 4, 385–409. http://doi.org/10.1080/09638199.2016.1260632

Bernadine Racoma. 2019. "How McDonalds Adapts Around the World." https://daytranslations.com/blog/how-mcdonalds-adapts-around-the-world/

Berrada, S. December 2015. "Capital One: Aligning the Organization through Data." https://digital.hbs.edu/platform-rctom/submission/capital-one-aligning-the-organization-through-data/

Bhagwaty, J. "CEE: Protectionism." *Concise Encyclopedia of Economics. Library of Economics and Liberty*, http://econlib.org/library/Enc/Protectionism.html

Birkinshaw, J., and K. Brewis, K. October 12, 2016. "Lessons from the World's Best-Known Fast-Follower: Samsung." https://london.edu/think/diie-innovation-icons-samsBofA Global Research. 2020. "Tectonic Shifts in Global Supply Chains." https://bofaml.com/content/dam/boamlimages/documents/articles/ID20_0147/Tectonic_Shifts_in_Global_Supply_Chains.pdf

Booker, B. November 2019. "Lego's Growth Strategy: How the Toy Brand Innovated to Expand." https://askattest.com/blog/brand/legos-growth-strategy-how-the-toy-brand-innovated-to-expand

Bové, A.T., and S. Swartz. November 11, 2016. "Starting at the Source: Sustainability in Supply Chains." https://mckinsey.com/business-functions/sustainability/our-insights/starting-at-the-source-sustainability-in-supply-chains

Brammer, S., C. Brooks, and S. Pavelin. 2006. "Corporate Social Performance and Stock Returns: UK Evidence from Disaggregate Measures." *Financial Management* 35, no. 3, pp. 97–116.

Branco, M.C., and L.L. Rodrigues. 2008. "Social Responsibility Disclosure: A Study of Proxies for the Public Visibility of Portuguese Banks." *The British Accounting Review* 40, no. 2, pp. 161–181.

Broda, C., J. Greenfield and D. Weinstein. 2006. *From Groundnuts to Globalization: A Structural Estimate of Trade and Growth.* NBER Working Paper No. 12512

Cahan, S.F., C. Chen, L. Chen, and N.H. Nguyen. 2015. "Corporate Social Responsibility and Media Coverage." *Journal of Banking & Finance* 59, pp. 409–422.

Cavusgil, S.T., G. Knight, and J. Riesenberger. 2012. *International Business: The New Realities*, 2nd ed. Pearson.

CDP. 2016. "From Agreement to Action: Mobilizing Suppliers Toward a Climate Resilient World." cdp.net

Chesbrough, H.W. 2006. *Open Business Models: How to Thrive in the New Innovation Landscape.* Harvard Business School Press.

Chesbrough, H.W. 2006. *Open Innovation: The New Imperative for Creating and Profiting from Technology.* Harvard Business School Press.

Cohen, R. 2019. "Here's How to Measure Corporations' ESG Impact." *Barron's*, 99, no. 46.

Coppola, M., T. Krick, and J. Blohmke. 2019. "Feeling the Heat, Companies are Under Pressure on Climate Change and Need to do More." Deloitte Sustainability Series, https://www2.deloitte.com/us/en/insights/topics/strategy/impact-and-opportunities-of-climate-change-on-business.html

Corbin, A. January 16, 2017. "Globalization, Localization and Rethinking What It Means to Go Global." Available at https://globig.co/blog/globalization-localization-and-rethinking-what-it-means-to-go-global

Cuervo-Cazurra, A., and L.A. Dau. July 5, 2008. "Structural Reform and Firm Profitability in Developing Countries." William Davidson Institute Working Paper No. 940, Available at SSRN: https://ssrn.com/abstract=1311928 or http://dx.doi.org/10.2139/ssrn.1311928

Daly, H. 2007. *Ecological Economics and Sustainable Development, Selected Essays of Herman Daly*. Northampton MA: Edward Elgar Publishing.

Davis, M. 2020. "Moody's Creates Global ESG Position." *Global Capital*, January 30.

de Kluyver, C.A. 2010. *Fundamentals of Global Strategy: A Business Model Approach*. Business Expert Press.

De Vault, G. October 2018. "How Starbucks Brought Coffee to China - A Case Study of Market Research." https://thebalancesmb.com/market-research-case-study-starbucks-entry-into-china-2296877

Defining Materiality: What Matters to Reporters and Investors. 2015. "Global Reporting Initiative." https://globalreporting.org/resourcelibrary/Defining-Materiality-What-Matters-to-Reporters-and-Investors.pdf

Desai, M.A. July-August 2008. "The Finance Function in a Global Corporation." *Harvard Business Review* 86, nos. 7/8, pp. 38–52.

Dewhurst, M., J. Harris, and S. Heywood. 2011. "Understanding Your 'Globalization Penalty.'" McKinseyquarterly.com

Dewhurst, M., S. Heywood, and K. Rieckhof. 2011. *Preparing your Organization for Growth. McKinsey Quarterly*

Douglas, S., C.S. Craig, and E.J. Nijssen. 2001. "Executive Insights: Integrating Branding Strategy Across Markets: Building International Brand Architecture." *Journal of International Marketing* 9, no. 2, pp. 97–11.

Douglas, S., C.S. Craig, and E.J. Nijssen. 2001. op. cit. p. 101.

Driving ESG investing in Asia: The Imperative for Growth. 2018. "Oliver Wyman and the Asian Venture Philanthropy Network (AVPN)." https://oliverwyman.com/our-expertise/insights/2018/jun/driving-esg-investing-in-asia.html

Duque-Grisales, E., and J. Aguilera-Caracuel. 2019. "Environmental, Social and Governance (ESG) Scores and Financial Performance of Multi-Latinas: Moderating Effects of Geographic International Diversification and Financial Slack." *Journal of Business Ethics*, pp. 1–20.

Eccles, R.G., and G. Serafeim. 2013. "The Performance Frontier: Innovating for a Sustainable Strategy: Interaction." *Harvard Business Review* 91, no. 7, pp. 17–18.

Eccles, R.G., and S. Klimenko. 2019. "The Investor Revolution." *Harvard Business Review.* Available at https://hbr.org/2019/05/the-investor-revolution

Edwards, J. 2014. "Mastering Strategic Management." 1st Canadian ed. https://opentextbc.ca/strategicmanagement/

Efrat, Z. 2020. *World's Top Global Megatrends to 2020 and Implications for Business, Society, and Cultures.* Frost & Sullivan.

Eklund, S., E. Woodcock, and M. Tam. 2018. "New Technologies, New Rules: Reimagining the Modern Finance Function." McKinsey & Company, https://mckinsey.com/business-functions/operations/our-insights/new-technology-new-rules-reimagining-the-modern-finance-workforce

Engelbrecht W., T. Shah, A. Schoenger, and M. Nevin. 2019. "Strategic Alliances for Competitive Advantage." https://deloitte.wsj.com/cfo/2019/09/08/strategic-alliances-for-competitive-advantage/

Eppinger, S.D., and A.R. Chitkara. Summer 2006. "The New Practice of Global Product Development." *MIT Sloan Management Review* 47, no. 4, pp. 22–30.

ESG and alpha in China. 2020. "Principle for Responsible Investing (PRI)." https://dwtyzx6upklss.cloudfront.net/Uploads/n/l/a/esgandalphainchinaen_90806.pdf

ESG Information is Now Critical for Investors. 2019. *FT. Com*, April 7.

ESG integration in Europe, the Middle East, and Africa: Markets, Practices, and Data. 2019. "Principle for Responsible Investing (PRI)." https://unpri.org/investor-tools/esg-integration-in-europe-the-middle-east-and-africa-markets-practices-and-data-/4190.article

ESG integration in the Asia Pacific: Markets, Practices, and Data. 2019. "Principle for Responsible Investing (PRI)." https://cfainstitute.org/-/media/documents/survey/esg-integration-apac.ashx

ESG integration in the Asia Pacific: Markets, Practices, and Data. 2019. "Principle for Responsible Investing (PRI)." https://cfainstitute.org/-/media/documents/survey/esg-integration-apac.ashx

Extracted with permission from Pearce, J.A., II, and R.B. Robinson, Jr. 2000. "Cultivating Guanxi as a Foreign Investor Strategy." *Business Horizons* 43, no. 1, pp. 31–38.

Ezell, S. January 12, 2009. "Benchmarking Foreign Innovation: The United States Needs to Learn from Other Industrialized Democracies." *Science Progress.*

Fan, Z., and C.R. Chiffelle. 2018. "How 5 Technologies are Changing Global Trade." *World Economic Forum*, https://news.itu.int/5-technologies-changing-global-trade/

Fariborz, G. 2006. "Conflict: Its Changing Face." *Industrial Management* 48, no. 6.

Fatemi, A., I. Fooladi, and H. Tehranian. 2015. "Valuation Effects of Corporate Social Responsibility." *Journal of Banking & Finance* 59, pp. 182–192.

Feenstra, R. 2006. "New Evidence on the Gains from Trade." *Review of World Economics* 142, no. 4, pp. 617–644.

Filbeck, G., R. Gorman, and X. Zhao. 2009. "The "Best Corporate Citizens": Are they Good for their Shareholders?" *Financial Review* 44, no. 2, pp. 239–262.

Ford Sustainability Report 2018/19. 2019. *Ford*, 25 https://corporate.ford.com/microsites/sustainability-report-2018-19/assets/files/sr18.pdf

Freund, C., A. Mulabdic, and M. Ruta. 2020. "Is 3D Printing a Threat to Global Trade, World Development Report 2020." Policy Research Working Paper 9024, World Bank, http://documents1.worldbank.org/curated/en/152701569432061451/pdf/

Friede, G., T. Busch, and A. Bassen. 2015. "ESG and Financial Performance: Aggregated Evidence from more than 2000 Empirical Studies." *Journal of Sustainable Finance & Investment* 5, no. 4, pp. 210–233.

Galema, R., A. Plantinga, and B. Scholtens. 2008. "The Stocks at Stake: Return and Risk in Socially Responsible Investment." *Journal of Banking & Finance* 32, no. 12, pp. 2646–2654.

Gartner. July 18, 2019. "How To Organize Your Finance Function." https://gartner.com/smarterwithgartner/how-to-organize-your-finance-function/

Ghadar, F., and E. Peterson. 2020. "Global Tectonics: "What Every Business Needs to Know." Available at https://smeal.psu.edu/cgbs/pubs/article

Ghemawat, P. 2007. *Redefining Global Strategy*. Harvard Business School Press.

Green, D.H., D.W. Barclay, and A.B. Ryans. 1995. "Entry Strategy and Long-Term Performance: Conceptualization and Empirical Evidence." *Journal of Marketing* 59, pp. 1–16.

Grossman, G., and E. Rossi-Hansberg. 2006. "Trading Tasks: A Simple Theory of Offshoring." NBER Working Paper No. 12721.

Gunther, M. May 2014. "The Base of the Pyramid: Will Selling to the Poor Pay Off?" *The Guardian*, Available at https://theguardian.com/sustainable-business/prahalad-base-bottom-pyramid-profit-poor

Gupta, A.K., V. Govindarajan, and H. Wang. 2008. *The Quest for Global Dominance*, 2nd ed, 28. Jossey-Bass, San Francisco.

Guthridge, M., and A.B. Komm. May 2008. "Why Multinationals Struggle to Manage Talent." *McKinsey Quarterly*, pp. 19–25.

Halkos, G., and A. Sepetis. 2007. "Can Capital Markets Respond to Environmental Policy of Firms? Evidence from Greece." *Ecological Economics* 63, pp. 578–587.

Hamel, G., and C.K. Prahalad. July-August 1985. "Do You Really Have a Global Strategy." *Harvard Business Review* 4, pp. 139–148.

Hamilton, S., H. Jo, and M. Statman. 1993. "Doing Well While Doing Good? The Investment Performance of Socially Responsible Mutual Funds." *Financial Analysts Journal* 49, pp. 62–66.

Helhoski, A. 2020. "SoFi Reviews: Student Loan Refinancing and Private Student Loans." *Nerd Wallet,* https://nerdwallet.com/reviews/loans/student-loans/sofi-student-loans

Henderson, J.E., C. Dhanaraj, and K. Avagyan. with M. Perrinjaquet. 2014. "Strategic Partnerships, IMD." Available at https://imd.org/research-knowledge/articles/strategic-partnerships/; http://mckinsey.com/insights/corporate_finance/avoiding_blind_spots_in_your_next_joint_venture

Henisz, W., T. Koller, and R. Nuttall 2019. "Five ways that ESG creates value – Getting your Environmental, Social, and Governance (ESG) Proposition Right Links to Higher Value Creation." Here's why. *McKinsey Quarterly,* https://mckinsey.com/business-functions/strategy-and-corporate-finance/our-insights/five-ways-that-esg-creates-value

Henisz, W., T. Koller, and R. Nuttall. 2019. "Five ways that ESG creates value – Getting your Environmental, Social, and Governance (ESG) Proposition Right Links to Higher Value Creation." Here's why. *McKinsey Quarterly,* https://mckinsey.com/business-functions/strategy-and-corporate-finance/our-insights/five-ways-that-esg-creates-value

Herbert, P. 2000. "Creating a Mindset." *Thunderbird International Business Review* 42, no. 2, pp. 187–200.

Holger, D. 2019. "Lyft, Zoom Mull ESG Disclosures." *The Wall Street Journal,* June 5. Available at www.wsj.com/articles/lyft-zoom-mull-esg-disclosures-11559750820?mod=searchresults&page=1&pos=2

Holt, D.B., J.A. Quelch, and E.L. Taylor. September 2004. "How Global Brands Compete." *Harvard Business Review,* pp. 69–75.

Horváthová, E. 2010. "Does Environmental Performance Affect Financial Performance? A Meta-Analysis." *Ecological Economics* 70, no. 1, pp. 52–59.

Hoti, S., M. McAleer, and L.L. Pauwels. 2005. "Modeling Environmental Risk." *Environmental Modelling and Software* 20, pp. 1289–1298.

Iansiti, M., and K.R. Lakhani. January 2017. "The Truth About Blockchain." *Harvard Business Review* 95, no. 1, pp. 118–127.

IMF World Economic Outlook. April 2018.

Jana, R. March 31, 2009. "P&G's Trickle-Up Success: Sweet as Honey." *Business Week Online,* Innovation Section.

Kahn, B.A. 2013. *Global Brand Power: Leveraging Branding for Long-term Growth.* Wharton School Press.

Kazemi, Y. 2019. "How the Modern Supply Chain is Evolving." https://forbes.com/.../2019/06/27/ (accessed June 2020).

Kell, G. August 13, 2014. "Five Trends that Show Corporate Responsibility is Here to Stay." https://theguardian.com/sustainable-business/blog/five-trends-corporate-social-responsbility-global-movement

Kell, G. July 31, 2018. "The Remarkable Rise Of ESG." *Forbes*, 4. https://forbes.com/sites/georgkell/2018/07/11/the-remarkable-rise-of-esg/#68f0712b1695

Kennedy, R. 2020. *Strategic Management*. Blacksburg, VA: Virginia Tech Publishing, https://doi.org/10.21061/strategicmanagement CC BY NC-SA 3.0

Khanna, T., and Y. Yafeh. 2007. "Business Groups in Emerging Markets: Paragons or Parasites?" *Journal of Economic Literature* 45, no. 2, 331–372. Retrieved September 13, 2020, from http://jstor.org/stable/27646796

Korn Ferry. 2015. "Leading through Ambiguity." https://focus.kornferry.com/leadership-and-talent/leading-through-ambiguity/

KPIs for ESG: A Guideline for the Integration of ESG into Financial Analysis and Corporate Valuation. 2009. "EFFAS: The European Federation of Financial Analysts Societies." https://greenfinanceplatform.org/resource/kpis-esg-guideline-integration-esg-financial-analysis-and-corporate-valuation

KPMG Survey of Corporate Responsibility Reporting 2017. 2017. Available at https://home.kpmg/be/en/home/insights/2017/10/the-kpmg-survey-of-corporate-responsibility-reporting-2017.html

KPMG: The Road Ahead—The KPMG Survey of Corporate Responsibility. 2017. https://integratedreporting.org/resource/kpmg-the-road-ahead-the-kpmg-survey-of-corporate-responsibility-reporting-2017/

Kyriakou, S. 2020. "ESG Investing has Moved to the Mainstream." *The Financial Times Limited*, April 24.

Lang, N., K. von Szczepanski, and C. Wurzer. 2019. "The Emerging Art of Ecosystem Management, Boston Consulting Group." https://bcg.com/publications/2019/emerging-art-ecosystem-management

Lee, D.D., R.W. Faff, and K. Langfeld-Smith. 2009. "Revisiting the Vexing Question: Does Superior Corporate Social Performance Lead to Improved Financial Performance?" *Australian Journal of Management* 34, no. 1, pp. 21–49.

Lee, H.L. October 2004. "The Triple-A Supply Chain." *Harvard Business Review*, pp. 102–112.

LEGO to open more than 140 stores in 35 Chinese cities. 2019. https://retail-insight-network.com/news/lego-china-denmark-opening/

Lemonade's European Expansion begins in Germany. n.d. *Insurance Journal*. https://insurancejournal.com/news/international/2019/06/12/528983.htm

Lessard, D., R. Lucea, and L. Vives. October 25, 2012. "Building Your Company's Capabilities Through Global Expansion." *Sloan Management Review*. Research Feature.

Lo, S.F., and H.J. Sheu. 2007. "Is Corporate Sustainability a Value-Increasing Strategy for Business?" *Corporate Governance: An International Review* 15, no. 2, pp. 345–358.

Lopez-Garcia, P., and F. di Mauro. 2015. "Assessing European Competitiveness: The New CompNet Micro-based Database." ECB Working Paper Series, No. 1764.

LSE. July 2019. "Global Trends in climate change litigation: 2019 Snapshot." http://lse.ac.uk/GranthamInstitute/

Luqmania, M., M. Leacha, and D. Jesson. 2017. "Factors Behind Sustainable Business Innovation: The Case of a Global Carpet Manufacturing Company." *Environmental Innovation and Societal Transitions* 24, pp. 94–105, www.elsevier.com

Lynch, R. 2008. *Strategic Management*, 5th ed. Financial Times/Prentice Hall, Chapter 19.

Maclean, J. 2016. "Globalization is Worsening the Effects of Climate Change, Study Says." https://cantechletter.com/2016/06/globalization-worsening-effects-climate-change-study-says/

Martin, M. 2018. "Keeping It Real: Debunking the Deglobalization Myth, Brexit and Trump: "Lessons" on Integration." *Journal of International Trade law and Policy* 17, nos. 1/2, 62–68. https://doi.org/10.1108/JITLP-06-2017-0020

McKinsey & Company. 2019. "Globalization in Transition: The Future of Trade and Value Chains." https://mckinsey.com/~/media/mckinsey/featured%20insights/innovation/globalization%20in%20transition%20the%20future%20of%20trade%20and%20value%20chains/mgi-globalization%20in%20transition-the-future-of-trade-and-value-chains-full-report.pdf

McKinsey Growth Institute. 2019. "Digital Identification: A Key to Inclusive Growth." https://mckinsey.com/~/media/McKinsey/Business%20Functions/McKinsey%20Digital/Our%20Insights/Digital%20identification%20A%20key%20to%20inclusive%20growth/MGI-Digital-identification-Report.ashx

McNulty, E.J. October 27, 2015. "Leading in an Increasingly VUCA World." *Strategy+Business*

Meenakshi, V.A. Febraury 26, 2018. "Nestle India to Adopt Regional Cluster Strategy to Boost Volume." *The Hindu Business Line*, https://thehindubusinessline.com/news/nestle-india-to-adopt-regional-cluster-strategy-to-boost-volume/article22859839.ece

Mehta, P. 2012. "Franchising in India." *Franchising World* 44, no. 7, pp. 55–56.

Mhugos. January 4, 2020. "Zara's Unique Business Model—Driven by Supply Chain Capabilities." https://scmglobe.com/

Mills, K.G., and others. 2008. "Clusters and Competitiveness: A New Federal Role for Stimulating Regional Economies." Washington: Brookings Institution, Available at http://brookings.edu/reports/2008/

Morschett, D., H. Schramm-Klein, and J. Zentes. 2015. "The Integration/ Responsiveness-and the AAA-Frameworks." *Strategic International Management*, 25–49. Springer Fachmedien Wiesbaden.

MSN. June 1919, 2020. "BP Plc. To Set Up New Global Business Services Centere in Pune." https://msn.com/en-in/money/topstories/bp-plc-to-set-up-new-global-business-services-centre-in-pune-to-hire-2000-employees/ (accessed June 19, 2020).

Muller, E.D. 2018. "Emerging Markets—Powerhouse of Global Growth, Market Commentary, Ashmore." Issued May 2018, http://ashmoregroup.com/sites/default/files/article-docs/ (accessed September 2020).

Myers, M.B., and M.S. Cheung. July 2008. "Sharing Global Supply Chain Knowledge." *Sloan Management Review* 49, no. 4, pp. 67–73.

NatWest. September 4, 2020. "ESG Essntials for Corporates: The Environmental Angle #5—Sustainable Supply Chains." https://nwm.com/insights/articles/esg-essentials-for-corporates-the-environmental-angle-5-sustainable-supply-chains

NextEra Energy assessed as having Best -in-Class Preparedness, According to S&P Global Ratings' Methodology for Environmental, Social and Governance Factors. 2019. NextEra Energy, Inc. *Cision PR Newswire*.

Norton. 2020. "13 ESG investing trends to watch for in 2020." *Barron's* (Online), January 30.

Norwich University Online. 2017. "International Business Strategies in a Globalizing World." https://online.norwich.edu/academic-programs/resources/international-business-strategies-globalizing-world

OECD Development Center. 2018. 'The Emerging Middle Class in Developing Countries." Working Paper No. 285.

O'Kelley, B. March 22, 2017. "Product and Platform." *Forbes*, https://forbes.com/sites/ciocentral/2017/03/22/product-and-platform/#65088af37c6e

Orlitzky, M., F.L. Schmidt, and R.L. Rynes. 2003. "Corporate Social and Financial Performance: A Meta-Analysis." *Organization Studies* 24, no. 2, pp. 403–441.

Ortas, E., I. Álvarez, J. Jaussaud, and A. Garayar. 2015. "The Impact of Institutional and Social Context on Corporate Environmental, Social and Governance Performance of Companies Committed to Voluntary Corporate Social Responsibility Initiatives." *Journal of Cleaner Production* 108, pp. 673–684.

Palzer, S. 2018. "Dialing Up Innovation - Taking Open Innovation to a New Level Through a Multi-Faceted Approach." https:// nestle.com/stories/research-development-open-innovation-multi-faceted-approach

Parks, R.M., J.E. Bennett, H. Tamura-Wicks, V. Kontis, R. Toumi, G. Danaei, and M. Ezzati. 2020. "Anomalously Warm Temperatures are Associated with Increased Injury Deaths." *Nature Medicine* 26, 65–70. http://doi.org/10.1038/s41591-019-0721-y

Pearce, J.A. II, and F.R. David. 1987. "Corporate Mission Statements: The BottomLine." *Academy of Management Perspectives* 1, no. 2, pp. 109–116.

Pearce, J.A., II, and L. Hatfield. 2002. "Performance Effects of Alternative Joint Venture Resource Responsibility Structures." *Journal of Business Venturing* 17, no. 4, pp. 343–364.

Pearce, J.A., II, and R.B. Robinson, Jr. 2015. *Strategic Management: Planning for Domestic and Global Competition*, 14th ed. Chicago, IL: R. D. Irwin, Inc.

Pearce, J.A., II. 1982. "The Company Mission as a Strategic Tool." *Sloan Management Review* 23, no. 3, pp. 15–24.

Pettinger, T. 2019. "Costs and Benefits of Globalisation." https://economicshelp.org/blog/81/trade/costs-and-benefits-of-globalisation/

Prahalad, C.K., and G. Hamel. May/June 1990. "The Core Competence of the Corporation." *Harvard Business Review*, pp. 79–93.

Prahalad, C.K., and K. Lieberthal. 2003. "The End of Corporate Imperialism." *Harvard Business Review*, https://hbr.org/2003/08/the-end-of-corporate-imperialism

Prahalad, C.K., and S. Hart. 2002. "The Fortune at the Bottom of the Pyramid, Strategy+Business." 26, and Prahalad, D. 2019. "The New Fortune at the Bottom of the Pyramid, Strategy+Business." 94, www.strategy.business.com

Rajesh, R., and C. Rajendran. 2019. "Relating Environmental, Social, and Governance Scores and Sustainability Performances of Firms: An Empirical Analysis." *Business Strategy and the Environment* 29, no. 3, 1247–1267. http://doi.org/10.1002/bse.2429

Ramirez, V.B. June 11, 2020. "New Record-Crushing Battery Lasts 1.2 Million Miles in Electric Cars." https://singularityhub.com/2020/06/11/

Randolph. 2019. "NextEra Energy, Inc. receive best-in-class preparedness assessment in S&P Global Ratings Evaluation." *Daily Energy Insider.*

Ricart, J.E., M.J. Enright, P. Ghemawat, S.L. Hart, and T. Khanna. 2004. "New Frontiers in International Strategy." *Journal of International Business Studies* 35, no. 3, pp. 175–200.

Rodriguez-Fernandez, M. 2016. "Social Responsibility and Financial Performance: The Role of Good Corporate Governance." *BRQ Business Research Quarterly* 19, no. 2, pp. 137–151.

Roll, M. March 2014. "Brand Globalization: Pitfalls to Avoid." Martinroll.com/resources/articles/strategy/

Roll, M. October 2019. "Uniqlo: The Strategy Behind the Global Japanese Fast Fashion Retail Brand." martinroll.com/resources/articles/strategy

Sallet, J., E. Paisley, and J. Masterman. September 2009. "The Geography of Innovation." https://scienceprogress.org/

Samuel, J. 2015. "First affordable, 'Made in India' CT Scan System Costs Less Than Rs.1 Crore." https://medindia.net/news/ge-launched-first-made-in-india-computed-tomography-147903-1.htm

Santos, J., Y. Doz, and P. Williamson. Summer 2004. "Is Your Innovation Process Global?" *MIT Sloan Management Review* 45, no. 4, p. 31.

Scaggs, A. 2019. "Those Socially Responsible ESG Ratings Don't Mean as much as you Might Think—Barrons.com." *The Wall Street Journal*, May 3. www.wsj.com/articles/those-socially-responsible-esg-ratings-dont-mean-as-much-as-you-might-think-barrons-com-11556890798?mod=searchresults&page=2&pos=14

Sheffi, Y. October 2005. "Building a Resilient Supply Chain." *Harvard Business Review Supply Chain Strategy* 1, no. 5, pp. 1–4.

Shu, C. 2020. "Sofi Goes International with Acquisition Of Hong Kong-Based Investment App 8 Securities." *Tech Crunch*, https://techcrunch.com/2020/04/21/sofi-goes-international-with-acquisition-of-hong-kong-based-investment-app-8-securities/

Silverstein, B. 2008. www.brandchannel.com, November 24.

Simanis, E. June 2012. "Reality Check at the Bottom of the Pyramid." *Harvard Business Review,* https://hbr.org/2012/06/reality-check-at-the-bottom-of-the-pyramid

Sofi. 2020. "SoFi Invest comes to Hong Kong." Sofi.com https://sofi.com/blog/sofi-invest-comes-to-hong-kong/

Starvish, M. 2013. "How LEGO Grew to Global Dominance." *HBSB Working Knowledge,* https://forbes.com/sites/hbsworkingknowledge/2013/03/18/how-lego-grew-to-global-dominance/

Statman, M. 2006. "Socially Responsible Indexes: Composition, Performance, and Tracking Error." *Journal of Portfolio Management* 32, no. 3, pp. 100–109.

Stranded Assets and Scenarios. January 2014. "Smith School of Enterprise and the Environment." Oxford University. https://smithschool.ox.ac.uk/research/sustainablefinance/publications/Stranded-Assets-and-Scenarios-Discussion-Paper.pdf

Sudha, S. 2015. "Risk-Return and Volatility Analysis of Sustainability Index in India." *Environment, Development and Sustainability* 17, no. 6, pp. 1329–1342.

Sull, D., S. Turconi, C. Sull, and J. Yoder. November 2017. "For Logics of Corporate Strategy." *MIT Sloan Management Review,* https://sloanreview.mit.edu/article/four-logics-of-corporate-strategy/#ref62

Syversen, C. 2004. "Product Substitutability and Productivity Dispersion." *Review of Economics and Statistics* 86, no. 2, pp. 534–550.

Temple-West. 2019. "Companies Resist Hong Kong ESG Disclosure Proposal." *FT.Com*, July 30.

The Liberty Beacon. January 6, 2014. "Ractopamine: The Meat Additive Banned Almost Everywhere But America." https://thelibertybeacon.com/ractopamine-the-meat-additive-banned-almost-everywhere-but-america/

The Sustainability Consortium. 2016. "Greening Global Supply Chains: From Blind Spots to Hot Spot to Action." sustainabilityconsortium.org

Thomas, L. 2019. "Lego Plots Global Expansion with Malls Hungry for New Stores." https://cnbc.com/2019/09/03/lego-plots-global-expansion-with-malls-hungry-for-new-stores.html; https://lego.com

Tschopp, D. 2003. "It's Time for Triple Bottom Line Reporting: Certified Public Accountant." *The CPA Journal* 73, no. 12, p. 11.

Van Agtmael, A. 2007. *The Emerging Markets Century—How a New Breed of World-Class Companies are Overtaking the World*. Free Press—A Division of Simon & Shuster.

Van Beurden and Gössling. 2008. "Corporate Social Responsibility and Shareholder Returns—Evidence from the Indian Capital Market." *Indian Journal of Industrial Relations* 44, no. 2

Van Duuren, E., A. Plantinga, and B. Scholtens. 2016. "ESG Integration and the Investment Management Process: Fundamental Investing Reinvented." *Journal of Business Ethics* 138, 525–533. https://doi-org.ezp1.villanova.edu/10.1007/s10551-015-2610-8

Vasal, V.K. 2009. "Corporate Social Responsibility and Shareholder Returns—Evidence from the Indian Capital Market." *Indian Journal of Industrial Relations* 44, no. 2.

VF Made for Change Report 2018. 2018. *VF Corporation*, p. 27. https://d1io3yog0oux5.cloudfront.net/vfc/files/documents/Sustainability/Resources/VF+2018+Made+for+Change+report.pdf

Wallens. 2016. "How the Paris Climate Agreement Impacts CSR and the Private Sector." *BusinessWire*. Available at https://blog.businesswire.com/how-the-paris-climate-agreement-impacts-csr-and-the-private-sector

Wang, Z., and J. Sarkis. 2017. "Corporate Social Responsibility Governance, Outcomes, and Financial Performance." *Journal of Cleaner Production* 162, pp. 1607–1616.

WebTimesMedia. December 18, 2013. "Les pôles de compétitivité ont désormais leur association." http://competitivite.gouv.fr/index.php?&lang=en

Woetzel, J., D. Pinner, H. Samandari, H. Engel, M. Krishnan, B. Boland, and C. Powis. 2020. "Climate Risk and Response: Physical Hazards and Socioeconomic Impacts." *McKinsey Global Institute*, January, www.mckinsey.com/business-functions/sustainability/our-insights/climate-risk-and-response-physical-hazards-and-socioeconomic-impacts

World Wildlife Fund and CDP. 2013. "The 3% Solution." thethreeperccent solution.org

wp-content/uploads/2019/07/GRI_Global-trends-in-climate-change-litigation-2019-snapshot-2.pdf

Yip, G. 1992. *Total Global Strategy: Managing for Worldwide Competitive Advantage*. Prentice Hall, Chapters 1 and 2.

Young, D., and M. Reeves. March 2020. *The Quest for Sustainable Business Model Innovation*. Boston Consulting Group, Henderson Institute.

Zimmerman, A., and E. Nelson. July 29, 2006. "With Profits Elusive, Wal-Mart to Exit Germany." *Wall Street Journal*.

About the Authors

CORNELIS A. DE KLUYVER

Dr. Cornelis A. "Kees" de Kluyver is a Professor Emeritus and the former Dean and James and Shirley Rippey Distinguished Professor at the Lundquist College of Business at the University of Oregon. He also is a former trustee of and holds an appointment as a Visiting Professor of Strategy at the Nyenrode Business University in the Netherlands.

His professional experience includes over 30 years in academe and management consulting. Prior to returning to Eugene, he was Dean and Masatoshi Ito Professor of Management at the Peter F. Drucker and Masatoshi Ito Graduate School of Management at Claremont Graduate University (1999–2010) and Dean and Professor of Management at the School of Management at George Mason University, in Fairfax, Virginia (1991–1999). Earlier in his career, he was a partner with Cresap Management Consultants, a Towers Perrin Company, with the firm's strategy and organizational effectiveness practice (1986–1999). In this position, he served a wide range of clients in the high-technology and service industries on a range of strategy issues, including the globalization of multinational operations.

He is a frequent speaker at executive programs and in board rooms around the world and has consulted with a wide variety of corporations and organizations, and serves/has served on and advises a number of corporate and nonprofit boards.

Dr. de Kluyver's areas of research include strategy and corporate governance. Authored books include *Strategic Management: An Executive Perspective* (with John a. Pearce II, Business Expert Press, 2015), *Strategy: A View from the Top* (with John A. Pearce II, Prentice Hall, now in its fourth edition and translated in Spanish, Portuguese, Japanese, Korean, and Chinese), *A Primer on Corporate Governance* (Business Expert Press, 2013, in its second edition), and *Fundamentals of Global Strategy: A Business Model Approach* (Business Expert Press, 2010).

Dr. de Kluyver holds a PhD in Operations Research from Case Western Reserve University, an MBA from the University of Oregon, and undergraduate degrees from the University of Oregon and from Nyenrode Business University in the Netherlands. Dr. de Kluyver is listed in Cambridge's *Who's Who*.

JOHN A. PEARCE II

Dr. John (Jack) A. Pearce II is the Distinguished Scholar in Residence at Eastern University, where he teaches and mentors doctoral students in the PhD Program in Organizational Leadership. In 2020, Stanford University rated him as a *Top 2% Scientist in the World* in an evaluation of the impact of researchers globally. Previously, Professor Pearce held endowed chairs at Villanova University and George Mason University and was a State of Virginia Eminent Scholar. He also taught at Penn State, West Virginia University, and the University of South Carolina. Dr. Pearce received a PhD degree in Strategic Management from Pennsylvania State University. He has worked in Canada, Germany, Malaysia, and Malta.

Professor Pearce has written 43 books. He has authored 132 articles, including 13 in law reviews, 50 business case studies, several practitioner articles, and 137 refereed professional papers. His groundbreaking article on product reconstruction appeared in the *Wall Street Journal* in 2008. Dr. Pearce received the Beckhard Prize from the *MIT Sloan Management Review* and the Best Article Award from *Business Horizons*. Sponsors of other recognitions include eight business schools, the National Association of Small Business Investment Companies, Association of Management Consulting Firms, and four divisions of the Academy of Management.

Dr. Pearce is a leader of executive development programs, an active management consultant, and an experienced expert witness. In 2009, he was identified as one of the top contributors to academic thought in the past 25 years. In 2014, he ranked in the 23rd position by *Google* for all-time contributions to the business literature. *Google Scholar* reports that his scholarship has been cited more than 25,000 times.

Index

OTHER TITLES IN THE STRATEGIC MANAGEMENT COLLECTION

John A. Pearce II, Villanova University, Editor

- *Sustaining High Performance in Business* by Jeffrey S. Harrison
- *How to Navigate Strategic Alliances and Joint Ventures* by Meeta Dasgupta
- *Strategic Management* by Cornelius A. de Kluyver and John A. Pearce
- *Strategic Management of Healthcare Organizations* by Jeffrey S. Harrison and Steven M. Thompson
- *Entrepreneurial Strategic Management* by Ken R. Blawatt
- *Developing Successful Business Strategies* by Rob Reider
- *Business Strategy in the Artificial Intelligence Economy* by Mark J. Munoz and Al Naqvi
- *Strategic Organizational Alignment* by Chris Crosby
- *First and Fast* by Stuart Cross
- *Strategies for University Management, Volume II* by Mark J. Munoz and Neal King
- *Strategies for University Management* by Mark J. Munoz and Neal King
- *Strategic Management* by Linda L. Brennan and Faye Sisk
- *Leading Latino Talent to Champion Innovation* by Vinny Caraballo, Greg McLaughlin and Heidi McLaughlin
- *Achieving Success in Nonprofit Organizations* by Timothy J. Kloppenborg and Laurence J. Laning

Concise and Applied Business Books

The Collection listed above is one of 30 business subject collections that Business Expert Press has grown to make BEP a premiere publisher of print and digital books. Our concise and applied books are for...

- Professionals and Practitioners
- Faculty who adopt our books for courses
- Librarians who know that BEP's Digital Libraries are a unique way to offer students ebooks to download, not restricted with any digital rights management
- Executive Training Course Leaders
- Business Seminar Organizers

Business Expert Press books are for anyone who needs to dig deeper on business ideas, goals, and solutions to everyday problems. Whether one print book, one ebook, or buying a digital library of 110 ebooks, we remain the affordable and smart way to be business smart. For more information, please visit www.businessexpertpress.com, or contact sales@businessexpertpress.com.

CPSIA information can be obtained
at www.ICGtesting.com
Printed in the USA
BVHW041838150322
631546BV00013B/464